POSSE
OF
THIEVES

Marc J. Reilly

The Thieves Press

Front Cover Photo by alphaspirit/www.123rf.com

Back Cover Illustration by Daryl Stephenson/www.caricatoons.ca

Title Font by Daniel Hochard/www.imagex-fonts.com

Printed in the United States of America

First Printing, 2017

ISBN 978-1-947107-00-7

The Thieves Press
www.crookbooks.site

Dedicated to Peg, who saved me from a life without true love.

Special thanks to the staff at the Nevada Historical Society and all the people who, over the years, have amassed an impressive collection of artifacts and historical documents. This book would not exist without the benefit of their wonderful research library.

Much gratitude is also due the curators and staff at the Nevada State Museum in Carson City and the Nevada Museum of Art in Reno.

The slogan, "If we can't make you look good...Your Ugly" is the official slogan of BJ's Hair Shop in Reno. It's where I get my hair cut and they manage to make even me look good, so please do not infringe on their rights by using or borrowing this slogan. They may take it out on me.

Thanks to Arthur Petron, MIT graduate and smartest person I know, for enlightening me as regards to the ins and outs of robotic technology, and the wonders of origami engineering.

I owe my inspiration for the Tinman Series to the late, great Donald E. Westlake. I only knew the man through his writings but he showed me a new path, and sent me on my merry way.

Last but by no means least, I thank the city of Reno for being such a wonderful character to write about.

ONE

AS HE SLIPPED ACROSS THE FAIRWAY he was wearing a grin, as he always did when working. He loved his job like most people love their firstborn. He especially loved it now that he'd become truly good at it. "The more I practice, the luckier I get," he thought, quoting Ben Hogan.

He was six when he stole his first thing. It was a peach and he got caught. He grinned wider at the thought. His birth name was Troy, but after the incident, everyone knew him as simply, Peach.

He was dressed all in black with a dark ski mask hiding everything but his green eyes and grinning mouth. The house he was fast-approaching in the dark was enormous and looked exactly like all the others in this gated golf community. They all bordered the eighteen-hole golf course located in the center of the development. This particular house, however, was considered special since the tee for the first hole was right out back. The lots were large, so there were no houses close enough to be of any worry.

A house on a golf course is about as ideal a setup as a burglar could want. Because wealthy people don't like living too near cities, there is no light pollution and the course is pitch-black at night. Also, the acreage is usually deserted.

Tonight, however, was a different story. He'd hidden behind a copse just off the first hole's tee box while several golfers began a round. Their presence did not alarm him. He was the cause of the nighttime event. Two weeks earlier he posed as a golf equipment salesman and visited the superintendent in charge of the course. As a welcome gift from his company, he gave the man several packs of glow-in-the-dark golf balls. He told him his patrons would love them and suggested he start an annual nighttime tournament.

Every night, Peach cased the place waiting for his opportunity. From the superintendent's enthusiastic reaction to his suggestion, Peach was certain he would jump on it. He also knew the wealthy residents would not be able to resist such a novel activity. Tonight, he hit pay dirt.

He reached the back of the house and turned to face the course. In the distance he saw a bright glowing green flash soar through the air, then another and another, like mini-psychedelic shooting stars. He could barely hear the squeals of delight from the titillated golfers. He figured they were just teeing off on the second hole. It gave him a warm feeling he could create such joy in others while on the job.

He stepped into the yard and lifted the lid on a valve box for the irrigation system. A brown valise was waiting for him. He hid his tool bag the first night he cased the joint. Possession of burglary tools was as bad as getting popped in the act. If something had gone wrong up to this point it would be difficult to prove he was intending on committing a crime with no tools.

He was, however, not at all worried about the cops. As always he had done his homework. He knew this was not a hot neighborhood because police records showed there had been no burglaries committed in the past five years. The cops wouldn't be looking for one now. He also researched the average cost of the houses and their tax valuations. This particular house he knew was owned by Marie and Daniel Simmons. Daniel was an up-and-coming trial lawyer who had just won a large settlement in a case involving a woman who sampled some perfume at a posh boutique in Newport Beach and claimed it created unsightly and painful boils on her neck which in turn caused her great emotional distress and mental anguish. "Man can I pick 'em," Peach thought to himself with no little amount of pride.

Most importantly, his research told him this was a perfect neighborhood because it was heavily secured with armed guards at the two entrance gates and cameras strategically placed throughout the community. Nothing works more in a thief's favor than people feeling secure. Unfortunately for the secure feeling people, the developers neglected to put cameras anywhere on the golf course.

He sidled his way down the side of the house until he reached the back door. He was pleased to see the windows were all alarmed because it meant the owners had something valuable to protect. The nice thing about alarms is they don't go off if you enter a house as if you have a key. He knew the type system and would have no problem disarming it if he chose, but it was far easier to just go through the door.

He examined the lock and saw it was a Baldwin Single Cylinder Combination Deadbolt and Handle Set. He noted the residents had not locked the handle, counting on the deadbolt to stop an intruder. Rookie mistake.

The lockset was rated Grade 2 according to the American National Standards Institute meaning it exceeded residential security requirements. There was one higher Grade, naturally Grade 1, and as Peach reached inside his bag he thought the Simmons may have wanted to go that extra step.

Not that it would have made a difference. He had a knack, and no lock had stopped him yet, at least not since he'd graduated from his formal training. He pulled on a pair of nitrile disposable gloves and selected his prized Fall Pick set made in England. It was, in his mind, the best pick set in the world. Handmade from stainless steel, it featured great tension tools that simultaneously grab the cylinder at the top and the bottom so there are no obstructions for the pick. The best part of the set, Peach thought as he inserted the correct tension wrench into the deadbolt, is the wrenches spread the torque evenly throughout the cylinder and are adjustable to fit almost any size lock.

Once he had the wrench inserted he decided not to take the time to pick the lock pin by pin. It's always a blast to do, of course, but time-consuming. Instead, he chose his rake pick, inserted it carefully, and, using his highly developed tactile sense, located all of the pins. Exerting just enough pressure on the wrench, he yanked the pick out of the lock, making contact with all the pins equally, and turned the cylinder.

"Bada bing, bada boom," he sang to himself as he pushed the door open and stepped inside. God help him how he loved his chosen career. The psychological state of mind is the most important thing in picking locks. You have to believe the lock is already open and you're just going through the motions.

Five minutes later he'd located the safe. Ninety percent of all people feel valuables are safer if they're closer to them. Usually, they choose the bedroom to hide their riches, and more often than not the safe is in the clothes closet.

Thirty seconds after finding it, it was open. "Will people ever learn?" he wondered. A fireproof safe is meant to keep out fire, not burglars. In this case, he used a rare earth hockey puck magnet stuffed in a sock to crack it. The flaw in most fireproof safes is in the use of nickel in the solenoid, in this case, an angle solenoid. A magnet placed directly over the solenoid and moved correctly will trigger it and activate the slide bolts.

Many wealthy people who can't figure out why they get paid so much, like movie actors, politicians, and especially lawyers, are afraid they'll be found out. Therefore, they always keep a cash stash buried away, like Linus with his security blanket. Dan Simmons, Esq. was no exception. There was a little over nine grand in cash and some interesting jewelry.

Peach pulled out his loupe and examined the bling. On the Blue Nile Floating Diamond Solitaire Pendant Necklace, he was specifically looking on the platinum chain for any laser inscription which is used for recovery in the case of theft. It requires high magnification to be seen and sure enough there it was. He tossed it back in the safe. On clean jewelry, his cut from a fence was only 30-50% of wholesale, much less for a piece that could be traced and had to be broken down. Not worth the hassle.

His discovery made him leery about the other pieces. He grabbed his UV flashlight and closely examined each item. As he suspected the light revealed forensic property markings. He dropped them back into the safe like they were hot coals. He admired the Simmons just a wee bit more than he had before. Still, not a bad haul, he thought as he shut and locked the safe, sans the nine grand.

Now most burglars would skedaddle, right? Well, one of the reasons Peach loved his work so much is it gave him the chance to learn more about people. He loved people and always wanted to experience a little of how they lived. He didn't want to be like them. He never wanted to be anybody but himself even when his life was in shambles when he was younger. No, he just wanted to be in their body if only for a short time, and see what made them tick.

With this in mind, after putting the hanging clothes back exactly where they had been hiding the safe in the closet he moseyed down to the finished basement. His examination of his victims' abodes always started from the bottom and went up.

Dan had done an admirable job in hiring the right people to turn the basement into a well-furnished game room. It was done in red oak paneling with stone accents. There was an eight-foot pool table and when Peach saw the manufacturer, knew he'd skimped a bit on it. Not that it mattered. He might have played on it once. There was a mobile bar made out of walnut and the top of a ping pong table that could be placed over the pool table. The paddles were cheap, however, and Peach's estimation of Dan dropped a little.

He proceeded upstairs to the formal dining room where he admired the long teak table no one was allowed to eat on. He noticed the smudged silver set and decided Marie was not as good as Dan at hiring help. He circled to the expansive kitchen in which Marie primarily used the coffee maker and the toaster. One look in their freezer showed they were frozen food eaters. Given all the money in the world, most people still chose to eat garbage.

He saved the best for last. The living room. Or from the size of it should one call it the great room? You could play a decent round of tennis in there. The furnishings were top-of-the-line, manufactured by the likes of Kelly Wearstler, Benetti's Italia, Oly, and E.J. Victor. It was definitely over the top. The Simmons were only in their late 30's but were obviously trying to demonstrate they were not new money. Peach knew money and what Dan and Marie didn't know is the trick to looking like old money is not to try.

There was a lot of artwork on the walls that showed their tastes leaned to modern with a dash of Native American. Nothing worth stealing. Even if there was, he was a firm believer good things come in small packages— mostly jewelry and cash.

At one end of the cavernous hall was the obligatory giant TV screen. In front sat a luxurious couch upholstered in cream white leather. He plopped down and grabbed the remote. He turned it on and it came up on the last channel watched, A&E. No surprise there. What else would they be watching, MMA?

Clicking it off, he leaned up to the coffee table. There were several art magazines covered in dust. Come on, Marie. Good help isn't that hard to find. He picked up a copy of this month's American Fine Art and settled in. The feature story was about Native American baskets. He was not crazy about baskets but he'd had a little experience with them when he was younger. Mostly he was intrigued by the cost of some. He suddenly shot to his feet like the SWAT team had burst through the front door.

A wide smile broke out. "Dat So La Lee you beautiful thing you!" he shouted. He shut the magazine and placed it exactly where it had been. The longer a burglar can keep his crime from being detected the better.

His fun was over here. His mind was focused on only one thing—time for a little visit back to his hometown. He grabbed his tool bag and trotted out of the living room and through the kitchen on his way to the backdoor. He spotted a calendar with all of Marie's appointments: Tuesday: spa, Wednesday: hair, Thursday: nails, Friday: tennis. Life's a drag. He tried to remember what day it was. Arriving at that, he checked the date. His eyes bugged. In a second he made the decision.

He turned and ran back through the house and up the stairs to the bedroom. He quickly opened the safe, grabbed the diamond necklace, and slammed the door shut.

A minute and a half later, he was letting himself out the backdoor. He disappeared into the darkness of the golf course. The nighttime duffers were nowhere to be seen. He jogged several acres until he reached a fence just off the fairway on the seventeenth hole. He squeezed through a slit in the chain link which he had cut two weeks ago.

He had a mile and a half walk through the surrounding woods to get to the car he had "borrowed" for the night's job. Before he started he pulled his shoes off and stepped out of the black jumpsuit. Underneath, he was wearing jeans, a flannel shirt, and a blue, zip-up nylon jacket. He wrapped the crepe shoes, ski mask, and jumpsuit in a plastic bag and stuffed it in a prepared hole near the base of a tree. From his tool bag, he pulled out a pair of low-top sneakers and put them on.

Peach was a careful burglar and knew the first thing you do when planning a heist is to plan the escape. All clothes must be immediately discarded. Clothes can leave distinguishing fibers and lead to a conviction if the burglar is still in possession of the garb should he be arrested. Shoes are also highly important. He always used the type he had worn tonight. They have virtually no tread, lots of people wear them, and they are difficult to trace. Just in case the cops did get a tread he always purchased the shoes one size too large to throw off any height and weight estimation they might make.

At this point, he would normally bury his tool bag and after the heat was off would return and retrieve it. But there was somewhere to be and to make it on time he had to start tonight. He decided to take the risk. The woods were inky black and if he heard anyone approaching he could drop it and run. It would be unlikely any pursuers would immediately find it.

He pulled off his nitrile gloves and wadded them into a ball. He walked several paces and bore a little hole in the forest floor where he buried them. Finished with his cleaning up, he started off at a fast clip. He estimated it would take him another fifteen minutes to get to the loaner car. From there, another twenty minutes would get him to the parking lot of the twenty-four-hour Walmart where he'd left his car.

The loaner car he'd taken from long-term parking at John Wayne Airport would not be discovered for at least a day or two. By then he'd be on his way. His heart was pounding with enthusiasm, not from the night's haul, it was a slightly above-average take for a residential heist, but nothing to get giddy over. The positive vibes came from the knowledge that in a couple of days he'd be sitting pretty.

TWO

HE WAS CALLED TINMAN BY THOSE IN THE KNOW. And until this very moment, he never realized how much he detested the smell of camel dung. Or maybe it was the camels themselves that reeked. He couldn't be sure. Did it make a difference? His soon-to-be violently ill stomach didn't think so.

He was also not very fond of their eyes, those deep, black saucers staring out at him like they knew exactly what he and his mob were up to. No, he was no friend of camels and this was the first time he was aware of it, mostly because he had never met any before.

Nor had he ever encountered any zebras, but he felt the same instant distaste. Their constant braying pierced his brain like giant porcupine quills wielded by an insane acupuncturist. It started low in the throat, like the growling of an angry cat, then soared upwards until finally exploding from the mouth in a high-pitched squeal much like a terrified pig who suddenly realizes that ax you're wielding is meant for him.

Sure, they were interesting enough to look at, but that's what photographs are for. Face to face was asking a little much of a city dweller, don't you think?

His main ire, however, was reserved for the ostriches. First of all, they were taller than he was—by a lot, and he felt it fundamentally unfair that a dumb bird could tower over such a statuesque human. And at least a cyclops had a proper head to match his one giant eye, not like this oversized evolutionary disaster with the largest peepers in the world that barely left enough room on his pinhead to squeeze in a beak. Which brought him to the most unnerving thing of all, the hissing. It was incessant and mean-spirited, meant to scare, at least that's how it felt to him.

Ostriches, zebras, and camels, oh my!

And that's why this was the last place on earth he wanted to be, perched on the side of a mountain, far from his notion of civilization, and surrounded by dozens of angry, exotic animals.

His sense of fairness to the animals returned when he realized they had every right to be angry. He would be livid if an untrained rider tried to race him around a track. He was not meant to be ridden and neither were these animals.

The thought made him look a little more kindly on these unsavory beasts. He still didn't like them, but he decided to reserve his displeasure for the humans who were participating in this outrage. And what a bunch they were. The novice jockeys were all wannabe cowboys and dressed like it. The audience, comprised mostly of tourists and drunken locals, was oblivious to the plight of the animals as they desperately tried to capture the event on their phones and tablets and pads and notebooks.

It was the age of mass distraction, and Tinman would have no parts of it.

The blaring of harmonicas and banjos alerted him to the start of another race. This time it was makeshift chariots driven by full-grown men and pulled unhappily by the hissing ostriches. The travesty began over fifty years ago when Bob Richards, the editor of a Virginia City newspaper, ran a fake story about upcoming camel races. Readers thought it was real, and Richards had to scramble to put together a bona fide race. As silly as it seems the idea caught on. So every year, the weekend after Labor Day, these poor animals were dragged up to the side of Mt. Davidson to put on a show. Hey, what the hell else is there to do in a mining ghost town turned tourist trap?

Reel in the suckers, that's what. Which reminded him why he was here. He checked his watch and realized break time was over. Time to go back to work—or back on the whiz as it's referred to by those in the game.

The races were being held at the town's fairgrounds just down from the main drag of C Street. After the mob's first go-around at the crowd, they'd decided to take a little break, then they would resume their business in the heart of town. They'd learned that when the races were finished, there would be a parade of sorts where the animals were marched up and down the streets with some of them poking their heads into various saloons to freak out the more intoxicated imbibers. Was that a camel I just saw? I don't know, was it the big thing standing next to the pink elephant?

Tinman heard the announcer start the last race and he abruptly turned from the disturbing sight and started up the hill to C Street. This was not how he normally spent his days. Usually, he would wake up late, spend an hour doing a combination of yoga, tai chi, and jumping jacks, then make a healthy breakfast. While he ate he would plow through several difficult crossword puzzles.

He was not an educated man and had never graduated from any institution of learning, be it higher or lower. He was, however, highly intelligent. His lack of formal education had only succeeded in driving himself to become self-educated. He was a wordsmith and had successfully read every entry in a 1972 edition of the New Webster's Dictionary and Thesaurus of the English Language—three times, he started young. He was a third of the way through his fourth reading and yesterday had tackled the words filicide and filiferous. He thought filicide was the far more interesting word of the two. Who wouldn't?

After the crosswords, he would dress and take a cab to his place of business. Often, he wouldn't return home until the wee hours of the morning. This went on for years, decades, ever since he was a teenager. Every day he could plan on clearing between $500 and $1000. That was then. That was when he still had a business. But his line of work was over and he was the only one who refused to accept it. Despite the fact the drought had continued nearly a decade, he firmly believed it was just a lull in the action. And now he was broke. Fifty plus years old and no other skills but the one which had made him a damn good living all his life, and that living was no more. In days past, he had a sense of humor, and would never have bashed on the poor animals at the fairgrounds. But his good-naturedness was all but gone and he was grumpy, at everything.

He was especially irked at having to resort to the whiz. He hadn't been in a whiz mob since he was a young man and he felt it beneath him to have to fall back on it. If it had only been money for food he needed he would have found another way. But there was an upcoming birthday party he was obligated to attend, and he knew it was going to cost him money. Lots of money. The birthday girl wouldn't have it any other way.

A tipsy, middle-aged cowgirl sporting a t-shirt reading, "I make inappropriate decisions when I drink," weaved her way into Tinman's path. She looked him up and down and saw a tall man, just over six feet, with a full head of prematurely silver hair—poorly cut in the style of a mullet, a small scar on the top of his forehead, veiled but piercing gray eyes, and unusually long arms tapering down to long thin hands with slender, delicate fingers. Though he'd been given his nickname as a boy, and not because of his looks, over the years his body had actually grown into a likeness of the metal dude from Oz. He marched rather than walked, and moved stiffly like life was an effort. When working, however, the oil lubricated his swimmer's body and he was a puma, swift, lithe, and lethal.

"Howsa bout a wowl in the hay cowboy," cooed the cowgirl, her watery green eyes melting all over him. He brushed by and continued up the hill. Along with losing his good-naturedness, he'd lost any interest in women— especially ones wearing self-debasing t-shirts. The cowgirl took a second to recognize the rebuke then erupted like a polecat, spitting and cursing and kicking at the dust-covered road. She ran after him and when in striking distance cocked her right leg back and let 'er rip. The heel of her boot caught her left ankle and she flipped into the air and landed on her ass. A vaudevillian could not have done a better pratfall, thought Tinman.

He didn't stop to help her up. He was nothing if not a gentleman and didn't want to draw attention to her drunkenness.

He climbed the last short rise to C Street, and there was Virginia City, Nevada in all its splendor. Well, not really. Not even close.

Tinman knew he was walking above 750 miles of tunnels that produced over 20,000,000 tons of ore. In its heyday in the late 1800s, the town boasted 40,000 residents, a population that rivaled Los Angeles at the time. There had been 100 saloons, four banks, twenty-two lodging houses, thirty-nine grocery stores, an opera house, and countless brothels. He knew all this, but to look at the present-day town it was practically inconceivable.

Now it consisted of a bazillion gift stores all seemingly selling the same kitschy stuff to tourists. There were still a lot of saloons, all desperately trying to appear the same as they did over a hundred years ago. One of the tricks in maintaining this appearance, Tinman mused, was to not fix, paint, or remodel anything.

Everything was in a state of disrepair and many of the buildings looked seconds away from collapsing. It was pure chaos, much like a beautifully constructed Lincoln Logs village looks after a five-year-old throwing a temper tantrum had smashed it into an unruly jumble of sticks.

As he looked at the dilapidated structures he came to realize the adage, don't fix it if it ain't broke, had been taken to a new level in Virginia City. Their motto seemed to be if it ain't utterly destroyed and razed to the ground, open up shop and milk the tourists.

And from the looks of it, they were doing a very good job of it. Even though the crowd from the races had not made it up here yet, the main drag was bustling. Places like The Super Chicken and the Comstock Bandito were doing a booming business selling the kind of stuff that would cause the buyers to wake up the next day and wonder what they were thinking.

Tinman was sincerely happy to see the prosperity. His business also involved milking the suckers and, though his particular line had fallen on hard times, he was glad to see other clever people were succeeding wonderfully in separating money from the gullible.

His mob was hoping to make a measly grand each today, and they were not even near their goal yet. The races were not conducive to their line of work because the crowd was penitentiary grift—just sitting on the bleachers watching the tortured animals be debased. The mob was hoping the parade would be their ticket—when the crowd was up and moving.

Tinman walked up to the Bucket Blood Saloon and quickly spotted Bones in front of a jewelry store, his attention fixed on something—or someone—inside. Catfish was idling across the street. A barely perceptible nod from Bones and they were back on the whiz.

THREE

WHILE ON THE WHIZ, the mob used what is called office. This form of communication could be either verbal code, or non-verbal signals, much like the way baseball coaches signal their players from the dugout. Catfish and Bones knew each other so well they could practically read each other's thoughts. But Tinman was out of practice so it was decided rudimentary office would be used for the day. None of the three made eye contact but both Catfish and Tinman were watching Bones closely for the important office that would tell them how the play would come down.

Anyone looking at Bones would have no idea what he did for a living—an absolute requirement for his chosen profession. He stood around 5'8" with a thin frame, black hair, olive skin, pronounced cheekbones, shoulders that pulled in and down, and no lips to speak of. He was in his early seventies but didn't look it. The only overt way age had affected him was periodic bouts of arthritis that afflicted his exceedingly long fingers. This was cause for much private concern because his fingers were his livelihood.

He was born in Alabama to a half white, half Chickasaw mother, who died giving birth. His grandfather raised him and taught him the tricks of his trade. He left home at thirteen and drifted to Chicago where he was taken under the wing of Catfish, a budding young conman who was trained by some of the top grifters in the country—back when the Big Con was still practiced. Bones would sometimes work as a shill for the con games but his true skill was in the high art of bodily theft.

It would not be fitting to say he was merely a dip, or a wire, for Bones was one of the last class cannons in the country, an elite pickpocket who had turned physical theft from a person into poetry. Any whiz mob he led was a class act. No rough stuff was ever allowed, even the act of bumping into a mark to position them. Everything was subtle misdirection, using physics and the mark's own momentum to lead them into the perfect frame for the touch to go down.

Entering the world of pickpockets is akin to falling down a rabbit hole and meeting up with the Mad Hatter. Their lingo is not found in any dictionary and is unintelligible—and unnecessary to know—for all but those involved. Tinman was essentially an outsider, but his early tutelage under Bones and Catfish had given him enough of the basics to get by. The lessons of his youth ran through his head as he waited for the signal the touch was going down.

A whiz mob is made up of the cannon, who is the boss and makes all the decisions from what mark to touch, to when and where the mob works. He acts in coordination with one to four stalls, each fulfilling a specific function. A stall's main job is to frame out the mark or put them in an advantageous position where the cannon can work without being seen.

Their second job is to make sure the cannon gets away if there is any trouble. If someone has to take the fall, it's the stall. The cannon is the lifeblood of any whiz mob. Without his sticky fingers, there is no money.

Sometimes stalls are asked to keep the mark in a stationary position. Other times they must attempt to get the mark in a good position while he is moving. The duties can vary from moment to moment, so they must be constantly aware of what the cannon wants and needs to make the touch.

To be a great stall one must have poise under pressure, be a consummate actor, be willing to improvise on the spot, and have absolutely no fear. They must spot a mark's weaknesses and work them to their advantage while maneuvering them into position. Most difficult to find is a stall who can follow instructions on the fly with no hesitation or ego. Thieves are inherently independent and often resist orders from anyone.

At best, a stall is a dancer in a crowd moving to the music of the cannon. When one can master all of these skills he is known as a bang-up stall. Catfish certainly fit this bill, and, normally, was the only stall Bones would work with.

Most cannons prefer at least two stalls, but Bones had tried adding other stalls over the years with little success. They had found one guy who looked like he might become a permanent fixture, but Catfish caught him weeding the pokes, or skimming the take, and the poor fella suddenly had a case of broken bones. You can't steal from your brothers, pal, it's against the code.

Eventually, Bones and Catfish decided to remain a two-handed mob, and they made a very good living at it for a long time. It's not true picking pockets has faded out because no one carries cash anymore. People carry a lot of cash. The reason the police no longer have specially trained whiz cops is that, much like the Big Con, the pros died out without passing on the knowledge and training. Consequently, there isn't enough of a problem for the police forces to worry about. For Bones and Catfish, this was a good thing. They could work practically unhampered by any fear of being arrested. The only recent worry was Bones' arthritis. How sad can it get, a pickpocket with bum fingers? But with enough pain killers in his system, he could still work when needed, and today his fingers were feeling just fine, thank you very much.

Tinman saw Bones was still studying the window of the jewelry shop, so he watched Catfish closely. He would be the one to feed him the signal when to get into position.

Catfish was of undetermined age, even to himself. Like Bones, he was one of those rare animals who once they hit a certain age seem to freeze in time. He stood just under six feet, with sandy hair, long eyelashes, grey steely eyes, full lips, and an imposing build. His ego was as big as his body but that was to be expected. Big-time grifters rely on their confidence to stay alive.

His ethnicity was also unknown. Mostly it was thieves' blood pumping through him. It's why he and Bones were brothers.

Catfish was an eight-year-old orphan living on the streets of Chicago when an old-time conman named the Hashhouse Kid discovered him. Hashhouse quickly recognized Catfish's innate grift sense and schooled him in playing a man against the wall or pulling off a con without the help of a mob. This involved learning every short con known, including The Hype, Up and Down Broadway, The Huge Duke, etc.

Catfish was indeed a natural. He had all the attributes required to be a class grifter. He was extremely intelligent and had a thirst for all things cosmopolitan: art, literature, music, business, and high-society gossip. Most importantly, he had a creative imagination. Con games are complex and most people wouldn't understand them even if they were told how they work. Catfish quickly became so good at mastering the short cons, Hashhouse turned him out as a big-time grifter. He had graduated to the Big Con.

By age twelve he was already roping for two mobs specializing in elaborate or long cons. His job was to locate loaded suckers and steer them to a big store—a fake front where the inside man or the boss of the mob would pull off the con. In exchange for his roping, Catfish received 45% of the touch.

He got his nickname when he was hustling as a young teen. He wanted to appear older to his marks so he manufactured a fake mustache using bristles from a scrub brush. The result was ridiculous, but the grifters admired his chutzpah, and the sobriquet, Catfish, stuck. From that point forward, he always wore a fake mustache when on the job and had amassed a collection of several hundred. Today he was sporting a petite handlebar, perfect for the setting.

Because of his genteel mannerisms and urbane ways, Catfish was like a magnet to the wealthy prospects. The façade of respectability worked like a charm and put the marks at ease. Consequently, mobs were clamoring to have him rope for them.

Touches from the Big Con commonly ran into the five figures and sometimes six. Given a game might only take a day or two to pull off, Catfish rose from a street urchin to a very successful confidence man in a few short years. By the time he was in his early twenties and met Bones, he had made and spent several fortunes.

But like all good things, the Big Con faded—fast. Mails-to-defraud laws, income-tax invasion, and a massive public education program took its toll. But the real death of the Big Con came from a dearth of class grifters. The old skills and knowledge were not passed down and no new blood took the place of the old-timers who either retired, died, or went to prison.

With little choice, Catfish and Bones hit the road working the trains with short cons. Soon, however, Bones convinced Catfish they would be better on the whiz. The Big Con had well-prepared Catfish for his new career as a stall, and he took to it like a cat to catnip.

To Tinman, Bones and Catfish were more than partners in crime; they were his uncles—not by blood, by consequence. And he knew today's invitation to this gig was more out of sympathy than necessity. They didn't need him to go about their business. They just felt bad because his vocation had tanked. Normally, he would not accept charity, but he was desperate, and he hated it.

So today they were a three-handed mob. Catfish would function as the front man and would primarily be in charge of positioning the mark. Tinman would be the shade or duke man. His job was to hide the act of picking the pockets from any onlookers. After the touch, the poke was handed off to him. He would quickly empty the wallet of any cash and promptly dispose of it.

Tinman suddenly saw Bones tug the left cuff of his windbreaker, then zip it partway up. He swept his thin hair back with his right hand and looked to the sky as if wondering what the weather held. He tucked his left hand into his left jacket pocket and stepped to a knickknack shop adjacent to the jewelers.

The office read: Turn the croaker in right and stick him for a left pit. Shade the right while I kick the poke.

Despite the time away from the whiz, Tinman translated the signals perfectly. It meant the mark was believed to be a doctor, probably because he was overdressed for the occasion as most doctors are prone to do. The wallet was in an inside left suit pocket. Catfish needed to turn the mark to his right then force him to stay put so Bones could get the correct slant and fork the leather. Tinman's job was to shade the right side of the mark from the street and sidewalk.

Catfish signaled Tinman and crossed the street heading straight for the jewelers. Tinman started across as well but on a more indirect path so he would come up behind Bones who was still in front of the junk shop.

Catfish reached the front door of the jewelry store and swung it inward just as a well-dressed, middle-aged man and his wife were coming out. Instead of getting out of the doorway, Catfish, with his hand still on the door, stepped back a little. He apologized to the doctor who impatiently brushed it aside. Realizing Catfish was not going to fully get out of the way, he turned to his right to slide by. His wife was still stuck inside the store, blocked by the jam.

As the doctor started to move, Catfish stopped him with a question about the quality of the jewelry inside. Tinman meandered down the sidewalk and stopped in front of the jewelry shop to look at a camel plodding by. It took a shade under three seconds for Bones to slide into the frame, slip his left hand across the mark's chest to the inside suit coat pocket, pinch the poke and move to the street, passing Tinman on the way and depositing the wallet in his waiting jacket pocket.

The doctor gruffly answered Catfish's question, grabbed his wife's arm, and squeezed out onto the sidewalk. Catfish decided he was no longer interested in jewelry and calmly strode away in the opposite direction. Tinman checked his watch, suddenly realized he had to be somewhere, he crossed over C street and marched up the short incline to B Street.

With everyone enjoying the festivities on the main drag, B Street was completely deserted, which is why Tinman chose it for his location to turn out the pokes (empty the wallets) and dispose of them. Prominent on the street was the old Storey County Jail, now the town's courthouse. Being so close to such a dangerous place gave him the willies. It was as bad as a stray dog hanging out in front of the pound. But he forced down his fears and went to business.

Across from the jail was a large steel drum on its side and raised by short metal legs. One end had a lever to open a small door. On the outside, stenciled in old paint, was, "1874 Virginia City Time Travel Machine. Discover the Future. 2 ½ cents per person." He grinned at the notion that thievery from the gullible was an age-old and proud occupation.

He flipped open the wallet and took out $320. There was a stack of credit cards, all claiming to belong to a Walter Cheny, MD, and all useless for the mob's purposes. He quickly skinned the poke by wiping both sides on his pants. He tossed it into the dead brush behind the magical time machine.

Back on C street, he caught up with Bones and Catfish and the whiz rolled on. The pickings were good and easy. Most of the men carried their pokes in their rear hip pockets—the candy pocket—so prat digging was the order of the day. Also, the vast majority of the marks were wearing jeans which tend to leave a bit of the wallet sticking out the top. If that wasn't the case, it was easy enough for Bones to top the poke or get it partly peeking out by using a light tap with his knee.

During the camel parade through the center of town, the mob hit its stride. A crush, or press means a crowd to a pickpocket, and parades provided the most lucrative kind. To a whiz mob, they were like gifts from Saint Dismas, the patron saint of thieves. All eyes and attention were on the parading animals and Bones only had to study the nape of the mark's neck. Most touches are done from the side or behind, so the ability to read the muscles of the neck was essential. This told the cannon if the mark was going to turn around. If it appeared the mark was going to spot his face, the touch was called off immediately.

Picking pockets works because of three truths: humans can only concentrate on one thing at a time, the sensation derived from a greater force nullifies that of a lesser force, and you can't steal a man's money when he has his mind on it.

They worked a little over two hours until Tinman gave the signal they had made their goal. Even if they hadn't, he was sure Bones would soon call off the game. It's never wise to hang around too long. Eventually, the loss of wallets becomes an epidemic and people start exchanging notes.

Bones signaled the end of play and Tinman chose his route back to the car. As he walked towards Washington Street where the car was parked he passed the Ponderosa Saloon and a boisterous crowd inside was whooping it up. An ostrich suddenly burst through the swinging doors, his tether flapping behind. He gave Tinman a desperate look and trotted onto the road where he bent over and with his beak scooped up a rather large stone.

He tilted his head back and the rock went slithering down his long neck. Tinman felt a surge of panic. Despite his distaste for the beast, he didn't want it dying on his watch. No one else had seen what had happened so he knew it was up to him to do something. He rushed up to the bird and grabbed its neck just beneath where he felt the stone slowly gliding to the stomach.

Squeezing tightly, he inched his hands up towards the head in an attempt to pop the stone out of the mouth. The ostrich let out a little croak and leveled his eyes with Tinman. The earlier look of desperation turned to ire, then outrage. Tinman met its gaze with equal irritation.

"I'm trying to save your life you idiot!" he growled.

The ostrich straightened, and Tinman squeezed up the neck like trying to get the last juice out of a Freeze Pop. The angry bird shot out a leg and it hit Tinman with a force of, oh, just around 2000 pounds per square inch, which even on a good day Ali couldn't manage.

The blow sent Tinman sailing through the air and down onto the dusty road. As he struggled to get his air back he heard applause from the appreciative audience who had quickly formed. They were rooting for the bird and this ignited something deep inside. He was not a violent man by any means, but to be taken out in the first round by a pea-brained, suicidal, oversized bird who's too dumb to even know how to fly was beyond the pale.

He struggled to his feet and a handful who were pulling for the dark horse let out some scattered cheers. Someone was betting on him! It gave him heart. He struggled to his feet, marched up to the ostrich, and raised his dukes.

What happened next is destined to go down in the annals of Virginia City history, surpassing even the great barroom brawls of boomtown days. Let it hereby be known as, The Rumble with the Ratite.

Spoiler Alert. The bird won.

FOUR

"SAY BONES, DID YOU KNOW OSTRICHES NEED PEBBLES in their stomachs to help them digest their food?" asked Catfish who always sounded like he was right out of a Damon Runyon yarn, except when he was playing a con when he could choose from a multitude of accents.

"No, I cannot say I did know that Catfish. Damn interesting," said Bones in his seductive Alabama drawl. He leaned over from the passenger seat. "Say, Tinman, did you know that? No, I guess you wouldn't, huh?"

"Enough," Tinman ordered as he concentrated on the narrow, winding road. They were only five minutes out of Virginia City and up till now it had been silent in the car. But he could feel the old men squeezed into his 1978 Datsun 280z four-seater were busting at the seams and the dam was ready to break.

Bones choked down a laugh and settled back. Catfish leaned up from the back seats. "I'll bet there's one thing you do know about ostriches."

"What's that?" Tinman grumbled.

"They pack a mean punch," said Catfish and playfully slapped him on his shoulder.

"Ow!"

Like two prepubescent boys hearing someone fart in church, Bones and Catfish erupted into uncontrollable giggle fits. Bones grabbed his stomach and rocked back and forth. Tinman had to keep pushing him away from the gear shift. Catfish pounded on the back of the front seats, snot threatening to spill from his nose.

"Howzabout when he tried to give it the Heimlich maneuver!" screeched Catfish.

"And the ostrich started doing three sixties with Tinman's legs sailing through the air!" shouted Bones. "It was like a drunken helicopter!"

"I was not doing the Heimlich. I was done trying to save the miserable thing. I just figured I'd have better luck wrestling than I was having at boxing."

"I can understand that!" cried Catfish. "Hell, that damn bird reminded me of Bad Bennie Briscoe. Bobbing and weaving. Christ, you couldn't put a mitt on him!"

"Except when Tinman landed that left jab on his ass. Boy did that piss it off," Bones howled. "I never knew anybody got pecked with a giant beak. How's your head feel?"

Up until now, Tinman's head was feeling fine, despite the pecking. But with help from Bones and Catfish, the pain he was feeling in his torso, as a result of the epic brawl, was indeed creeping into his brain in the form of a migraine.

"Please tell me no one took pictures," said Tinman.

"You kidding? Hell, I wouldn't be surprised if you weren't on the local news tonight!" said Catfish.

"Wonderful," Tinman groaned. He had spent all his life successfully staying under the radar. Now he was famous for getting KO'd by a dumb bird.

"Well, after this, Virginia City is out for you Tinman, at least as far as the whiz goes," said Bones. "You're a celebrity. A real legend in your own mind."

"Knock it off."

Bones continued unabated. "I overheard people talking seriously about setting up more bouts for you. You know, like a tourist draw. Fact is, one guy said he has an emu he wants to line up against you right away."

"I'm warning you guys."

"That's on the straight!" said Bones.

"Christ."

"Say, maybe there's a real future in this," Catfish piped in. "You know, wait until the odds are right then lay down bets on the birds! Hell, it's a no-brainer! We'd clean up!"

Tinman tried to block them out as he concentrated on maneuvering through a near 360-degree hairpin turn at Geiger Point. As the road straightened out he could see a stretch ahead with no guardrails. Just to shut these two guys up, he was tempted to pull a Thelma and Louis, plummeting the car into the ravine below. But he was certain it would be a clear case of cutting off his nose to spite his face.

Bones glanced at Catfish and silently told him enough was enough. Catfish shrugged his shoulders in compliance.

Bones said, "Actually, it was a stroke of pure genius, brother."

"I'm telling you one more crack and we'll take the shortcut," Tinman threatened.

"On the up and up! You pulled off the best diversion I've ever seen any stall do."

Tinman was confused and had to think about this. "You mean you stayed on the whiz during all that?"

"Hell yes!" said Catfish. "You created the perfect moving crush! Every time the crowd would get static you kept them moving. It was Candyland!"

"It was particularly clever when you about pulled his tail off and he went nutso and chased you into that saloon," Bones mused.

"Downright brilliant!" Catfish agreed.

"Yeah, I'm really glad I thought of that," added Tinman.

"Sure. With all them drunk rufus' just waiting to be touched it was easy pickings. People were laughing so hard, the prat pokes were practically falling out on their own. All I had to do was collect 'em all up and pass 'em on to Catfish for the turnout."

"You're saying we harvested more than we originally thought?" asked Tinman.

"A lot more, pal," said Catfish. "I figure the knock-up increased maybe 30-35%."

The car fell silent with the news. Bones and Catfish grinned privately. They saw a little relaxing in Tinman's forehead and they knew he'd be just fine. It's one thing to make a fool of yourself and quite another to make money doing it.

"Well, then. I guess that's okay," said Tinman as he pulled out a wad of cash from his jacket and tossed it into Bones' lap. "This is the earlier take."

Bones reached a hand out to Catfish who obediently handed over his wad from the second half of the whiz. "Alright gentlemen, let's see what we have here," Bones cooed. As the cannon, it was his right to count the knock-up and split the take. His nimble fingers wasted no time in sifting and sorting the cash.

Before his arthritis, Bones' specialty was making a touch, turning out the wallet for valuables, and returning it from whence it came. All within four seconds or less. He would no longer attempt that move now, but Catfish once told Tinman that Bones could pick anything from anyone, anywhere, anytime. Tinman had no reason to doubt this.

But what always amazed Tinman was Bones' uncanny ability to read the eddies and movements of a crowd. He saw things others could not—mostly where the money was. He could glance at a gathering of fifty people and pick out the fat marks in seconds. He claimed people with money walked differently than those without. He would watch the rhythm of people's strides, their stance and build, their type of clothing and its fabric, and quickly determine if they had money, and if so, where it was on their body.

As a youth, Tinman often thought of it as X-ray vision but it was more than that. Bones had thieves' blood coursing through his veins. This only comes when you've been raised to be a thief by a thief, who was in turn raised by a thief, and so on. You had to have thieves' blood to sense the worth of a mark, otherwise known as grift sense.

The most important skill Bones had, however, was the ability to be invisible in a crowd. He was always meticulously rung up while on the whiz, his garb carefully chosen to fit in with whatever particular crowd he was working. He had an ease of manner and an air of confidence that belied his criminal intentions.

Once, as a young man and in a particularly foul mood, Tinman made the mistake of belittling Bones' skills and the whiz in general. It hit Bones hard. Catfish had taken Tinman aside and if it were not for their "family" relationship would have beaten him senseless. Instead, he impressed upon him in no uncertain terms exactly where Bones stood in the hierarchy of thieves.

In general, heavy-gees, or people considered to be in the upper echelon of crime, looked down on pickpockets. Catfish explained that in Bones' case his high level of skill was so admired if he were to walk into a room full of the country's top ten heavy-gees everyone there would jump to attention and offer their seat out of pure respect. From that day forward, Tinman never looked at Bones in the same way. He'd even discovered a descriptive word for him during one of his times through the dictionary: prestidigitator, a sleight-of-hand artist, a magician. Though Bones never could figure out how to spell it, he was honored, and Tinman was forgiven his transgression.

As they weaved down Mt. Davidson, the Great Basin Desert, the largest desert in the country, yawned at them from below. To the south was Mt. Bullion, no doubt named by some hopeful miners in the 1800's. Many towns and landmarks in this state were named similarly: Silver City, Eureka, Goldfield. The boom or bust mentality reigned mighty in Nevada. As a native, Tinman had it in his blood and he dutifully followed the siren's call when riches were to be had, regardless of the risk.

By the time they reached the bottom, Catfish and Bones were happily punching gun. Pickpockets never tire of retelling their conquests. "When you reefed the kick from that pappy I thought sure he was ranked and was gonna beef gun." "Hell, I was safe as Kelsey. No chance I was going to the floor with it. Now the bates with the dipsy in the britch kick, that was a helluva sneak job." "Can you believe no sucker trouble all day? Not a single dead skin, no pieces, smash, dribs, or drabs. What a beautiful day."

It was the height of criminal argot only the initiated could decipher. If he concentrated, Tinman could make out what was being said, but his mind was elsewhere. He was thinking about work and whether or not tonight would be the time when the tides would turn and life would get back to normal.

His given name was Trey Harrigan and he was born and raised in Reno. Before he was twenty he was on the road. He'd seen most of the big cities in the country and more than a few small ones. He liked the lifestyle, but circumstances forced him from it. The slow decline of his business had clipped his career short. He only returned to his hometown ten years ago, a disillusioned man in a crisis.

To avoid the dreaded Interstate 580, he took old Route 395 which somewhat followed the historic Virginia and Truckee Railroad line that had been used to transport miners and ore from Virginia City to the railroads in Reno.

It's not that he didn't like driving on highways, but the car he was piloting, which he'd bought when times were high, had not been legally registered for almost as long as he'd been back in the state. Instead, every year, some poor resident would wake up and find their tags had been carefully detached from their license plate. As far as he could remember, this year his Datsun was sporting tags from an Isuzu Trooper—a secret that would not be hidden long if a real trooper pulled him over. As long as he was a good boy on back roads, he was reasonably safe. Around town, he usually took cabs, or buses if he was really broke.

They passed the Bowers Mansion, a classic casualty of the boom or bust mentality. Eilley Bowers, The Queen of the Comstock, ran a boarding house for miners. When her boarders were unable to pay for their lodging she would accept payment in the form of mining claims. Unlike so many others, Eilley's claims hit pay dirt, producing $18,000 every week in gold and silver, roughly half a million at today's currency value. She and her third husband spared no expense building the Georgian mansion which had views of the mountains that had made her fabulously wealthy.

Shortly after the construction was completed, the mines went bust. The house was foreclosed on and Eilley spent the rest of her life drifting around the West telling fortunes with a crystal ball. She died a pauper in 1903. Boom or bust.

After traversing the ranch country, they entered the southern outskirts of Reno where the newly built cookie-cutter condominiums reigned supreme. They filled the valley like a bivouacked army of wealthy suburbanites preparing for the final onslaught on the dwindling territory of the poor urban dwellers.

It was always hard for Tinman to witness change. He had a distinct disdain for the modern world, and could never understand why things couldn't be left the way they were. He shared this notion with Bones but not Catfish. Conmen don't let the passing of time bother them. For their grift to stay viable they must change with society and remain young in spirit. They never live in the past and Tinman envied this.

Route 395 had now turned into Virginia Street, the main north-south road in Reno. They approached a bus stop at the intersection at McCarran, and he knew it as the former location of Lips, a shady bar frequented by criminals. In his late teens, he had attended a party there that became infamous in the annals of Reno crime. It was a happening that shaped his future and one he wished he could forget.

The humongous, glittering blue Peppermill Casino loomed a few blocks ahead. Tinman was always amused by the name and wondered why the gamblers never caught on to the allusion. Just like a real peppermill, the casino ground up the suckers and turned them into dust.

They moved into midtown on their way downtown. Despite its many changes, this was the Reno Tinman loved, as it still retained some degree of seediness, while much of the city was in the process of being prettified. When he was a kid he found a stack of old magazines in an alley behind a drug store. They were early editions of American Magazine. In one of them from the 30s a writer had described Reno as "a boil that's giving America a pain in the neck, or the last stand of individualism and right thinking."

He'd never forgotten it and liked to think of himself as the same thing. He grinned, knowing they can tear down all the buildings and paint pretty murals on walls and modernize all they want but they can never change the heart and soul of his hometown.

As they neared the new Virginia Street bridge spanning the Truckee River, Bones nudged him and he pulled over and parked. "What's the verdict?" Tinman asked.

Bones passed him a sheaf of neatly stacked bills and said, "Thirteen hundred and change." He handed Catfish his share and opened the door. "See you two at the birthday party tomorrow night. Don't be late, you know how she gets."

Catfish and Tinman groaned in unison, and they pulled back onto the road. An idiosyncrasy of pickpockets is they never tell even their closest associates where they live and it is considered rude to ask. Tinman knew damn well Catfish knew where Bones lived and vice versa. He, therefore, thought it was a little silly, but he recognized it as part of the code and never broke the rule. He assumed it had originally started as a way to protect oneself from the cops if a partner was picked up. What they didn't know didn't hurt you.

Catfish got out across from the Club Cal Neva. None of them were gamblers, so Tinman imagined he must be crashing in one of the many transient motels encircling the downtown casinos.

He turned east on Fourth street and headed for Sparks, Reno's sister city. This stretch of road between Reno and Sparks used to be a very busy thoroughfare. It was centrally located, so visiting gamblers could move between casinos in both cities. It was also part of the Lincoln Highway, the first transcontinental route in the country. Anyone driving from New York to San Francisco went right through the middle of Reno. Despite all the misplaced hype over Route 66, this was the original, "Main Street Across America," and it was over a thousand miles longer and more than a decade older.

Eventually, Interstate 80 was built and the Lincoln Highway crumbled. Consequently, East Fourth street was mostly deserted. Many of the old brick hotels built to house the soon-to-be-divorced who had come in the 40s, 50s, and 60s to get the "Reno Cure" were now abandoned and crumbling.

There were a few strip clubs, some dive bars, and lots of motels built during the heyday of the city's gambling era. Reno was filled with these old motels: the Castaway Inn, the Ho Hum Motel, the Wonder Lodge. Tinman knew them all. As a kid, he had lived in most. All of the establishments had seen better days.

None, however, were as bad as the All Inn Motel, he thought, as he turned into the deserted parking lot. He wondered—not for the first time—how he had sunk so low.

FIVE

THE ALL INN MOTEL had originally been called Everybody's Inn Motel, but when the present owner acquired the property she'd changed the name. It was apt since she was a poker player and had won the fleabag going all in during a high stakes game of Texas Hold 'em.

The parking lot featured two very lonely, dying trees. To the left was a used tire business, the office mostly invisible behind giant stacks of rotting tires. In the rear of the motel, a vacant lot held abandoned trucks and heavy construction equipment. The railroad tracks lay farther behind. It was not a pretty sight.

The current owner had no interest in running a motel and primarily kept it as a tax write-off. Tinman had an arrangement with her whereby if he paid the annual property taxes he could live there rent-free. Now all he had to do was figure out how he was going to scrape up this year's way overdue taxes.

The one-story motel was built in the classic L-shape design. All of the twenty guest rooms were boarded up except one at the far end. In front of this room were several stolen grocery carts piled high with bags of aluminum cans. They were owned by Rudy who occupied the room. He was the general of a small army of can collectors. He ruled the dumpsters of Reno and any collector who wanted to work his turf had to pay a tariff.

He also ran a bi-weekly poker game underneath the I-80 overpass, a short way up from Tinman's motel. The currency of the game was cans and from the new mountains adorning the front of his room, Tinman could tell Rudy must have had a good night with the cards.

They'd first met when Tinman moved into the motel. Tinman had immediately admired Rudy's initiative and they had worked out an agreeable arrangement so Rudy would not be homeless. At first, his minuscule rent was pocket change, but now Tinman looked forward to the first of the month.

At the far end of the L was where the original office was located, now sporting an illegible No Vacancy sign on the front window. Some clever manager had also decided to squeeze a little more change from the patrons by adding a small store called Everybody's Mini-mart—now obviously nobody's mini-mart.

Where the lines of the L met forming the corner of the building, a previous owner built a second-floor unit functioning as the manager's apartment and accessed by an outside staircase. It was one large room with various areas segmented into a kitchen, bedroom, living room, and attached bathroom. After Tinman moved in, he built a little sun deck and in good weather spent much of his time out there watching the trains. It was an abode but would never be home.

When he first left the road, he was able to afford a very nice apartment right next to Virginia Lake in southwest Reno. Within a year, he couldn't afford the rent and was forced to move. A consolation was that out of all the motels he lived in as a kid, this was not one of them. It was a small thing but meant a lot. He didn't like going backward.

To keep it away from the prying eyes of the cops, Tinman pulled his car around to the back. The sun was starting to fade as he stepped inside his unit. The place was sparsely furnished with a single bed, a bedside cabinet, a card table, two metal chairs, and a ratty recliner with a floor lamp next to a bookcase. A fourteen-inch television sat on top of the refrigerator but it was rarely used.

The bookcase housed his Webster's Dictionary, the Morris Dictionary of Word and Phrase Origins, the Prentice Hall Encyclopedia of World Proverbs (for kicks on a rainy day), and a worn copy of Roget's The New Thesaurus.

He didn't enjoy reading fiction though he did have two novels, On The Road and The Grapes of Wrath. He found Steinbeck's masterpiece in a motel room when he was still on the road. After reading the first page he couldn't put it down and blew off three days of work to finish it. When he reached the final word he sobbed like a baby and it was the first time he could recall ever crying as an adult. He just couldn't get over the selflessness of Rose of Sharon, losing her baby yet giving her mother's milk to a dying man.

Tinman thought of himself as a hard person with little compassion for others, his occupation demanded it. Yet here this little girl held a mirror up to him and he was ashamed to look. From that time, he'd try to spread a little goodwill if he could. It was most likely Rose of Sharon who had persuaded him to give Rudy a break.

He bought his copy of On the Road because he thought it would be something he could relate to. He'd had it for twenty years and had yet to finish it. Kerouac's vision of being on the road was nothing like his. He didn't do drugs or abuse alcohol which pretty much ruled out going on a road trip with Dean and Sal.

He did have a vice. He was a closet smoker when he could afford them, but never at work and never in public. He was afraid if some kid who looked up to him saw him smoking he would think it was a cool thing to do. Why any kid would look up to him was a question he had not yet dared to ponder.

The place was meticulously kept with everything in its proper spot. The kitchen was particularly well-equipped. He was a scratch cooker, having learned when he was very young. It was a matter of survival then, but now he truly enjoyed it.

He opened the refrigerator and lifted out a large container. When money was tight he would make a vat of soup. If he could afford ham he opted for a hearty thirteen bean soup. But these were lean times indeed and he was forced to settle for miso, using tofu, ginger, and various vegetables. For bulk, he threw in several packs of Ramen noodles without using the little packets of faux seasoning. He'd been subsisting off the same batch for over a week now and, though it was good, he was getting sick of it. He made a mental note to get groceries before he spent the rest of his whiz money at the birthday party the following evening.

While he ate, he let his mind go blank in preparation for the night's work. It was a ritual he always followed. He was a very disciplined man and normally his days ran like clockwork. He needed things to follow set patterns and he resisted any variance.

He allowed himself very few idle pleasures. One of them was baseball. He was obsessed with the pitching and loved to watch how spin affected the movement of the ball. He could watch an entire game and not know what the score was, his concentration never wavering from the pitcher's mound. Reno had a minor league team, the Aces, and the ballpark was just a short distance away. He used to have season tickets, but this year he couldn't afford them and it was breaking his heart.

In the closet near the bed was a collection of several kites: stunt kites, box kites, high-flying kites. It was his one secret pleasure and perhaps the only thing he did purely for fun. Just like everything in his life, however, even that became a competition. Take on Mother Earth and beat the wind. Still, he thought of it as fun. As long as he won.

He finished his soup and prepared himself for the evening. He changed out of his whiz outfit, transforming from a wannabe cowboy to something resembling a delivery guy at UPS. Because of their line of work, Bones and Catfish had extensive wardrobes and could dress up to fit in any crowd. For his job, Tinman preferred his everyman work clothes. Just another guy punching the clock.

From the closet, he retrieved his tool case which was a three-foot cylindrical tube. He locked the front door and started down the stairs. His cab was already waiting. He had a longtime deal with Garshasp, an Iranian cab driver, who agreed to give him a low weekly rate for transporting him to and from his workplace. They couldn't understand each other past "Hi" and "Here's your money." The arrangement suited them perfectly.

On the way to work, Tinman fought to keep down the creeping depression that comes from knowing one's endeavors are fruitless. He had to remain hopeful. It was the only thing keeping him going, and sane.

In Midtown, just off Virginia, Garshasp stopped in front of a brick building with plate glass windows painted black. Above the door, a neon sign read, McCue's. Tinman hated the name. To him, a pool hall is a church, a sacred place. Any decent hall deserved a name that honored the greatest game ever devised.

Pool was his work, his life, his religion, and the only thing he was ever really good at. And he was very, very good. In truth, Tinman was quite possibly one of the greatest pool hustlers ever to wield a stick. The problem was he was born twenty years too late. For several years after he hit the road, the game was alive and well. Now pool was dead. And whether he liked the name of this hall or not, it was the only place in Reno that could even be remotely considered a pool hall, and, so, it was home.

There were pool tables in bars but they were not regulation size and usually, the cloth was paper-thin, the rails soft, the pockets weak and they were not level. He sighed and climbed out of the cab. The biggest problem, however, was the lack of players. No one aspired to master the game anymore. It required concentration and patience which was unacceptable to the distracted society of today. Those that did achieve any proficiency were hesitant to bet big money.

He stepped inside the empty hall and waved at Amber. The place was owned by a rich guy from Truckee but he could care less if it made a profit as it was a tax break, and he had only visited twice in the last five years. Amber ran the operation. She was in her 40's and plump in all the right places. When she first started working there, she'd had a fling with the owner and threatened to tell his wife if she didn't get complete control.

She and Tinman had a very copacetic relationship. They enjoyed fake flirting but nothing serious had ever happened. This was mostly Tinman's doing. He knew if he had a fling and later things soured, he'd still have to see her every day and it could make things very uncomfortable in the hall. It may even throw off his game which was not worth the fleeting pleasure an affair would provide.

Amber instinctively knew Tinman's reasons why their relationship remained platonic but didn't hold it against him. She'd even given him a key to the place so he could practice during closed hours. She also usually waived the regular table rate during open hours. In exchange, he cut her in on any action she steered his way. If she saw a loaded mark, Tinman would get a call and immediately drop what he was doing and race to the hall. These days, however, the action was so off she was forced to charge him the regular hourly rate of four dollars. He usually hit the hall in the early afternoon and practiced until dark. If there was going to be any action, that's when it would show up.

"You're late," Amber shouted.

"I was whizzing," Tinman replied.

"It took you four hours to take a leak?"

"I was taking my time."

Amber nodded knowingly. "Bum prostate, huh."

"Yeah, but it didn't affect my performance."

"That's good . . . but, hey! Then why did it take you so long? I mean the prostate's connected to—"

"The neck bone," Tinman warbled.

"Huh?"

"And the neck bone's connected to the toe bone."

"It is not!"

"And the toe bone's connected to the head bone. Now hear the word of the Lord!" He finished with a flourish.

Amber flung a cube of chalk at him which he deftly caught. "I hate when you're in a good mood," she said and spun around heading for the far end of the bar.

"Dem bones, dem bones, dem dry bones."

"SHUT UP!"

The hall had twelve tables and a large wraparound bar. There was also a foosball table, air hockey table, and two pinball machines that, fortunately, had been broken for over two years. Amber suspected it was Tinman's doing but had no proof. The worst thing was a digital jukebox dominating one corner. The volume was purposefully set at high and he thought its very existence in the hall was an abomination.

McCue's had started out attempting to be a real pool hall but as the players dwindled it crept ever closer to being just a bar that happened to have some pool tables. The cloth was quality—five years ago. But it was sorely in need of replacement. Fortunately, the tables were all regulation size Brunswick with one Olhausen Grand Champion Tournament Series, which was Tinman's table. It was left covered unless he uncovered it. Amber made no exceptions.

Tinman opened his cue case. It was designed to hold two cues. He slid out his practice cue. He'd bought it when he was really rolling and it was a true work of art. Custom-made to his specifications by McDermott, perhaps the best pool cue manufacturer in the country, it weighed 21 ounces with a shaft diameter of 13mm, and the handle was beautifully inlaid with turquoise, silver, snakewood, and ebony.

Twenty-five years ago, it cost him eleven thousand dollars. No matter how bad things got financially he would never sell it. It would be like cutting off one of his limbs. Ironically, he never used it when working because it would scare off the marks. He screwed the two pieces together, uncovered the Olhausen, and leaned his cue against it.

He opened his case again and slid out his work cue which was a Meucci, another fine brand. This one was completely unadorned and referred to as a Sneaky Pete. It was the preferred type of cue for almost all good hustlers. In quality, balance, and power the cue rivaled his practice cue but it looked exactly like any cheap house cue so it didn't alert the suckers.

He placed the cue in the cue rack closest to him and stowed his case behind the bar. Amber smacked his butt. "You are one crafty bastard, Tinman."

"Takes one to know one," said Tinman.

He retrieved his practice cue and starting gliding balls around the table. As he shot, his body and movements changed. He became fluid, his stroke smooth as silk. He stalked the table looking for the geometric patterns formed by the balls' random positions, always seeking out the proper way to clear the table.

He was a natural and completely self-taught. In his bedside cabinet, he had a weathered 1968 copy of, Willie Mosconi on Pocket Billiards. It was a small manual with just over a hundred pages. Catfish and Bones bought it new for a buck and gave it to him on his ninth birthday. It was the only formal training he ever had.

When he was ten he ran a hundred and twenty-two balls straight. It was at his favorite hall back then, The Silver Cue, and the owner was so impressed he called the local newspaper. Bones and Catfish had to pay the sports reporter $50 to kill the story before press time. They had foresight and didn't want anybody to know how good he was. The lesson was embedded in Tinman. The pool hustler's mantra: never show your speed.

The front door swung open and four punks in their early 20's strode in like they owned the place. Tinman had never seen them so he knew they'd never been there. Amber distracted them by asking for their IDs while Tinman quickly stashed his practice cue behind the bar.

As he went back to his table he could tell with a glance there was only one player amongst them, the guy with the oversized pants and his butt crack showing. He was eying Tinman as his pals ordered beers. He figured him for a penny-ante player but hoped he was wrong.

Tinman acted as if he'd just showed up at the hall and made a big deal of sizing up the house cues. He selected his Sneaky Pete and started missing balls. Butt Crack wandered over and leaned on the pocket Tinman was aiming for.

One of his buddies turned on the jukebox and some rapper with misogynist tendencies started screaming out obscenities in an infantile attempt to debase women while sounding sexy. It made Tinman's head hurt, but he stood up from his stance and waited for the play.

"Yo! You just beating off or you want to play for real?" asked Butt Crack.

Tinman said, "Well, I'm not sure I know what you mean by for real."

Butt Crack and his crew snickered like a pack of hyenas. "Yo, what I mean is you wanna play a man's game?"

"Oh, geez, I don't know. I just play to relax after work. What do you have in mind? I don't know many games."

Butt Crack grinned like he was reeling in a twenty-pound trout. "Yo! Eight ball. What other game is there dude? I play you for three dollars a game. Hah!"

Sigh.

Tinman looked to the ceiling like he was calculating if he could afford the stakes. It was low points in his life like this when he wondered, "Where in the hell is Peach?"

Six

IT WASN'T THE RUMBLE OF THE TRAINS that woke him so early. It was The Feeling. He'd first felt it when he was very young, maybe even in the womb of his mother—whoever that was. He learned what it meant at an early age. It was primal. But this time he just couldn't believe it. It didn't make sense and he couldn't stand things that didn't make sense. He'd been lying in bed for the last two hours wondering if he'd truly felt it. He was sure he had. But why now?

He couldn't think of it anymore. He climbed out of his single bed and hit the shower. Perhaps he could wash it out of his mind. As he bathed he did his best to block it out. Normally, he prided himself in taking a three-minute shower. After all, this was the West where drought was a persistent concern. This morning, however, he took extra time cleansing every part of his body. He even hooked each foot up over his knee for a proper scrubbing. First, the right one where he discovered he would soon need to clip his nails. Then the left where he discovered— AGGHH.

Like most people who grew up with little access to hospitals, doctors—even Band-Aids, Tinman was a hypochondriac. Some people like to flaunt their imaginary illnesses but he thought it was a sign of weakness so he was a closet hypochondriac. Still, any itch, twitch, blotch, or glitch in his physical state of being, gave him a bad case of the jitters.

Even if he had the money and the inclination to get health insurance, he would never ever let anyone poke and probe and know things about his insides that he could never fathom. In his estimation, going to a doctor was a form of rape, an involuntary baring of one's insides to a perfect stranger. He would not be a party to it. Fortunately, the issue rarely came up because he usually came to his senses and realized the evil spot of melanoma on his neck was merely a harmless spider bite.

That's why when he found the strange growth he panicked. This was no figment of his imagination. This was real, tangible. A bump on the bottom of his left foot. It was beyond his knowledge and experience and, though he couldn't face it, may require the intervention of another person. An intrusion into his private life. The thought was unbearable and he quickly discarded it. There had to be another way.

Naturally, the first option was to go into denial. Let the subconscious mind fret while sleeping, thereby leaving the conscious mind blissfully and ignorantly free of any fear. The second option was to cut off the foot to save the rest of the body. His left foot was only used for his stance at the table and he was fairly certain some form of prosthetic would do the trick. He imagined if he strapped on a block of wood to the stump he would still be able to shoot. The third and final solution—always the final solution—was to simply succumb. Let the freakish growth take over his body, his mind, his soul, and he would pass into the other side.

It came to him that option one and three were similar, if not identical, in that the ultimate result would be the same. But he had no patience for the meanderings of an addled brain. He needed a distraction. He didn't feel like working and hadn't planned on it anyway. The birthday party was tonight and there was no point spending the day at the hall.

He quickly dressed making pains not to touch the mysterious bump for fear of it spreading and expediting his imminent demise. Baseball. That was it. The Aces had made it into the Pacific Coast League playoffs and were scheduled for a Sunday day game. Most of the whiz money was earmarked for the party and the rest for food. Yet he figured the scratch he'd taken off Butt Crack would buy him a general admission ticket for the common grassy area. The Cracker Jacks, however, were out. As suspected, Butt Crack was not a high roller.

A Quick March at 140 beats per minute got him to the ticket counter in twenty minutes. The ballpark was part of a downtown renovation and it was one of the few additions to the city of which Tinman approved. Before the stadium, a fire station and a dirt lot were the only features. He couldn't quite get his brain around the design. It was sort of "Modern Abstract Erector Set," but it didn't bother him. It held just over nine thousand people and he could tell from the lines today's game would be at capacity. Baseball was his only activity that involved being around lots of people but for some reason, it didn't produce a headache.

Once inside, he shuffled along with the crowd and became instantly envious when some lucky person with a ticket for an actual seat peeled off down one of the aisles. In the distance, was his destination. The general admission ticket allowed him onto the grassy berm located behind right center field. The only saving grace was it overlooked both bullpens and he was able to watch the pitchers warming up during the game.

He continued around the concourse with the luxury skyboxes overhead. Below was home plate and in between, his old seat, Section 110, Row 6, Seat 1. The seat he'd had since the stadium opened. The seat that had a perfect view of the ball as it released from the pitcher's hand. He tried to resist the urge to look but failed. An old biddy who would've looked more at home at a knitting bee was perched on the seat like a false goddess. He'd be willing to bet all his whiz money the Queen of Sheba couldn't tell the difference between a low outside fastball and a slider. It made him sick. Life is not at all fair. Fare is what you pay the cabbie, or the bus driver if you're broke.

He lumbered past first base and the concession stands and an eternity later reached the common grassy area. People had brought their lawn chairs and children were racing around with absolutely no interest in the upcoming game. "Don't the parents realize they'd rather be playing video games?" he muttered to himself. "Let them rot their eyes at home. Why bring them here to screw up the game for serious fans?" In his view, children were not considered desirables.

"Hey old man, you stepped on my foot!" yelped one of the brats. Tinman walked on. The hell with the kid. Nobody could prove he did it on purpose.

He muscled his way through the rabble and secured a place at the railing directly over the bullpens. With great fanfare, the playoff game began. The Aces were playing the Fresno Grizzlies. Most Triple-A games featured several pitchers because minor league teams rarely had great pitching. Though Tinman was too far away to see the mound, he felt certain he would be able to spend the afternoon happily observing the relievers as they warmed up.

He was wrong. Because it was an important playoff game, both teams had sent out their aces and they were both pitching gems with no need for relievers. It was a pitching duel and Tinman couldn't see a damn thing.

His fascination with pitching began shortly after he discovered the use of spin in pool. He saw the similarities between the effect a pitcher's release has on a baseball to the English a pool cue has on the cue ball. The game of baseball held little interest but he never tired of analyzing the pitching.

Much of the first half of the game he spent growling at children who came too close to his personal space. This pleasant diversion helped him temporarily forget the dreaded protuberance on his foot but he was still having trouble with The Feeling.

It was like waking up with "Muskrat Love" in your head and no matter how much it mangles your soul you just can't shake it. Worse yet, it was getting more pronounced. While he was considering this a long ball heading directly for him threatened to clear the wall. He was oblivious to it and the roar of the crowd. Seeing the trajectory of the ball, several children clustered around, hoping to catch it. Tinman barked at them and the ball landed smack onto the back of a departing youth.

As the hapless kid wailed, Tinman slipped from the crowd and ended up on the back walkway that ran from right center to left center field. Standing directly behind the mound, it seemed a million miles away. He strained his eyes but could barely make out the next pitch. He guessed maybe it was a fastball only because of the awkward swing by the batter. He was just thinking of leaving when someone gave him a noogie.

He turned around and there was Peach. Sure, he was a little shorter and thinner than Tinman, their eyes were different colors and Peach's hair was light brown but one look at their faces and there was no doubt they were twins—fraternal, to be exact.

"Want some?" Peach asked, offering a half-eaten box of Cracker Jacks.

"I already had a box," said Tinman.

"What was the prize?"

"A ring whistle."

"Oh, you hate those things."

"Yeah."

The two stared at each other. They had once been inseparable. Now both wondered what relationship was left.

Peach said, "You don't seem surprised to see me."

"Very funny," said Tinman.

Peach grinned. He knew all about The Feeling. There was a time when their two minds practically worked as one.

"Yeah, I knew you were coming. But how did you know I'd be here?" asked Tinman.

"I nosed around. You know, finding where the best tables were. Got steered over to McCue's. Man, what a dump. But that Amber, she's a real sweetheart, and she loves you!"

"Sure," said Tinman. "Who doesn't."

"Right. So when you weren't there I figured you were killing time before mom's birthday party tonight. No wind so I knew kites were out. Then I saw the new stadium and figured you had to be here."

"I'm surprised you even remembered Dez's birthday. And she's not our mom," said Tinman, turning back to the field.

"I say tomato and you can say whatever. Anyway, how could I forget?" said Peach and he leaned against the railing, their shoulders barely touching.

"I don't know, Peach. It's only been, what, fifteen years," snarled Tinman. "You sure you're even invited?"

The crack of a bat resounded throughout the stadium. A player for the Grizzlies slid safely into second.

"Hell, I'm always invited! I'm the life of the party!" declared Peach.

"Not for a long time," Tinman muttered.

Both of them were at a loss for words. Peach stared into his box of Cracker Jacks and located the prize. He excitedly dug it out and found a miniature magnifying glass. He held it up to one eye and closely examined Tinman's ear.

Tinman swatted it away like a gnat. "You should hold that up to yourself."

Another crack of the bat and the Grizzlies have men on first and third.

"You think she's mad at me?" asked Peach. Tinman stared at him as if to say, "Are you really that stupid?" Peach grinned stupidly as if to say, "Probably." Tinman leaned back onto the railing.

Peach straightened up and examined the stadium. "They did a nice job with this place."

"Uh-huh."

"Sure beats the Moana Municipal Stadium," Peach continued.

"Uh-huh."

"Remember when we used to sneak in there to see the Silver Sox play?"

"Uh-huh." Tinman, determined to give the cold shoulder, peered out over the field trying desperately to see what the next pitch was.

"I figured you for season tickets right behind home plate," said Peach, attempting to break the ice.

"Used to. Every year since they opened. I was, uh, late this year and they sold out."

"Huh. Say these guys are getting clobbered," said Peach. "Let's go do something else."

"There's still time," said Tinman leaning farther over the railing.

"You ever think about getting binoculars?"

"Knock it off!" Tinman snapped, swinging around to Peach. He was actually more irked at himself for not thinking of binoculars. Damn it to hell.

The batter for the Grizzlies connected solidly and the ball soared towards center field. Tinman stared angrily at his brother who was ignoring him as he studied the sky. Peach suddenly dropped his box of Cracker Jacks and adroitly caught the home run ball. A kid ran up with hopeful eyes.

"Here you go, pal," said Peach tossing the ball to the kid. He turned back to Tinman and grinned. "Cute kid, huh?"

Tinman grimaced. "Let's get out of here."

SEVEN

OUTSIDE, THE TWO BROTHERS WALKED SIDE BY SIDE, Peach bopping along to a happy song and Tinman marching to a dirge. "You hungry?" Peach asked.

Tinman saw him looking across the street in the direction of the old Santa Fe Hotel, owned by a Basque family who had been serving authentic food for over fifty years. Over those years, Harrah's Casino had mushroomed and now owned everything in the block but the old brick building built in the 1900s as a boarding house for Basque immigrants. It was now sandwiched in between parking garages. "Haven't been in there for a while. I'm glad to see they haven't sold out. Best tongue stew and Picon Punch west of the Pyrenees."

"Eh, never could stand Basque food. I was thinking of that place," said Peach.

He pointed at a large sign hanging over the entrance to one of the parking garages, advertising, "Harrah's Hash House a Go-Go."

Tinman sighed. "I lost my appetite."

"Oh. Okay. Say, I got it! Let's go play some golf," said Peach. "I can't tell you when the last time was."

Tinman was determined to find out why his brother had chosen this moment to show up. And he knew he was only going to find out when Peach got his way. "Fine, I know a place," said Tinman. "It's new."

"Aw, man. What about our old course?" Peach complained.

"It's too far away."

"Hell, I got a car," Peach countered.

Tinman stopped walking and examined him. "You have a car?"

"Sure, doesn't everyone? Say, you still have the 280Z?"

"Yeah. Come on, this place is near the Grand Sierra," said Tinman. Peach was perplexed but tried to hide it. "Used to be the MGM Grand, then Bally's, then the Reno Hilton, remember?"

"Right, right. Things sure do change," said Peach.

"I know. I hate it."

"Hey, all things gotta change."

"Why?" asked Tinman.

Peach cracked up. "All things but you, brother, all things but you. Come on, car's over here."

* * *

Peach's car, if it really was his car, was a 2004 Ford Taurus Wagon, painted in Arizona Beige Metallic. It was not what you would call flashy. There were no dings or dents and seemed to run like someone was actually taking care of it. The back seats had been removed to increase the wagon area. A brown tarp covered what appeared to be a large rectangular box that filled the rear space. The side and back windows were tinted.

Tinman's doubts over ownership of the car came because he had never known his brother to own anything. If it was his, he wondered what he was doing that would allow him to afford it. He decided to let it rest for now. He needed to know if his presence in Reno was a prelude to some disaster or if the disaster had already struck and he was here for help.

"I just can't get over this town!" said Peach. "I always remember it as being so gritty. Now it's bright and, well, it feels reborn."

Tinman said, "I prefer gritty."

"Look! There's another one," said Peach. "I love those things!" He was pointing out a five-story high mural painted vertically on the side of a parking garage next to the Bowling Stadium. It showed a young woman's shoulders and head, painted in blue, with a giant red rose blooming where her brain should be.

"It's graffiti," said Tinman. "The tagger should be arrested."

"They're so creative. And they're everywhere. When I was in Midtown looking up McCue's I saw one that really knocked me out. It was in this alley, see, behind some tattoo shop. Just a dumpy little alley with garbage cans and—"

"Rats and pigeons and bums and—"

"Lo and behold, there's this mural! I mean it's inside the alley filling up one entire wall. It must be twenty feet by fifty or something," Peach continued. "And the crazy thing is you wouldn't even see it unless you were in the alley—"

"Shooting up heroin, or taking a leak, or rolling a drunk—"

"And it's a masterpiece, I tell you. The centerpiece is this monster-like creature that looks like a cross between a dragon, a tiger—"

"And Dez when she's pissed off," added Tinman.

"Sort of, yeah. Say you seen it already?"

"No. But I saw where you were going."

"Right. Anyway, it's painted these vibrant colors, neon blue and orange with purple highlights, and the fangs are bright yellow and it looks like this thing could come alive any second and leap off the wall and eat you. A real thing of beauty."

"In the eye of the present beholder."

"Exactly! But the mysterious thing is this artist puts it in a place where you have to find it. It's not out in the open, saying, "Here I am!" I think that's amazing. Art for art's sake."

"You've changed," Tinman observed.

"Thanks!" said Peach. "What's the fastest way there?"

A quick jog down Second Street brought them into the Grand Sierra sprawl from the north, where Grand Adventure Land was located. In general, casinos can no longer rely on gaming receipts to remain viable. To fill the coffers, they've come up with all kinds of hooks to lure the people in: arcades, laser tag, climbing walls, anything to bring out the kid in all of us.

It took no prodding for Peach to find his inner child. As soon as they hit the parking lot, he jumped out of the car and began to explore. Grand Adventure Land boasted four separate tracks for go-karts, a miniature golf course, and The Ultimate Rush which was restricted for the legally insane. It consisted of several giant poles on which a body sling was attached to long straps. For a mere $25 you could risk your life by being hoisted to the top of the swing and released, sending you swooping down 180 ft. at a speed of 65mph.

Peach was eager to try it, but Tinman insisted on the saner activity of mini-golf. The course was only six dollars a round. Peach offered to pay for both of them but Tinman insisted on covering his own. Still, the offer to pay was strange and he was quite sure he'd never experienced such a thing from his brother. His suspicions were definitely on the rise.

They walked around the go-kart tracks and headed for the course which sat just off the launching pad for The Ultimate Lunacy. They stepped into a little building where they picked out clubs and got a scorecard. Once on the course, Peach was dumbfounded.

"Where are the windmills and the waterwheels? Jeez! There's no clown where you have to get the ball in the mouth! What is this place?" Peach asked.

"It's a new kind of course. No gimmicks. The holes are laid out like a real golf course with little rolling hills, doglegs, and traps. It's supposed to be more challenging."

The crestfallen look on Peach's face showed he was not impressed. Nevertheless, he quickly shook it off and placed his ball at the first hole. "Remember when we used to play on the South Virginia course. We always talked about owning our own mini-golf." He gently tapped the ball and got a good lie on the pocket sitting just behind a rock strategically placed in the center of the fairway.

Tinman placed his ball on the tee box. "As I recall, all you talked about was how we could rob the place."

"Well, naturally that too."

"Which we did."

"Sure, so we could have the cash to build our own. Why else?"

Tinman firmly hit his ball which just as firmly smacked into the center rock and rolled back to the tee. He sighed and leaned over for another try. "I see. And what about the grocery store and the five and dime we hit?"

"Sue me. I wanted to be a merchant. You need money to buy a store. By the way, that's one stroke."

"Thanks for keeping count." Tinman shot again and hit the rock with similar results. "And I suppose you wanted to be a banker, too."

Peach smirked. "Remember that! I go in all gung-ho and then realize it's closing time and they lock the door on me. I had to get the assistant manager to let me out! Thank goodness I hadn't got to the teller yet."

"Yeah, then I had to go back the next week and get it right," said Tinman as he lined up his shot again.

"Hey, we cleared three grand as I recall."

"And made all the papers. That was loads of fun."

"You need to hit it softer with a little angle if you're going to clear that thing," Peach offered.

Tinman waved him off then did as he was instructed and was rewarded with a decent lie. "Look, I don't want to talk about old times and how close we were to spending our youth in prison."

"Sure thing," said Peach, sinking his ball. Tinman followed suit and they moved to the second hole.

Behind them, a recent escapee from the mental institute was being suited up in the sling for The Ultimate Stupidity. Once strapped in, the attendee slowly hoisted him up into the air.

Tinman was struggling with a hole where the ball had to jump over an opening in the fairway which spanned a little creek. His ball had fallen into the water four times already and the hole was a par three. Peach had birdied the hole and was leaning on his club, admiring his hero.

From as early as he could remember, Tinman was his idol. For some people, it can be tough growing up with a wunderkind. Peach, however, had never resented the fact Tinman was born with uncanny skill and natural talent. There was no rivalry, only a desire on his part to somehow make his brother proud. Indeed, Tinman had been the main motivation for them parting ways and Peach learning a real trade. He wasn't sure his brother would approve of his chosen career, but he knew he owed him for what he had become and he would never forget it.

"So tell me about your latest conquests," said Peach. "I always loved hearing how you took out some chump on the table."

Tinman was concentrating hard on his next shot. The maximum number of strokes for any hole was seven and he was getting close. He pretended he hadn't heard Peach.

"Come on, man! Give me the skinny!" Peach urged.

Tinman stroked, the ball glided down the fairway, went aloft over the creek, hit the far edge, and plopped into the water. He looked to Peach. "You want to know?! I haven't tapped serious money in five years, maybe longer. Pool is dead. My action is over."

The madman in the sling was released and with a bloodcurdling scream plunged headfirst to the ground. It unnerved Peach but not as bad as Tinman's revelation. He had always been the stable one. Always the one with money and action. The man who walked into a pool hall and slew all those silly enough to take him on. It hit Peach like one of those giant mallets Wile E Coyote bought from the Acme Company. His brother's mood and behavior suddenly made sense, and it about brought tears.

"Why aren't we playing at our old course?" he asked.

"Because they charge $12 a round, okay!" Tinman retrieved his ball and again placed it on the tee box. He lined up his shot and decided the hell with it. He swung his club back and banged the ball out of the course, across the road, and into the Grand Sierra parking lot. "This is stupid, let's get out of here."

He flung his club away and marched through the course. Peach chuckled as he followed. "You know, I almost forgot how much fun it is hanging out with you."

As they approached the car Peach called out. "I meant to ask you, what's with the hair?"

Tinman spun around. "It's always been like this since I was sixteen. Or did you forget that too?"

"No, not the white—"

"Silver."

"Silver, right. I mean, the mullet."

"What are you talking about?" Tinman sputtered.

"Who's been cutting it? You look like MacGyver."

Ouch. It was a low blow and Tinman's proud countenance finally collapsed. "I've been doing it myself. I can't reach back there."

Peach covered as quickly as he could. "Damn, you do a pretty good job! Maybe you could just get a little trim to even things out, you know, you want to look good for the party, right?"

Tinman's embarrassment was palpable and he was having no luck hiding it. Peach stepped up and put an arm around him. "You got a regular place. I mean, you used to go to?" Tinman nodded weakly. "Okay, then, let's go have a visit. My treat."

"I got it covered!"

"Okay, okay."

"I was on the whiz Saturday with Bones and Catfish."

Peach couldn't help himself and let out a guffaw. He quickly regretted it as he felt Tinman's shoulders slouch. "Hey, you gotta do what you gotta do. But let me tell you something brother. Things are about to turn around for us."

"How do you know? You suddenly become a psychic?"

"I just know. Leave it at that for now. Come on, let's go get you prettified. I think that's a word."

"Yes, it's a word. Right after Pretorius and before prettily."

"Is that a fact! And what is a Pretorius?"

"It's not a thing it's a guy."

"Interesting. You can tell me all about him on the way there."

They took Kuenzli St. east back into downtown where it met Lake St. near where the Truckee River bends. In the wild, old days, this area had been home to The Stockade, perhaps the country's most notorious legal whorehouse. Reno had never been shy about bucking the system. Perhaps it's one of the reasons why many of its longtime residents lived, shall we say, alternative lifestyles.

Heading north on Lake, Peach continued to marvel at the transformation of his home town. It irritated Tinman to no end that his brother apparently liked what had occurred. He knew, however, it wouldn't last. There were a few changes he was certain would burst his brother's happy bubble.

Their destination was BJ's Hair Shop at the corner of Fifth St. and Evans. As they drove, Peach tested his memory of the city.

"Okay, now I remember. So if we were to continue on Lake and take a left on Seventh St. then a right on North Virginia it would take us up the hill past the university and the planetarium and of course the Historical Society Museum. Remember that place."

"I'd almost forgotten. Thanks a lot," grumbled Tinman. "Just turn here, will you. It's a block up on the left."

BJ's Hair Shop sat in the middle of a small, single-story row of mostly empty storefronts. On the front window, their motto read: "If We Can't Make You Look Good, YOU'RE UGLY." Tinman had to sock Peach to stop him from laughing as they climbed out of the car and crossed the street.

"I should have made an appointment," said Tinman. "You usually need an appointment."

"Don't fret it. They'll take one look at you and immediately clear their slate."

This deserved another sock in the arm but Tinman resisted. A pool player must protect his hands at all costs. A little bell rang when they stepped inside. In the center of the room was a barroom-sized pool table with excellent felt. Along the far wall were six chairs, all full. The haircutters were all women. They all wore t-shirts proudly declaring, I Love BJ's. Each of them gave a cursory glance at the newcomers.

When the stylist working station two looked over, the scissors she was wielding froze mid-air. She slowly turned and approached, her eyes widening in rage. The place became silent as the other cutters watched the impending showdown. Tinman instinctively backed away until the front counter prevented any further retreat. When she was just a foot away, she bellowed, "WHAT HAVE YOU DONE!"

Tinman tried to respond but making excuses was never his strong point. "Do you know that you are a walking billboard! How many customers am I going to have if they see you looking like that!"

"I'm sorry Lucille," he mumbled. It was Lucille and God help you if you called her Lucy, despite her flaming red hair. She also sported a set of boobs you could use as a bean bag chair if you were gutsy. "I've been a little short lately."

"That is not an excuse to ruin my business! Sit down, grab a beer, and shut up." She whirled around and stomped back to her station.

"Beer?" asked Peach.

"They're only for customers!" ordered Lucille over her shoulder. She had very good hearing to boot.

"Sounds good!" Peach piped in. "Sign me up!"

"Ginger, he's next," Lucille called to the pretty blonde stylist at the end of the row.

"Check," said Ginger.

Tinman and Peach grabbed two Sierra Nevada ales from the small refrigerator and retreated to the bar stools near the pool table. "This place is beautiful!" said Peach. "I never seen a barbershop like it!"

"Yeah, I keep telling them they should get a regulation table, but no one listens to me," said Tinman.

"Eh, you're just a pool snob," Peach said as he stood and headed for the pool cue rack.

Lucille quickly wrapped up her client and snapped her fingers in the direction of Tinman. With head bent, he shuffled over to her station and sat down. He was hoping his punishment was over. It wasn't. As soon as he was settled, Lucille head-slapped him not once but three times. She was that overcome with grief.

A few minutes later, Peach was beckoned by Ginger and he skipped her way. As the cuttings proceeded, Peach spent his time flirting with his lovely stylist and thinking about his brother's situation.

It's a matter of pride to class thieves to always look good. First, it shows other thieves you're doing well, even if you're not. And second, for cover, it was necessary to look as good as the normal Joe. You had to blend in to throw off any suspicion. If Tinman had come so low he couldn't even swing for a decent haircut, it meant times were tougher than he'd let on.

Tinman noticed that at first, Lucille was being a little rougher on him than usual. Normally she would ask him to turn this way or that, now she just grabbed his head and yanked it to the position she wanted. He did not dare complain.

As the cut went on, however, she softened and became the gentle expert she was. When Tinman found the place, he knew right off it was a gem. All the stylists were pros and they were serious about their motto. And let's face it, what barbershop has a pool table, regulation or no. If forced, they would accept women but mostly it was a guy's place and that was that.

As Lucille neared the end of the cut she wrapped a warm towel around Tinman's neck. She broke out her old fashioned flip-open razor and honed it with a strop. When it was sharp enough to slice through bone, she whipped off the towel with a flourish and placed the razor under Tinman's neck.

"Don't do this ever again," she hissed in a voice only he could hear. Tinman gingerly shook his head, careful not to upset the razor. "Promise?" she asked with a sweet smile. He nodded his head lightly.

It was difficult to get Peach out of the place. He and his stylist were whooping it up, giggling and making funny faces at each other. Tinman had to intercede and managed to get him to the front counter. He reached for his wallet, but Peach was quicker. He peeled several bills from a healthy wad and plopped them down. With all the girls around, Tinman was not in a position to argue, especially when Peach told them he was covering the cuts to pay off a debt.

When they hit the light of day, they were indeed looking sharp. BJ's had done its magic and they were styling once more. They also looked even more like twins—except for their clothes. Tinman had thrown on a t-shirt and jeans to go to the ballgame while Peach was dressed in black, sateen pants from Calvin Klein and a lilac, linen, sport shirt.

"Man, that place is the deal. I never looked so good," said Peach as they got into his car. "So what do you say, let's go see mom."

This urgency to face the music with Dez perplexed Tinman. He knew Peach must be nervous, so why so anxious to get on with the thrashing? "We've got at least a couple of hours before we need to be there. What's the rush?"

Peach looked away and started fumbling with his keys. Something he had not done up to this point. Tinman noticed his hands were shaking a little. "No rush! It's just, you know, been a long time and well, it was just that—"

Tinman calmly let him babble on for a while, never quite completing a sentence and not quite getting the ignition key in the cylinder. When his patience had run its course he grabbed Peach's hand.

"Why are you here?" he asked. He was wearing a look Peach was very familiar with. It said, "Lie to me and you're toast."

Peach could hardly contain himself. He'd been wanting to tell him all day but couldn't find the perfect moment. One look at Tinman told him that perfect or no this was the moment.

"Okay, take a step back in time with me," he began. Tinman's eyes narrowed. "The year is 1978."

"I remember it like it was yesterday—unfortunately."

"Specifically, December."

"Yeah."

"Does the name Dat So La Lee ring a bell?"

"No. Should it?"

"How about baskets?"

Tinman thought hard. "You mean the Christmas baskets we stole?"

"Bingo!" Peach cried.

"What about them?"

"Those puppies are worth a million bucks a pop right now," said Peach, dropping the bomb.

Tinman relaxed his grip on Peach's hand. The two met eyes and the sparkle lit up the car.

"Let's go see Dez."

Peach barked out a laugh and fired up the car. He stopped and looked Tinman up and down. "Don't you want to change? I mean to go with the new cut?"

"You're right."

"Where do you live?"

"A hole in the wall."

"Street Journal."

"Huh?"

"You remember," said Peach. "Before and after. You said 'A hole in the wall' and I said 'Street Journal.' So it becomes 'A hole in the Wall Street Journal.' "

"You still doing that?"

"The show's still on. Why wouldn't I?"

Tinman sighed, a silly grin creeping onto his face for the first time in years. And why not? In a few short hours, he was going to be sitting pretty.

EIGHT

WHEN PEACH FIRST SAW WHERE HIS BROTHER was living he found it hard to hide the shock. In fact, he laughed so hard Tinman had to pummel him with a pillow to shut him up. Tinman kept the details of his arrangement with the owner vague. He was hoping the basket money would allow him to find a new place before Peach found out the truth. Once properly attired for the occasion in his only pair of dress pants and a partly-wrinkled, button-up shirt, the two-headed for the party.

The neon lights adorning the casinos were ablaze but the streets were mostly empty of gamers. There was a time when even on a Sunday evening the gaming tables and slot machines were full. The hit on the economy, however, had taken its toll.

Peach and Tinman were very familiar with the ebbs and flows of a casino town. Neither were gamblers but their connection to Dez had provided easy access to all the casinos and the secrets upon which they made their fortunes. As children, they were even allowed to wander the makeshift grid high above the gaming floor in Harold's, which the forerunner of the "Eye in the Sky."

They watched how the cheats worked and how they got caught. They studied the tricks casinos used to extract the maximum amount of money from patrons. Though neither had attended school, they were well trained in the ways of the world.

As family legend has it, a young, unwed barmaid had given birth to them on top of a pool table in the now defunct Colony Club which sat right next to Harold's Club. Bones and Catfish assisted Dez in delivering the babies. The mother was close friends with Dez who was then a dealer at Harold's. Bones and Catfish just happened to be in the wrong pool hall at the wrong time. When the mother promptly skipped town shortly after the birth, Dez felt obligated to take over the raising of the orphans.

Catfish always believed Tinman's extraordinary skill at pool started the minute he left the womb. He was the first of the twins to slide out and when Peach followed soon after he shoved his brother forward causing his head to hit the three ball which promptly sank in the corner pocket. Apparently, that's why he was dubbed, Trey, though no one used it anymore. His lifelong moniker came later and for a different reason.

Dez would not reveal the identity of their true mother, explaining it would serve no purpose trying to track down a lady who had voluntarily turned her back on them. The logic made complete sense to the boys and they never thought of her again. Their surname, Harrigan, was concocted by Dez and the phony doctor who provided the birth certificates.

Anyway, that's how the story goes. There was no reason to doubt. Right? Peach happily accepted the tale outright. Tinman, however, always thought there were a few sections of the coloring book conveniently left uncolored.

Dez never professed to be a good mother, and she wasn't. She kept a roof over their heads—barely, and provided foodstuff which Tinman cooked. She only worked as a dealer when she really needed the money. Her chosen career was in poker. As she struggled to perfect her play in all-night games, the boys were given carte blanche. Enrolling them in school was too much paperwork, so she took it upon herself to teach them street sense and how to survive by their wits. She called it home-schooling, the law considered it contributing to the delinquency of minors and truancy.

Left to their own devices, both found plenty of trouble. Tinman less so. His problem was mostly getting booted out of pool halls he was too young to be in. Peach was a different story. He'd try to steal anything he could get his hands on. It wasn't that he needed all the stuff he tried to steal. It was more of a game. He usually got caught and it was usually Tinman's job to figure out how to bail him out. As surrogate uncles, Bones and Catfish, when they weren't on the whiz somewhere else in the country, often helped to clear up any mess before Dez got wind.

As is often the case, the wayward child is the most beloved and this was true with Peach. He was Dez's favorite. Tinman was too absorbed in pool to care much, but every once in a while, he had to bite his lip when the two would fawn over each other.

In Dez's mind, Tinman was the more stoic and responsible of the two and she felt if she doted on him he would soften up. In truth, they both loved each other madly, but neither of them could show it. Mostly because neither of them would show it. They were both too stubborn to be the first to show weakness through love.

She had always hoped Tinman would follow in her footsteps and become a poker player. She recognized and admired his skill in pool but felt it was a dead-end, and the game would fall out of popularity. It was a sore point for Tinman her prediction proved correct while she, in her seventies, was still making bank at cards.

Whether they realized it or not, their life growing up was difficult. When the cards were cold, Dez would pack them up and move a block or two to another seedy motel. When she was on a roll, they might not see her for a week at a time. Oddly enough, the brothers never thought of their life as bad or out of the ordinary. They knew nothing else and took it as a matter of course this was the way a family lived.

There's no denying Dez was partly responsible for the way they turned out. Neither of them resented it. They both loved her and were grateful to her for raising them. By the time they were teenagers, Dez had become a professional. She was a "DP" or dangerous player and began to make a very decent living at her chosen profession.

"So how's her game these days?" asked Peach as he maneuvered his wagon through the heart of downtown.

"She really hit her stride about ten years ago. Now she's unbeatable."

Peach sighed. "Oh great."

"Yeah, wait until you see where she lives."

"Hey that dump you're in, we never lived there did we?" asked Peach.

"No."

"Well at least that's a good thing," said Peach. He knew how Tinman felt about going backward.

They were attending the birthday party empty-handed. There was no need to race around looking for the perfect gifts. The only required gifts were their presence and loaded wallets. This was necessary as the main activity at the annual party was a high-stakes poker game. And all the invitees were obligated to play. They weren't obligated to lose and none of them went with that intention. Everyone knew, however, the results were inevitable. Dez was that good.

One might wonder why anyone would attend such a party and the answer is simple enough. At some point in each of their lives, Dez had come to the rescue, saving them from catastrophe. Attending the party was like paying off a perpetually regenerating IOU. She was the grand dame of their makeshift family and always would be.

"So is she working private games or the card rooms?" asked Peach.

"Strictly private. Six nights a week. Usually held at her place. Sundays are Sabbath Day, reserved for counting her loot. She won't touch the casino rooms since they went strictly Texas Hold'em."

"I thought she loved that game!"

"Not when it's every hand. She does employ a little army of cardroom players to steer high rollers her way. But that's as far as it goes with casinos. Take a left on Sierra."

They drove past Circus Circus, the Silver Legacy, and the El Dorado which were now all under the control of the Carano family. It was like a mega-mall of gambling where people went to spend their money but got no pretty packages in return.

Just before they reached the Truckee River, Tinman told Peach to park. They found a spot on the street and climbed out.

"Tada," said Tinman, flatly, as he gestured to a towering high-rise sitting right on the river between the Virginia and Sierra Street bridges. In the center of the L-shaped, ivory-colored tower was a rooftop swimming pool overlooked by the floor-to-ceiling windows featured in the luxurious condominiums above. It was The Palladio. Peach nearly choked with glee.

"She's in one of those things?!" he cried.

"Welcome to home sweet home," Tinman answered. "Let's go."

"Hold on a sec. So how are we going to handle this?"

"What are you talking about?"

"Come on, this is Dez. If she finds out how much those baskets are worth she's gonna want a cut for sure."

Truer words had never been spoken and Tinman swallowed hard at the notion of giving up a cent to Dez. "We just have to lose big. Soften her up. Then slip it in when she's not expecting. As soon as they're in our hands, she can't do a damn thing."

"Clever. Okay, from what you say they'll be no problem losing," said Peach.

Tinman said, "Yeah, I got about a grand to dump."

"Nice. Say. How was it being on the whiz after all these years?" asked Peach. "Any troubles?"

"None to speak of," Tinman lied.

"Remember when they first taught us to stall? Hell, we were only eight or nine, no?" he laughed.

"Then Dez found out and threatened to turn the old guys into eunuchs." Tinman couldn't resist a smile at the thought but soon got back to business. "How much you holding?"

"Believe it or not, I'm flush. So I tell you what. I'll take the brunt of this. Hold back a little of your stash for essentials. I noticed your fridge is empty and I'm in need of a little home cooking."

For Tinman, attending this annual bloodbath was like going to the DMV every year and paying his dues, when he used to be able to afford them. The only difference was he didn't have to stand in line. He resented the fact Peach had been able to escape it for all these years. "Deal. After all, you're due."

"Okay, when I'm ready to make the move, I'll office you. This is our time in the sun brother," said Peach with a grin, and he strode to the entrance where a doorman awaited. Tinman followed slowly. This show of magnanimity from Peach was so foreign he was taken aback. He wondered again what the cause of it was and where all the wampum was coming from.

A quick intercom call from Dez to the doorman allowed them entry and they took an elevator to the top floor. On the way up, Peach admired the artwork. "After we're rich we should live in a place like this."

"After we're rich, we should buy a place like this," said Tinman with a wink. The prospect of a big payday had caused the brothers to revert to their childhood relationship when they were the Dynamic Duo. As they reached the top floor and stepped out, Tinman grabbed Peach. "What have you been up to? Anything I should be aware of?"

"What are you talking about?"

"The big wad, the nice clothes, it's not like you."

"You got that wrong, brother. This is the new me. You're just getting reacquainted," Peach answered, straight-faced. Tinman wasn't buying it and Peach knew it. "Don't worry about it. We'll talk later."

Actually, Peach was hoping the basket money would allow him to retire and Tinman wouldn't have to know about his new career. He was proud of what he'd become, but Tinman had a thing about theft and prison. In truth, he was a bit of an elitist. Even though he hustled money from people on the table he refused to consider it stealing. He believed his gig was above thievery and Peach was not in the mood to get into the old argument. There were more important things to worry about.

Dez's unit was on the corner, the largest on the floor. At the front door, Tinman turned to Peach. "Remember, don't call her mom. You know she doesn't like it." He rang the bell.

From inside he heard Dez call out, "It's open!"

Tinman opened the door and saw Bones, Catfish, and Dez, all wearing stupid party hats. They were seated at a poker table and Bones was doing some fancy shuffling. "Hey everybody, I found a fifth player," Tinman said.

"Fresh blood! Perfect! I can't stand a four-person game," said Dez, rising to her feet. She was tall for a woman, had natural, ginger red hair, green eyes, and her original gleaming teeth. Even as a septuagenarian, her figure was the sort that would drive almost any happily married man to infidelity. There was something about her, though, that spoke of ruthlessness. It took a strong man indeed to stare her down when she was preparing to strike. She stepped to Tinman and looked over his shoulder. "Well, where the hell is he? Did you leave him in the elevator?"

Peach stepped into the doorway and there was a collective gasp. He threw open his arms. "MOM!"

Dez ran to him and the two crashed into each other. As they embraced they turned in a slow circle, cooing and giggling. Tinman was startled and aggravated at the warm welcome. It made him feel a little better when he heard a "thonk" and Peach's head snapped forward, his shoulders shuddering.

He knew Dez had just slammed a knuckle into the soft spot under the back of his skull where the spine connects. Properly placed and with the correct velocity, the "brain bash," as it was called in the family, sent shockwaves from the toes to the crown of the head. He and Peach had received many of them over the years. It was an unspoken scolding and meant, "I've told you not to do that and you refuse to listen so now you're going to pay."

The embrace ended and Peach instinctively rubbed his wounded brain. "Dez! Gosh, it's good to see you!"

"That's better," Dez said. "Bones, Catfish, look who's here!"

The next few minutes were spent slapping Peach on the back and probing into his whereabouts for the last fifteen years. Peach expertly slithered around the truth, giving just enough information to sate everyone— temporarily. Tinman knew he would eventually have to spill the facts. These were hustlers and thieves, after all, and they knew when they were being conned. As Tinman expected, however, everyone momentarily let him get away with his yarn.

When Dez and Peach were busy yammering at each other, Tinman took the opportunity to pull Bones and Catfish aside. He asked them not to mention anything about the whiz or the ostrich brawl. There were definite reasons why he didn't want Peach or Dez to know the dirty details. The two old guys initially resisted. They thought it was unfair to stop them from relaying such juicy anecdotes, especially at a party. But in the end, they grudgingly agreed.

Dez became aware of Peach's garb. "Well, well, aren't we looking dapper these days!" Like a debutante at a coming out ball, Peach spun slowly around showing off his duds. Bones and Catfish whistled appreciatively. "And your hair is so nice and neat," Dez continued.

"Say, that looks like a BJ's cut!" Bones declared.

"You know that place?!" asked Peach.

Catfish said, "Only true cutters in town."

"I got my hair cut too," Tinman mumbled, but nobody noticed.

"So Dez, geez what a joint!" Peach said in a deft attempt to divert attention from himself.

"This old hovel?" Dez said, sliding onto a luxurious couch. Peach noticed it was a Chesterfield Grand Sofa, upholstered in emerald velvet with oak frame and hickory finish. The rest of the place was similarly furnished, the color scheme mostly tasteful greens and cream. Dez had struck a Garboesque pose. "I've seen better."

"Yeah, and I've seen worse," said Peach, admiring the Tahoe-inspired artwork. "Much worse!"

Dez looked at Tinman. "Speaking of which, have you paid the taxes on the motel yet?"

"We'll talk later," Tinman said quickly, hoping Peach hadn't heard, even though one look his way told him he had.

"Later nothing! I keep getting letters from the city. For crying out loud kid, it's not like you're paying off the federal debt. And what's with the shirt? For God's sake, take it off, I'll give it a quick iron."

Peach came to the rescue. "I thought we were here for a party! So let's party! Break out the cards!"

There was only one way to shut Dez up and it always worked. She kicked off her shoes, leaped from the couch, and raced to her preferred seat at the poker table. "Give me those cards Bones. You know you're not allowed to deal."

Bones' skill on the whiz was nearly matched by his ability as a card manipulator. Dez was well aware of this and under no circumstances would she let him handle the cards other than looking at his hand. Catfish always dealt for him.

The game was dealer's choice, no limit, anything goes. This included such monstrosities as Seven Stud Low-Card-in-the-Hole Wild, Six Stud with a twist of either down card at the end, Five Card Roll-Your-Own Mexican Stud, and just about anything a demented poker mind could come up with. Dez liked to keep her competition off-balance: wild cards, twists, shared cards, smoke, and mirrors. Anything to make them forget it was all the same game—best hand wins. It was one of the secrets to her success, among many.

It was strictly a cash game. This was another of her tricks. She'd learned people play differently with cash than they did with chips, especially when calling bluffs. And when it comes to poker, bluffing is the name of the game, brother.

There were no IOUs, chits, floaters, or otherwise. If you went bust you were a kibitzer for the rest of the game. From past experience, everyone knew at least a grand was needed to have a respectable showing, and last more than an hour. The ante started at ten bucks and went steadily up. This was last man standing, winner take all.

"Okay boys, let's see the green," Dez demanded. "I want to see how much I'm gonna haul in tonight."

The guys pulled out their wads and placed them on the table. The money was no longer theirs and they knew it. Fond farewells were made and Dez passed out beers in a show of commiseration. She was surprised to see Peach holding the largest stack of bills, nearly twice what the other guys showed. Truthfully, she was amazed he had any money at all but chose not to mention it. When she saw Tinman's wad, however, her eyebrows lifted. "Well, well, Mr. Rockefeller, I thought there was no money for the taxes."

"Look, you want me to pay the city or you want me to pay you?"

"Screw the taxman, let's play," said Dez, giving the expected response. "Wait a minute! You two need hats." She grabbed two stupid party hats and strapped them on Peach and Tinman. "That's better. Okay, birthday girl deals first. Any complaints?"

Nary a peep. "Good. Let's start with The Works, Five Card Draw, deuces, one-eyed jacks, and the suicide king wild with a twist at the end." And with that, the bleeding began.

The first three hands went to Dez. Bones won the next pot only because the birthday girl bowed out to go to the bathroom. When she got back she promptly won the next two.

Peach said, "So Dez, seriously, what's with the posh digs? You used to be so frugal."

"Think of it as a business expense. After all, this is where I work. If you're trying to reel in the high rollers you have to keep up appearances."

"A very wise observation, my dear," said Catfish with a wink. "And may I say you are looking particularly yummy this evening." She was wearing a navy, tulle, Marchesa Notte dress with gunmetal and silver embroidery. Her only jewelry was a pair of diamond stud earrings. She was indeed a knockout and the other men nodded in agreement.

Catfish had always had a thing for Dez and the same was true for her. The problem was neither of them had the selflessness to endure a real love affair. As a solution to their mutual attraction, they had tacitly agreed to conduct a near fifty-year fantasy affair, replete with flirtation, innuendo, and for titillation, the occasional brushing of private body parts. For two hustlers, it was a match made in heaven. No guilt, obligations, restrictions, or any of the other pesky drawbacks that come from being in love.

As the game proceeded, it didn't take long for the others to see the change that had overcome Tinman. For so many years, he'd been a grumpy Gus, and now he was grinning and cracking jokes, even laughing heartily when he lost a hand. Dez couldn't stand it anymore.

"Are you on drugs?" she asked in all seriousness.

Tinman howled, then quickly swallowed his private thoughts. He had a secret and he sure as hell was going to keep it to himself. He wiped the smirk from his face and stared back at her. "Worse. I'm pregnant."

Dez froze for just a split second then threw the deck she was holding. The cards scattered mid-air flitting this way and that like a swarm of butterflies with their heads cut off. The guys cracked up while Dez pouted a bit. The moment quickly passed but she started watching him a little closer, searching for a crack in his armor. It didn't faze him. He knew the routine and had long ago learned how to protect himself from her X-ray vision.

Two hours later, Bones was the first to go bust. He was down to his last hundred and fifty bucks and mistakenly went for an inside baby straight. He caught the card and ran hard with it right into the brick wall Dez was holding: a ten-high club flush.

"How many times I gotta tell you chumps? Do not go for any straight that isn't full of a lot of faces!" Dez reprimanded. Bones good-naturedly laughed it off and grabbed another beer. He kicked back in his chair and sighed, finally freed of the pressure to survive Hurricane Dez.

A little over an hour later, Catfish followed suit, victim of Dez's trip nines to his three eights. Dez felt it was a bad beat and offered to let the hand pass, but Catfish was far too much a gentlemen to accept.

A tick before midnight, Tinman went belly up during a game of Seven Stud Follow the Queen. The card that follows an up Queen becomes wild. But if another Queen comes up then the next card up is wild and the original wild card is no longer wild. Naturally, a late Queen canceled out the wild card Tinman was holding and his hand collapsed. Dez raked in the pot with what appeared to be even more glee than she had shown throughout the night. Tinman let it slide. It was now down to Peach and Dez and that's how they planned it. Now all he had to do was wait for the signal.

The two went back and forth with Peach amazingly holding his own. Then Dez got serious. She nailed him good in a hand of Iron Cross, then proceeded to fleece him in Black Mariah and nearly wiped him out with Burn the Biffel. She eyed his depleted stack and smelled blood. She called for a game of Five Draw Lowball with a one card optional twist at the end.

Low Ball is where the worst possible hands wins. Ace is considered low. The nut, or perfect hand, is 6-4-3-2-A, unsuited. And this is exactly what Peach drew. As soon as he saw his hand he knew the moment had arrived. He leaned back in his chair and rubbed his eyes with his thumbs. Tinman picked up the office and knew the game was on. Bones and Catfish saw the signal as well but didn't know what the brothers were up to. They decided to keep mum and watch the fun.

Dez drew 10-8-5-3-2. Peach bet a C-note and Dez called and raised the same. Peach called. When the draw came he declined.

"What do you mean you don't want a card?" cried Dez. "If you don't need any cards why didn't you re-raise like I taught you?

Peach said, "Maybe I'm rusty."

"Whatever. You can't beat these. I'll hold 'em, same as you," Dez declared.

She grinned like she'd caught the immaculate. Peach grimaced and checked. Dez slid out two C-notes. Peach studied his hand. "Damn, maybe I should have taken the draw."

"There's always the twist," Dez offered. "Believe me, you're going to need it."

Peach shrugged and called the bet. It left him with only a handful of twenties and some tens in his stack. Dez asked if he wanted a twist and he immediately threw the 6 and drew a Jack. Dez stayed pat, she twitched and weaved around in her seat, like a cobra preparing to strike.

Peach said, "Well, the twist definitely helped."

"Yeah, I'll bet. How does five hundred sound to you?" she said, smiling ever so sweetly.

"Okay," said Peach, and he nonchalantly reached in his pocket and peeled off the bills from a fresh wad. "There's the five and I'll raise you the rest of what I've got here. Let's see, looks like it comes to a hundred fifty more."

Everyone sat up and started paying a lot more attention. Tinman in particular. He had no idea his brother was this flush. Dez scrunched her eyes, sniffing for a trap. She decided he was just playing stupid and called then re-raised a grand.

Peach sighed, looking oh so dejected. "Well, that taps me out. Cash only, huh?"

"You know the rules. If you can't meet the bet, you're out."

"I remember, I just thought this might be enough to cover it," said Peach, reaching into his pocket. He pulled out the Simmons' Blue Nile Floating Diamond Solitaire Pendant and placed it gracefully next to the pot. The second collective gasp of the evening occurred, this one included Tinman.

Dez was the first to recover. She picked up the necklace and felt its heft. "Ouch, it feels hot. Who'd you mug, Peach? The Queen of England?"

"It's not like that anymore, I tell you! And I never mugged a woman in my life!"

"Uh, huh. You wouldn't be trying to mug me would you?" Dez asked, staring at the back of his cards.

"You accept the bet, and you'll find out," said Peach.

The necklace was making its way around the table. Catfish eyed it carefully. "It's real alright. And I think it's worth a heckuva lot more than seven hundred fifty clams. You sure you want to do this Peach?"

"Shut up! Of course he does," said Dez, hoping not to let Peach off the hook. She was already imagining the bling around her neck. "Okay, you're on, what have you got?"

Peach said, "I called you."

Dez shrugged and flipped her hand. "Ten high."

"Damn, I shouldn't have taken that twist. Jack high. You win. I thought you were bluffing."

"Ten high is a bluff! What have you grown stupid?" she blurted out.

"Well, you bluffed me too good. Made me take that twist. Before then I was at eight high. Eh, easy come, easy go!" said Peach with a laugh. "Happy Birthday, Dez. It's all yours."

Dez knew there was some trickery going on but couldn't figure it out. She quickly tossed off her suspicions and snatched up the necklace. "Oh my god! Look at the filigree on the platinum chain. And the rock! Catfish, be a dear and clip this thing for me. Come on, come on! What are you waiting for?"

Dez held the necklace up to her neck and Catfish dutifully fastened it. Like a school girl having just received her first kiss, she pranced around the apartment. Peach glanced at Tinman with a little nod.

"It sure looks more beautiful on you than off, Dez," said Tinman. "It's like it was custom designed."

"You're right!" exclaimed Dez, studying herself in a floor mirror. "Now, who's the Queen of England?"

"You've always been the queen of this family, Dez," Tinman continued buttering up. "Now you've got the crown jewels to prove it."

"Oh, thank you, Peach!" Dez cried as she ran to him and planted a big smooch on his cheek. "Hey, you earned it," said Peach.

"I know, but it's worth way more than that bet!" said Dez. "I almost feel like I owe you and that's a very foreign emotion for me."

"Nah, you don't owe me anything," said Peach. "But I was wondering about those baskets."

Dez continued strutting around the apartment, doing her best imitation of royalty. "Huh?"

"You remember," said Tinman. "Those baskets we gave you for Christmas one year. Right before we all went on the road."

"And left me here to fend for myself," said Dez as she once again admired herself in the mirror. "You know that really wasn't nice of you guys. All four of you taking off at the same time. It brought me bad luck, did you know that? I had a run of cold cards that lasted so long it was like the second ice age."

"Dez! The baskets. You remember?" Tinman repeated.

"Of course I remember. Those Indian baskets. I used to have them on the windowsill at my old place."

Tinman looked to Peach for help. "You think maybe we could take a look at them? Bring back old memories, you know," said Peach.

Dez, still in front of the mirror, spread her arms wide to get a better view. "I gave them back."

Tinman involuntarily rose. "You gave them back."

She stopped her preening and turned back to the table. "Yeah, I found out you two stole them so I gave them back. Purely for your protection."

"You're telling me you, yourself, Deziree Hartman, walked in there and gave them back," intoned Tinman, sinking deeper into a stupor of despair.

"Well, no, naturally I used a subsidiary," said Dez.

"The word is surrogate. And who was the surrogate?" asked Tinman

"Just some guy. And don't correct my words! Even if they are wrong! Look, I'm not going to say any more about it. They were a gift. You can't give a gift and now question what the recipient did with it. As far as the giver is concerned, they're gone. I'm allowed to do whatever I want with them. And it was all for your benefit anyway. To take the heat off."

Tinman's head which had slowly been sagging now dropped completely, his jaw scraping his chest. He reached up and pulled off his stupid party hat. He dropped it on the floor and drifted towards the door, a man without a paddle.

As he shuffled past Dez she recoiled. "Hey! Back off! They're where they belong." She looked to Peach for help.

"Dez, um, those baskets are now worth a cool million apiece," Peach said with great gravity.

The air was sucked out of the room. Dez spun around just in time to see Tinman disappear out the door. "Tinman? Come back!" When there was no response she whipped around to Peach, fear in her eyes. "Did you know that when you gave them to me?!"

"We love you, Dez, but come on. I just found out," Peach explained.

Dez's hands clutched the pendant. Her mind racing around in circles desperately looking for words. "Go with your brother! He needs your help! NOW."

Peach kicked back his chair and darted out the door. Dez looked to Bones and Catfish who stared askance back at her. "Stop it! How was I to know?"

* * *

Tinman was in a fog as he stepped out of the lobby into the clear night air. He barely felt Peach's arm as it draped around him. They were halfway back to the motel before he could manage a word.

"I guess that's it," he said. "I imagine you'll be heading out of town now. I can fix you up for the night. I've got some old mattresses in one of the motel rooms."

"Thanks so much for the offer, but I've got a date," said Peach.

It took several seconds for this to sink in. "You've got a date."

"Yeah, with Ginger," said Peach brightly. "Well I call her Ginger Snap, but that's just a pet name."

"You have a pet name for some girl I never heard of and you just hit town today? Who the hell are you talking about?" Tinman demanded.

"The stylist! The lady, the cutie who cut my hair. She asked me over to her place tonight."

"Ginger Snap."

"Now you got it. I told her about the party and she said she'd wait up. It was kind of like mutual lust at first sight," Peach explained.

"Figures. Well, if you get the chance, stop by and say goodbye before you head out."

"Eh, I think I'll stick around for a little bit. It's not that I don't trust Dez, I just don't trust her. I want to do a little nosing around. See what's what. I have a hunch this thing isn't over yet."

Tinman lifted his heavy head. He didn't want any hope. Hope led to anguish, despair, and ultimately, misery. Still, as he looked at his brother through part of one eye and saw him bopping along to a tune only he could hear, he wondered if maybe, just maybe, there was light on the dark side of the moon.

NINE

Elite Art Magazine Feb. 2003

The Abominable Basket Burglary

By

Florence Whittenheimer

One of the most famous Native American basket weavers was Dat So La Lee, a member of the Washo Tribe. Much has been written about her weaving techniques and personal history but little about an infamous burglary where four of her baskets were mysteriously stolen from a museum in Reno, NV. This is due, perhaps, to the fact there is very little information about the theft and the thieves were never apprehended. What follows is a collection of the known facts.

The Nevada Historical Society in Reno is located up a steep road in the northeast corner of the University of Nevada, Reno campus. It was a snowy day just before Christmas of 1978. The museum had very few visitors due to weather and slick roads. There must have been, however, at least two. For at some point around midday, four degikup baskets, woven by Dat So La Lee, were removed from their glass cases and vanished.

There was no damage found in the display and no locks had been tampered with. It is believed recent renovations allowed the thieves to simply lift the Lucite enclosures and remove the baskets because the cases had not yet been properly secured. How the criminals could walk out of the museum unhampered, however, has never been discerned.

It would have been difficult to smuggle them out of the building as they were all approximately one foot high and 15 inches in diameter. One hypothesis is the thieves struck around noon when most of the employees were at lunch. On top of this, in 1978 there was no admission charged so it would have been easy to enter the building without being identified. Also, the building had little to no internal security.

Surprisingly, it was not until the following day the baskets were discovered missing. Since the theft fell under the designation of Art and Cultural Property Crime, the FBI was immediately notified. A massive search ensued. With the help of local police forces, the FBI rounded up and questioned all known thieves in the Carson/Reno area. From the beginning, there were few clues and no leads. An in-depth investigation of the museum employees led nowhere and no arrests were ever made. It was speculated the crime may have been a "contract" crime whereby an unscrupulous collector had arranged for the theft with the intention of possessing the baskets for a private collection. This theory, however, met with little success.

After months of intensive searching, it was believed the baskets were gone forever. Two years later, however, the Historical Society was contacted by a California attorney representing a person or persons who claimed to have two of the baskets. This anonymous person offered to return the baskets for a finder's fee of $2500 per basket. Representatives of the museum traveled to Santa Cruz and viewed the baskets but determined only one of them to be authentic. The finder's fee was paid for the one and it was returned to the museum.

After this event, the trail again went cold. Seventeen years later a Tucson art dealer sent three unidentified baskets to a Canadian basket expert for identification. The expert immediately recognized the baskets as the stolen Dat So La Lee baskets and notified the FBI. An investigation cleared the Tucson dealer of any wrongdoing. He stated he bought the baskets through a surrogate of an undisclosed art collector for the price of $45,000. The FBI confiscated the baskets and retained complete legal possession for over a year before the investigation was closed. They were stored in a locked metal cabinet at the Historical Society and the FBI held the only set of keys.

The art dealer, claiming ownership of the baskets, sued the State of Nevada. Later in 1998, the Nevada Attorney General's Office settled the case for $55,000 and the baskets again became the official property of the state.

Upon examination, art experts found faded areas that may have demonstrated the baskets were exposed to direct sunlight, possibly by being placed on a table near a window. Wear on the inner rim of each basket suggested they were periodically lifted from their setting. It was imagined this was for cleaning purposes.

It was some time before the baskets were put back on display. This time the museum took every precaution, claiming to have spent over $300,000 on security for the new exhibit. When asked about the security level, a museum representative claimed anyone attempting to steal the baskets again will be "cut in half by a laser beam."

Such precautions are not surprising. The original baskets were purchased by the Historical Society in 1945 at an approximate cost of $75 each. In today's market, they are worth well over 10,000 times that amount.

The baskets are now back where they belong but mysteries still linger. Did the thieves have inside information about the unsecured cases and lack of security or was it simply a stroke of dumb luck? Was there an inside accomplice who facilitated the theft? Where were the baskets kept for twenty years and why were they ultimately sold to an art dealer in Tucson at well-below their market value?

These are questions to which we will most likely never have answers. But one thing is clear. The theft of historic and cultural artifacts is an abomination and it is up to us to protect our national heritage from the lower depths.

TEN

"OKAY, LET'S GO OVER IT AGAIN. The Philosophy of Pool Hustling 101. There are two ways to hustle someone: take advantage of their pride or their greed," Tinman said.

"I already know all that!" fumed Tek, a fifteen-year-old boy with a light, olive complexion, long, dark hair, and brooding eyes. His given name was Thomas Edison Kager but he hated it. Tinman, Bones, and Catfish also hated it and for a while after meeting him they called him Alva, after his namesake's middle name. But the kid hated that even more than his given name and so he created his own nickname. He settled on Tek because he was a bona fide computer prodigy, and it happened to be the first three initials of his name. The guys liked it and it stuck.

"Well you're not acting like you know it," said Tinman. "I told you to almost pot that ball and you sank it clean."

"I don't like hiding my skill. I worked hard to play good," Tek argued.

"Hiding your speed is just plain survival in this job. If you start out showing everybody in the room how good you are you'll scare the money away before you can say rack 'em."

"Yeah, yeah. Tell me something else I don't know."

"Look, we'll get to avoiding tush hogs, picking your marks, using your weak hand and stuff like that. But first, you need to learn to camouflage your juice!"

Tek said, "I don't know, man. It sounds like cheating."

Tinman's frustration was quickly turning to anger. "Cheating, or sharking, is when you intentionally throw a guy's game off. Like talking while he's shooting or doping his drink. I don't do that. I'm an honest hustler and don't you forget it!"

"I'm starting to wonder if you're as good as you claim," Tek challenged.

Tinman turned away and slid his cue onto the pool table. At the bar, Bones and Catfish shook their heads. Amber was nowhere in sight as it was early and the hall was not officially open. For extra money, Tinman had agreed to teach Tek to hustle. This was their fifth class and it wasn't going the way either of them had planned.

Tek, however, thought he'd made a point against Tinman. He grinned and turned to the two old guys.

"Tek, you got this all wrong," said Catfish. "A pool hustler has to be the best in the room. He has to be able to sink any ball at any time. Now you can believe this or no, but I've never seen anyone shoot stick as good as Tinman. He's maybe the best hustler of his era."

"Then why doesn't he play in tournaments?!" Tek demanded.

Catfish sighed heavily and began to explain. Bones stopped him and took over the lesson. "If he played in tournaments, he'd win." Bones held up a hand to stop Tek from talking over him. "So he wins. Maybe the prize is a few C notes, big deal. In reality, he loses, big time. Word spreads fast in the pool world. Pretty soon everyone knows his speed and the action fizzles, for good. At all costs, a pool hustler must never let the world know just how good he is."

Tek let this sink in. Tinman watched, wondering if he would finally come around. "I guess I get it," said Tek slowly. "But I don't think I can do it." Tinman's shoulders sunk.

Tek walked over to him. "I'm sorry. About what I said. I know you're great. I just know myself and when I'm good at something I can't hide it." Tinman nodded his head and Tek continued. "So, I guess the lessons are over. Thanks anyway. Here's for today."

He handed Tinman fifty bucks who for a second thought about waiving his normal fee but the growth on his foot had mushroomed and he needed money for the impending amputation. He shoved the bills in his pocket.

Tek asked, "No hard feelings?"

Tinman looked down at the kid and a wry grin came. He knew what he did was not for most. He'd tried training guys with twice Tek's skill and they just couldn't wrap their brains around it.

"No, kid, no animosity. You'll find something you like. There are plenty of ways to fleece suckers." He picked up his cue and started his regular practice session.

Tek wandered over to the bar and sat next to Bones and Catfish. "Hey Bones, show me again how you top a prat poke."

Bones asked, "You been practicing?"

"A little, but I still think I'm using too much pressure," answered Tek. "It's tough to know because I'm using the dummy I made to practice on like you told me."

"Okay, let's go over it again. Catfish will be the mark."

"With pleasure," said Catfish and he stood up and Bones placed a wallet in his hip pocket. Bones then proceeded to show Tek how to gently use a knee to slide the wallet up the pocket so part of it was poking out the top and could then be picked.

None of the guys thought it was wrong to teach such things to Tek. They would never corrupt a kid if he wasn't one of them, that would be immoral. But if a person has thieves' blood in them they didn't consider it bad at all. In fact, they felt they were obligated to train him. A person with thieves' blood is going to learn about crime somewhere. As class criminals, they felt it would be wrong if they didn't teach him the right way. They would never forgive themselves if he turned into one of the many modern-day thugs who stuck up convenience stores or mugged drunks and had the audacity to call themselves true thieves. They wouldn't even share a cup of coffee with such punks.

In between shots, Tinman glanced over and shook his head. He was disappointed Tek couldn't take to hustling because he felt it was better than most thievery. But if the kid wasn't cut out for it, he had to learn some kind of trade. He knew Bones and Catfish had good intentions and he hoped Tek would find his way with them.

The reason Tek had such stature amongst the guys was because of his parents. He inherited his criminal predisposition from both his mother and father. His mother had been a dancer in a bar in Bangkok's notorious Patpong "entertainment" district. She had a good thing going fleecing the tourists who came to get laid. One of these tourists had been Tek's father. His mother made her biggest score by getting him to marry her and take her back to the States.

She had expensive tastes and her husband, never one to shy away from breaking the law, turned to embezzlement to keep the money train rolling. His position as an investment advisor provided him with plenty of opportunities. Unfortunately, he got a little greedy and was arrested on twenty-five counts of fraud. He still had several years to go at Otisville Federal Correctional Institution before he paid off his debt to society. Fortunately, Tek's mother was smarter than his father and had been methodically siphoning off money and stashing it away. When he went to jail, she was sitting on a very tidy sum.

She divorced her husband and moved Tek out of their tony neighborhood in Nassau County, NY, and moved to Reno. Until then, Tek had been educated in exclusive private schools and shown his genius with computers. Now, to save her money stash for partying, he was enrolled in the public school system. For kicks and extra cash, she worked as a dancer at the Wild Orchid Cabaret. She still spoke broken English and had little concern for the rules and regulations of proper citizenship so she didn't really care if Tek didn't attend regular classes. As long as his grades were okay she left him to his own devices.

Tek kept his grades good and his attendance record clean by hacking into the school's computer system and making the necessary adjustments. For spending money, he'd discovered a wormhole in an online app store and arranged for a small amount of money to be deducted from every transaction and deposited into an anonymous account. The little amounts added up and he was never without ready cash. The guys didn't understand how he was doing it but they admired his initiative and he was welcomed into their little clan.

The front door suddenly swung open. Everybody was a little startled because it was always locked during off-hours. Peach strode in.

"Hey! This place is closed!" shouted Tek. "How did you get in here?"

"Just walked right in," said Peach.

Tinman said, "That's strange, I'm sure I locked it when we came in."

"You'll have to do better than that," Peach said. Tinman raised his eyebrows but Peach diverted him. "Who's the kid?"

Tek strutted up to him. "Question is, who are you? This is a private party."

Peach grinned, immediately taking to Tek. "Oh yeah? Well, that's my brother and I always have an open invitation to any of his parties."

"Tinman has a brother?" Tek asked in awe. "Are you a pool hustler too?"

"Hell no," said Peach. "When you grow up with him you realize you better find another path in life. Why compete? He's the best there is."

"So everyone keeps telling me," Tek said, retreating to the safety of the bar.

"I thought you left town," said Tinman. "Where you been for two days? Eating ginger snap?"

"Some of the time," said Peach. "The rest, well, let's just say I've been doing some research. I got something you should read."

He pulled out a folded sheet of paper and handed it to Tinman. He opened it up and studied the title. "Florence Whittenheimer? Is this a joke?"

"Uh, uh. Facts," said Peach. "I found it when I was poking around the UNR Library. Ginger's a part-time student and got me a visitor's pass."

Tinman spread the article out on the table and began to read. Peach went to the bar. Bones and Catfish introduced him to Tek and gave him a quick rundown of his background and why he was permitted access to their den of thieves.

"Dat So La Lee. That's where you got that name," said Tinman, looking up from his reading.

"That's our gal. Keep reading, it gets better," said Peach. "So Bones, Tinman tells me you guys were on the whiz. Give me the skinny."

Bones and Catfish proceeded to tell Peach and Tek about their trip to Virginia City. When they told them the camel races was the draw, Tek was envious. He'd never had a chance to see them and immediately whipped out his phone in a search for YouTube videos of the event.

Tinman shot upright. "The FBI! Christ, we were lucky we got out of town when we did. I had no idea some dumb baskets would cause such an uproar."

Peach moved his way. "I thought you'd be interested in that. But keep going. There's even more juice."

The very mention of the FBI drew the attention of Bones and Catfish. They left the bar and leaned over Tinman, reading along with him.

"Is that really true? You guys just walked in and lifted the cases?" asked Catfish. "Or was there an inside man helping you out?"

Peach laughed. "Hell no! Like the lady says, pure dumb luck. We didn't know about any renovation or lack of security. We were just looking for something to give Dez. You know, to take away the sting that we were going on the road with you guys."

"And you just walked right out with them?" Bones asked.

"The place was deserted! I don't think we saw a single person from the time we went in, to the time we strolled out. Isn't that right?"

Tinman nodded slowly. He was going back in time, remembering the snowy day and the mentality he and Peach had back then. There was nothing too crazy for them to try. "Not a soul. As I remember, the way it started was Peach bumped into one of the cases and the damn top almost fell off."

"Hey! I forgot that part!" Peach shouted with uncontained mirth. "Then it just came to us. If they were going to leave those things so unprotected, they deserved to be stolen. So, rather than put the case back on we just lifted it up and did the snatch."

"Right. But I can't remember why we took four of them," said Tinman.

"I do. Because there were three other cases just like the first. Therefore, the same principle applied."

Bones nodded sagely. "Makes perfect sense."

All four leaned back in and continued reading. When it got to the part about an anonymous person returning one basket for a finder's fee of $2500, there was a collective groan.

"Oh man," Tinman moaned. "How could she have been so dense? With all that heat on, she must have known by then they were worth more than that."

"Remember. She said after we left she had a run of bad cards," said Peach.

"Right. That explains it," said Tinman. "She'd sell her soul to get a poker stake."

"Yeah, well, keep reading. I don't think you're going to like what happened next."

They all kept reading and got to the section about the art dealer. Catfish said, "Uh-oh. Bad girl, Dez."

"She owes us money! I'm going over there right now!" Tinman yelled, unscrewing his cue.

"Will you just read the rest," Peach pleaded.

Tinman exhaled angrily. He quickly finished the article and looked at Peach. "So what? All that tells us is those baskets are in Fort Knox, Reno."

"Eh, I'm not so sure about that," said Peach.

"Look again, brother! Three hundred thousand dollars spent on killer lasers!"

Peach said, "You can't believe everything you read. We should at least go have a look-see."

"To see if we can steal them back again? Heaven forbid! That would be an abomination perpetrated by members of the lower depths!" Tinman snorted. "I'm going for the sure thing."

"I do not think I would necessarily refer to Dez as a sure thing," Catfish warned. "You know how she is about the green."

"He has a point," said Peach. "You don't really expect her to fork it over, do you? After all this time?"

"Well this is our money, not hers," said Tinman, shoving his cue in its case.

"Hey Tinman!" shouted Tek. "You're famous!"

"Not now," said Tinman. "Look. I'm going over there and demand what is rightfully ours. You coming? Because if you don't and I get the money, I'm keeping all of it."

"Guys, you gotta see this! This is dope!" Tek squealed.

"Okay, okay, I'm right behind you," Peach said to Tinman. "But I really think we'll have more luck at the museum." He turned to Bones and Catfish. "You guys feel like tagging along? For moral support?"

As one, Bones and Catfish threw up their hands, palms out. "I'm old," said Bones. "I can't afford to get beat up."

"Ditto," said Catfish.

Tinman said, "Alright, lock up when you leave."

Tek ran up and blocked his path to the door. He held his phone up. "Over a half million hits! You've gone viral, Tinman!"

Tinman peered at the video playing on the screen. The ostrich was pecking away at his head. Peach leaned in to get a peak.

"What the heck is that?" Peach asked.

Tinman grabbed him by the arm and pulled him to the door. "Simple explanation," he said. "It's my doppelganger."

"Huh?"

"It's like a body double. Someone who looks exactly like you. Has to be. Only a fool would take on an ostrich."

"Or Dez," said Peach, and Tinman shoved him out the door.

ELEVEN

"SO HOW ARE WE GOING TO HANDLE THIS?" Peach asked as they waited for the elevator door to open.

"With a distinct lack of finesse," answered Tinman.

They stepped into the hallway and started for Dez's apartment. "You know, she did say she was trying to protect us, what with all the heat on," said Peach.

"That's a crock. We were a thousand miles away by then. And she didn't sell the first basket for almost two years and the other three went twenty years later. I doubt there was any heat on."

"True. I still think she had our best interests in mind."

Tinman wheeled around. "Is that right? Well, I've been back here for years scraping like a pauper and she never even mentioned it or offered me a cut." He waited for a comeback but Peach could only shrug.

As they approached the apartment they heard moaning and groaning coming from inside. They placed their ears to the door and listened. "It sounds like someone's torturing her," said Peach.

"Somebody beat me to it," said Tinman. A loud wailing broke out and his ire quickly turned to concern. Dez may have stolen from him but he would fight to the death if she was threatened. He pounded on the door. The moaning quickly stopped.

"When the door opens, we'll have to act fast," said Peach. "We'll do like the cops do. You rush one side and I'll rush the other. Stay low. They may have guns. If there's only one of them we hit him from both sides. If there's two, you get the big guy."

The door slowly opened but one look at the doorman forced a change in their plans. They froze. He stood well over six feet with a physique that would make most bodybuilders weep from shame. His features spoke of Latino ethnicity but his coloring was anything but. He was white, from the hair and eyebrows to the skin. His eyes were pale with a tinge of pink. He was wearing a pair of boxer shorts with "Beef, It's What's For Dinner" printed on the front and nothing else. On his chest, he sported a large tattoo of an ascending angel. Arched across his pectorals, in flowing script, read, "Angel de la Muerte."

Peach decided he was a shoo-in for the role of Mr. Clean's evil twin. Tinman was thinking of Brobdingnagian, the mythical land of giants. Both wisely kept their thoughts to themselves.

After the initial shock, they peaked around the colossus and saw Dez, completely nude, lying face down on a long, low table. A small towel barely covered her buttocks.

"Are you hurting our mother?" asked Peach in such a way as to imply he was just curious and whatever the answer was, it would not concern him in the slightest.

"Your mother?" The voice did not match the body. It is was squeaky high and quite comical. They both, however, decided they would wait until they got to know him quite a bit better before telling him he sounded like Speedy Gonzalez.

"I swear Peach! If you do that one more time I'm gonna box your ears!" yelled Dez. "Now get in here!"

Peach and Tinman squeezed by the behemoth and dutifully scooted over next to Dez. "What took you so long?" she asked.

"You expecting us?" asked Peach.

"I knew it wouldn't take long before you found out."

Tinman snorted. "Is that why you enlisted the heavy? For protection?"

"Angel? He's no heavy, he's my neighbor," Dez explained. "He's just giving me a massage. The game went until four last night and I'm as stiff as a plank."

Tinman looked at the albino. "You live here?"

"Next floor down," squeaked Angel.

"And you can afford a place like this as a masseuse?" asked Peach.

"Oh, this is just a hobby. I like the feel of skin. I only do close friends though. I make my money in drugs," said Angel.

"Pharmaceuticals, huh," said Peach.

"No, the illegal kind," said Angel.

Tinman caught Dez's eyes and shook his head in shame. "It's not what you think, stupid," said Dez.

Angel picked up on the insinuation. "I'm no drug dealer if that's what you think. I hate drugs. In fact, I started my business by robbing dealers but I figured out I could make more through protection."

"From the cops? Other gangs?" asked Peach.

"From me," said Angel with a cherubic smile. "Most of the dealers around here are Latino and the albino thing really freaks them out. And they're all very superstitious.

So the name Angel of Death puts the fear of God into them."

"Clever," said Peach, really warming up to Angel. "Did you come up with that? Very nice. I bet the rippling muscles don't hurt the shakedown either."

Angel agreed. "I try to keep in shape."

"And you're doing an admirable job of it, pal," said Peach as he patted one of Angel's rippling pecs.

Angel giggled. "Oh, you're hands are cold."

"You run this protection racket by yourself?" asked Tinman.

"I have a partner who helps," said Angel.

"Hm. I guess it's time I give up my street corner nickel bag gig," Tinman quipped.

It fell flat on Angel who narrowed his eyes and took a step toward him. "Just kidding big guy!" said Tinman. "Relax. I never touch the stuff." Angel finally caught up to the quip and backed off.

"Angel, these are my two dear friends. The grumpy one is Tinman and the happy one is Peach," said Dez.

"It's a pleasure," said Angel sincerely.

"All mine," said Tinman with more than a hint of attitude.

"Okay, enough of the introductions," said Dez. "Now, you two are wasting your time."

"I told him so," said Peach.

"Well, he obviously didn't listen. I am not now or ever going to give back any of the money I got for those baskets. End of debate. See, wasn't that fun?"

"Goddammit, Dez! This is not fair!" shouted Tinman.

"Fair? Hell, I practically gave you the motel. I never asked for that back have I?"

"It's entirely different!" Tinman bellowed, even though her dig definitely took some of the steam out of his argument.

"Calm down everyone! What's the beef here?" asked Angel.

"You be the judge, Angel," said Dez. "If a person gives you something and then wants it back what are they?"

"Indian giver," said Angel.

"Right. And what do you think of Indian givers?"

"They're scum. Worse than drug dealers."

"See. Angel agrees. Now get out of here before he gets pissed off. I want everyone to be friends. I'm sure you two smart kids can find your own way to get those baskets back."

"And how are we supposed to do that?!" Tinman demanded.

"I don't know. Steal them back," said Dez. "Come on, Angel. I've got a knot under this shoulder that's threatening to propagate."

As Angel resumed his massage, Tinman stared down at Dez, face turning red, breathing labored. His mouth twitched and contorted like he was trying to find a way to kill her with words. Peach gently turned him toward the door.

He managed to get him to the foyer when the light in the doorway was suddenly blocked by a faceless shadow, like a lunar eclipse. Their eyes focused and saw what appeared to be a sumo wrestler filling all but a few inches of the entranceway. The human mountain had on a giant pair of Jersey Shorts and bunny slippers. His skin was island brown and on his impressive forehead a tattoo read, "Your Worst Nightmare." Around his feet, two Chihuahuas ran in circles, yipping and nipping.

"Hey, Angel," spoke the monster. Peach and Tinman were shocked the thing could actually speak, much like the way Dr. Frankenstein must have felt. "Kutchy and Koo need to go pee-pee. I'm gonna take them to the park."

"Okay, Malice. I'll be down in a bit," said Angel, and the titan disappeared from the doorway, footsteps thundering down the hall.

"Malice?" Peach asked.

"That's my roomie. His real name is Malosi. He's from Samoa. But I call him Malice. He's also my business partner and the name helps the effect," Angel explained.

"Why does that not surprise me," said Tinman, and he marched out of the room with Peach at his heels.

"Moody guy," observed Angel.

"Eh, he's been that way since he was a child. A little lower, honey. That's the ticket."

* * *

Peach decided not to tell Tinman where he was taking him. He knew if he did he would never get him there. It didn't take much not to tell him. Ever since they'd left Dez, he'd gone comatose. He stared out the window of the wagon, glazed eyes seeing nothing. Peach was beginning to worry about him.

He knew if they were ever going to get their hands on the baskets, Tinman would need to get his brain right. He would have to remember their roots and how at one time nothing was unattainable. He would have to rediscover his thieves' blood.

It's no surprise the brothers were into crime. When they were kids, there was plenty of inspiration. In 1978 alone there were several high-profile heists that had fascinated and inspired.

There was a million-dollar heist of an armored car in New York that was never solved. A week later another armored car was hit for two million. A month earlier, some guys in a van pulled up to the Lufthansa cargo hangar at LaGuardia Airport and stole five million dollars from the vault.

In the middle of the country, three Cezanne paintings were stolen at the Art Institute of Chicago. It was their second burglary in ten days. Also, forgers started to use color copiers for the first time, creating bogus money orders that were nearly impossible to detect.

On the other coast, thieves dropped through the skylight of a San Francisco museum and made off with a Rembrandt worth a cool million. In San Diego, Stanley Mark Rifkin pulled off the first heist using computer transfers. By memorizing the daily transfer code he was able to wire himself over ten million dollars—the country's largest bank heist. He made the mistake of trying to liquidate the cash by attempting to exchange the money for diamonds through a Russian merchant and was eventually caught. But Rifkin was an early hero of Peach and Tinman.

The brothers studied these crimes and learned. They went to the hit movie of the day, The Brinks Job, and sat through two showings to make sure they hadn't missed any details. Other movies were, Up In Smoke, Every Which Way But Loose, Animal House.

The country seemed awash in illegal activities. Hunter S. Thompson was busted in Pismo Beach CA with an ounce of pot. Dan Haggerty was pulled over in a Ferrari going 100mph and tossed away a bag of white powder before the cops could stop him. Shame on you, Grizzly Adams.

In 1978, Reno's crime rates were up 29% from the previous year. Neither was into drugs but they were surrounded by the associated activities. Drug trafficking was so bad the sheriff appealed for a special drug squad. Reno was a big drop-off point because the small airport had a casual atmosphere with a limited number of customs agents. The surrounding desert and dry lake beds also provided ideal locations for private planes to land and unload contraband.

Reno was also a known gathering spot for career criminals: bank robbers, jewelry thieves, heavy gees. The police held an annual conference in Sparks to discuss the three to four hundred known criminals who passed through town as they crisscrossed the country pulling heists.

Peach and Tinman's first introduction to professional criminals came in January of 1978. Until then, they had specialized in petty crime and it was no more than a lark. The party at Lips changed all that. The party was the brainchild of three thieves who hung around Guys and Gals, a bar on South Virginia known to be a hangout for criminals. They decided it would be fun to hold a large gala and invite big-time crooks from around the country. The idea was to give people in the rackets an opportunity to rub shoulders, exchange notes, and possibly set up future heists.

Tinman used to play pool at Guys and Gals and was invited by one of the party hosts after Tinman took him for $500. The guy thought it would be funny to bring him in as a ringer to beat some of his fellow crooks. Peach was allowed to come along. On January 23, two hundred criminals descended on Reno. They flew in from San Francisco, New York, Los Angeles, and as far away as Hawaii. Lips provided limousine service from the airport and valet parking. It was quite the underworld extravaganza. While Tinman shot pool, Peach hobnobbed with as many of the attendees as he could, soaking up knowledge.

By the time the affair was over, his direction had changed. He now saw crime as a career. The effect it had on Tinman was more through osmosis. After the party, Peach went on a tear, and to keep him safe, Tinman was forced to come along for the ride.

In the months following the party, several arrests were made across the country. Many involved crooks who had attended the event. It was later discovered the three guys who set up the shindig were undercover agents for the Washoe County Sheriff's Office. The party and ensuing stings were financed by the U.S. Justice Department.

Peach and Tinman were too small-time to be of any bother and escaped blowback from having attended. They were free to continue their explorations into crime and took full advantage.

During that summer, there was a rash of burglaries in the Carson area. Thefts included radios, stereo equipment, auto parts as well as jewelry stolen from the Lucky Spur Casino. In September, they tried to get into a safe at the Ormsby House. They had no safecracking tools and no idea what to do with them even if they'd had any. In the end, they had to take it along with them, still unopened. They never did manage to open it and it ended up in a landfill. The manager later stated he was perplexed why anyone would want the safe as it was empty.

On the morning of October 18, a very polite man robbed Czyz's Men's Clothing Store in Tahoe. The take was $43. Around lunchtime, it was reported that two polite young men pulled up to a lady in a bank parking lot. She was about to make a deposit for her business. They asked her nicely to give them the money and she handed over $2000. Three hours later, at a different bank, another depositor was relieved of $4500. Later that evening, at the Arco on Keystone Avenue, a polite man robbed the clerk for $65. It was just one of those days. Why quit when you're ahead?

By the time December rolled around, they thought they were invincible. The basket theft was a natural result. They did have a plan behind all of this. The idea was to make enough money to go on the road. In that, they succeeded. The day after giving Dez the baskets, they split town with Bones and Catfish.

Once out of Reno, Tinman discovered he could make far more money hustling than he could pulling small heists. At first, Peach agreed and became his steerer. His job was to locate a mark and set him up for Tinman. When action was slow they would go on the whiz with Bones and Catfish. But after five or six years, Peach got bored. He started pulling lone wolf robberies: convenience stores, bowling alleys, pedestrians. He was anything but a class act.

Bones and Catfish did not approve and took off to sunnier locales. Tinman put up with it for a long time, but he refused to take part anymore. His stature as a pool hustler rose and he felt Peach's activities were beneath him. About twenty years into their time on the road, Peach's luck ran out and it nearly cost both of them several years in the pen. Only Tinman's quick thinking saved them. After that, it was mutually decided they should part ways.

Tinman hustled solo for a while until his action died and he returned to Reno. Peach took a long look at himself and went about learning his current trade. Now he knew the best way to pay his brother back for all he'd done was to convince him to join forces, and the Dynamic Duo would be reborn.

* * *

"Why are we here?" asked Tinman

"That's an age-old question, brother," Peach said. "You'll have to ask a philosopher."

"No! Here!"

"I figured it would be fun to at least have a look at our baskets," said Peach. "For old times' sake." He leaned over and unlatched the glove box. Reaching in, he grabbed an impressive looking high-tech digital camera with a zoom lens.

Tinman asked, "What's that for?"

"To take pictures."

Tinman sighed heavily. "Where did you get it?"

"Oh, I picked it up someplace."

"And you know how to use it?" asked Tinman.

"Why would I have it?" asked Peach, looking strangely at him.

"Well, why do you need it now?!"

"I love museums. I want to take pictures of my favorite displays. Come on."

Peach climbed out of the car and started toward the Historical Society Museum. From inside the car, Tinman watched. Peach stopped and impatiently beckoned him with a wave. Tinman groaned and got out.

The museum sat halfway up a steep grade on the east side of the UNR campus. Just down from it was a small building housing the Transportation Services Dept. for the university. In front, a security guard/parking attendant sat in a golf cart eating a hoagie. Behind the building was the Fleischmann Planetarium, bordered by a large parking garage. On the other side of the garage was the approach to the Mackay Stadium where the school's football games were played. Here and there were posters and plaques with a snarling blue wolf on them. This was Wolf Pack country and you best not forget it, grrr.

The "tilt-up" concrete and steel building that housed the museum was plain with no distinct architecture except interspaced, narrow concrete buttresses jutting out along the length of the building. The only decorative elements were elongated diamond shape cutouts on the outer walls, painted orange. It was built in 1968 and though a new addition had been added in the early 80s, it looked like it was time to build a new museum.

Tinman and Peach walked up the ramp to the front doors which had been salvaged from an old bank. They were large and impressive. To Tinman's eyes, they were impregnable if secured. Peach, however, eyed the locks and figured on about a minute or so to pick, maybe two.

They stepped inside through two more automatic doors. A hallway ran down the middle of the building. To the right, just inside the front doors, was a small gift shop. Also on the right, farther down the hall, was the entrance to the research library. Across from the gift shop was a teeny office for the director of the museum. The entrance to the displays was just next to this office.

A thirtyish, buxom lady with a killer smile and dark skin trotted up to them. "Hello!" she chirped. "If you're here to see the museum it will be five dollars apiece."

Tinman turned to go. Peach grabbed him and handed over a ten spot. "Have you ever been to the museum before?" the lady inquired.

"A very long time ago. It was a memorable moment," said Peach, showing off his equally killer smile. "But I forget a lot of it. Maybe you'd like to show us around."

"I'd love to!" squealed the lady. "My name is Pepper. I'm a graduate student and I'm here working on a research paper about the history of Reno. So I'm not a regular docent. If you'd like me to get you one I can. But I'm sure I can do a good job." She looked at them with hopeful, eager eyes.

"I'm sure you do a great job," said Peach. "Lead the way, Pepper."

As they followed her into the display area Tinman whispered to Peach, "What's her pet name going to be? Peppermint?" Peach thought about it, raised his eyebrows, and gave the thumbs up.

Just inside the entrance, to the left was a short, curved hallway leading to a display of Reno history. To the right, the room opened up showing several display areas each one featuring a different part of Nevada history. Directly in front of them was the new Dat So La Lee display.

Ten of the famous weaver's baskets were on display in Lucite cases mounted on green, waist-high cube stands. Behind the cases was a blown-up photograph of the mountains around Virginia City. It was nearly seven feet high and arced behind the entire display. Across from this were baskets by weavers from other tribes.

As Pepper babbled on about the history of basket weaving Tinman surreptitiously examined the cases. He saw locks on the sides of each one and his heart sank. Peach was inwardly taken aback by the poor quality of the locks which were more used for filing cabinets not million-dollar baskets. He added another twenty seconds each to his time count.

Above and to the left of the display was a small round box mounted to the ceiling and facing the cases. Tinman imagined it must be the laser beam. He instinctively stepped out of its range. Peach, on the other hand, was stunned there was only one video camera and it was not of the rotating sort. From his experience, it meant it was more for show than anything and most likely not monitored regularly but rather stored footage for later examination should a burglary occur. Which is a little bit too late, don't you think?

Disheartened, Tinman fled the display hoping never to set eyes on it again. He wandered away from Peach and Pepper and headed into the main display room. When he didn't see any more of the laser boxes, he began to relax. He spent a few minutes looking at the display on cheating, featuring juiced dice, marked cards, and a mechanical vest "holdout" that allowed a cheat to slip a card into play without being seen.

He perused the old slot machines in the gaming display and checked out the cowboy exhibit. He admired the large, red and white neon sign featuring two martini glasses complete with multi-colored olives. It used to hang in front of The Phone Booth, a bar that was right next to the old Bell Telephone Building on N. Center. All the telephone company employees used to hang out there after work. Now it was the Cal-Neva Parking Stadium. The thought depressed him. Whatever happened to parking garage?

Just off from the neon sign was a small display honoring Miss Atomic Bomb. The center photo showed a lovely blond posing in the desert, her arms spread wide and a cardboard cut-out of a white cloud covering her private parts. The caption declared she "radiated loveliness instead of deadly atomic particles." Tinman shook his head. Only Nevada could turn a nuclear holocaust into a tourist draw.

He meandered around a corner and found himself facing a stuffed two-headed calf and that did it for him.

He saw Peach and Pepper down by the bootlegging display. They were giggling like a couple of schoolgirls. He high-stepped over to them and tapped Peach on the shoulder.

"It's time to go," said Tinman.

"Actually, Pepper is about ready to cut out of here in a few minutes. We were thinking the three of us could have a drink somewhere."

Tinman shook his head. "Not in the mood. I'll take the bus home." He turned to go.

"Wait a minute, honey," said Pepper. "Don't I know you?"

"I doubt it," said Tinman with a shrug.

Pepper closed in and peered at his face. "Where have I seen that face before?"

"Maybe you're thinking of him," said Tinman. "We're twins."

"Don't be silly, I knew that. No, it was somewhere recently. I know it was you."

"Maybe it was his doppelganger," offered Peach.

"Ooh! You have one of those?" Pepper asked Tinman.

"Apparently so," said Tinman. He spun around and marched out of the place.

As he walked past the Transportation Services building he saw the security guard still sitting in his cart. He thought to himself it must have been a helluva big sandwich to take that long to eat. He hit the sidewalk along North Virginia and saw a bus stop a few blocks down.

Inside the museum, Pepper told Peach she had a few things to wrap up in the research library before she could leave. She told him he could wait in the gift shop but Peach said he'd wait for her outside and headed for the front doors.

When he got outside he began to take pictures. He took several of the front doors and walked around and shot the back and side entrances. He stepped into the side parking lot and took photos of every angle and aspect of the building. He was just wrapping up when he felt the presence of someone behind him.

He turned around and saw a young security guard who he imagined was the same guy in the cart. The kid had that look about him like he held his position in way too high regard. "What do you think you're doing?" he asked.

Peach smiled but received none in return. "Architecture. I'm way into it. Just love anything out of the ordinary. I have a whole library of photos."

The guard furrowed his brow and looked at the plain building. He was just about to object when Pepper came bopping out of the side door and practically jogged over to Peach. He threw an arm around her and they swayed over to his car. Peach gave the security guard a friendly wave and the guard narrowed his eyes.

TWELVE

THE VERY ACT OF EATING DISGUSTED HIM. It reminded him he was human, just another animal forced to rely on primal needs. He stared at the hoagie sitting next to him on the electric security cart. Eating involved masticating and that reminded him of another word that started with "mast." He could barely think of the word much less say it. It represented another activity the weak human body often succumbed to. Not that he ever would. When the urge came he immediately doused it with a cold shower. He was stronger than that. He didn't need what other humans needed.

His stomach growled. He slapped it angrily. Another reminder that eating was a reality even he couldn't hide from. He lifted the hoagie from its resting spot and with a scowl raised it to his mouth. The name tag on his uniform showed he was referred to as Hobie. As he forced the food into his body he thought about the repugnant process he was beginning. Put the food in the body, the body turns it to waste and the waste is ejected through defecation. On and on. Over and over for an entire lifetime. What was the point? The human body was flawed, its systems redundant and its makeup weak.

Hobie thought of himself as a machine. A fighting, killing machine who's only mission was to root out evil and annihilate it. His hero was the Gunslinger in the movie, Westworld. Yul Brynner played the android who went around the futuristic amusement park killing human visitors in what were supposed to be mock gunfights. Hobie always thought he was justified in his actions because of the way the androids were treated by the humans. The director of the movie had no such vision and no sane audience member would ever think of the Gunslinger as the guy in the white hat. Hobie didn't care. People didn't see reality. At least not his form of reality. They were blind.

An alarm went off in his head signifying the presence of evil. Hobie believed he had a sixth sense regarding evil. He could sniff it out from a distance and had proof this mystical sense worked. When he was just a boy he became certain his father was stealing canned food products from the grocery store where he worked stocking shelves. Hobie had reported this to the manager and his father was fired. He began to drink heavily, Hobie's mother divorced him and he eventually took his own life out of despair. Mission accomplished!

In the winter of his senior year in high school, he discovered the school's old janitor had run an extension cord from a tool shed to a homeless couple's encampment in some trees at the edge of the property. The couple was using the stolen electricity to power a portable heater. One night, Hobie broke into the shed and caused a short circuit in the fuse box. The shed caught on fire and burned to the ground. The homeless couple was arrested for vagrancy and destruction of public property. The old janitor was forced into early retirement. Another evil pursuit thwarted!

There were many other successful pursuits because Hobie was always vigilant. As he saw it, his function in life was to save human civilization from itself. When left to their own devices, humans reverted to their bestial beginnings. All humans were just one small step away from embracing their depraved, primitive instincts. Fortunately, Hobie was put here to save them by eradicating their sinful ways. He alone could smooth the fabric of society and avert ultimate destruction.

He looked up from his hoagie to see what had caused the bat signal to go off in his brain. Immediately, he spotted the beige, station wagon as it drove past the Transportation Services Building and turned into the Nevada Historical Museum's parking lot. There was something about that car that wasn't right. First of all, who drives a station wagon anymore? He would watch to see who got out. If it wasn't a family of four, there was mischief in the doing.

He grinned when he saw a very shifty looking man in his fifties climb out of the driver's side. This was no family man. Hobie could see another person still in the car. The driver waved his arm impatiently and the other person climbed out. This guy was even shadier. He had a banner attached to his back saying "hardened criminal." Hobie watched as the two disappeared into the museum.

He immediately smelled big trouble. The museum housed many valuable things and he was certain these two guys were out to take them. He decided to take a closer look at the car. He'd have to move fast before they came back out again. He didn't want to tip them off to the fact they were under suspicion. He flipped his disgusting half-eaten hoagie onto the ground and started the cart. Hobie to the rescue.

He was fairly certain they wouldn't try to rob the place in broad daylight. He hadn't seen any bulges in their pockets indicating they were packing. Still, he couldn't be sure. He instinctively patted the portable Taser attached to his belt. Not that it would do much good in a gunfight. He hated the fact they wouldn't let security guards wear guns. How can you really hurt someone with a Taser? Hell, just for kicks, he had tried it out on himself several times. Sure, it stunned you a little bit and momentarily scattered your brain waves but then it went away. There was no permanent damage. No maiming, mangling, or mutilation of any kind. What good was that? There was no permanent reminder to the villain that their behavior was unacceptable and never to be repeated.

He'd suggested to his boss they be allowed to carry nunchucks but that was shot down. He then asked about machetes. Wouldn't that be something! Strap a machete to your belt and these little punk college kids would know who's boss. The proposal had landed him in parking duty, handing out tickets to cheap bastards who refused to put enough money in the meters.

He'd thought about bringing one of his guns to work but had not attempted it yet. There was no sound reason why he shouldn't be allowed to carry one. He was very adept with guns. For fun, he spent his free time at the Big Shot Shooting Range. He was at home there. For a measly $50 or so he could rent a fully-automatic tommy gun and blast away at the imaginary malefactors. For the same amount, he could also practice with an Uzi, a Russian Saiga, or the .50 IMI Desert Eagle with the largest centerfire cartridge of any magazine-fed self-loading pistol. To him, the shooting range was heaven on earth.

He reached the wagon and quickly jumped off his cart. He peered into the windows and didn't see anything amiss. Of course, it only meant he was dealing with professionals. He squished his face against the tinted glass of the rear wagon area and saw a tarp covering . . . something. He leaned back and thought. Probably burglar tools. That would explain it. They weren't doing the heist today, they were only casing the joint. He got back on his cart and wheeled around to the front of the Transportation Building. He didn't want to arouse their suspicions by being too close. Now he would wait and see.

He knew this job was only a holding pattern. There were great things in store for him if only he could pull off a major coup. All he had to do was be the hero and stop some nefarious act and he would be off to bigger and better things. This was no place for one such as him, even though others along the way had been too blind to see it that way.

After he barely graduated high school with no chance of getting into college, he tried enlisting in the army. They turned him down as did every other branch of the military. It had frustrated him to no end. The unfairness of it all angered him. All over one failed test. There had been many placement tests in the process of enlisting, mostly to see what job fit the enlistee. He had done fine with all of those. And then he failed the one test and was denied. One test! And it was some silly psychological test which made the unjustness even greater. How can one fail a psychological test? How can what you think be wrong?

Ever since he decided not to tell people what he thought. They were too blind to understand and it led to trouble. He still held a grudge against the military but after a while, he figured it was their loss. Eventually, he would end up in some shadowy, secret department buried deep in the NSA, the sole purpose of which was to infiltrate the bowels of the world's greatest evil empires and implode them from within. He felt his loins stir from the thought and forced it from his head. There was no cold shower anywhere nearby.

His reverie was broken by the appearance of the guy who was in the passenger seat of the wagon. He was surprised to see the man start walking across the grassy area in front of the museum. Was this crook on to him? He was coming his way. He needed a cover. He quickly reached down and picked up his squashed hoagie from the road and acted like he was eating it. It did the trick. The no-goodnik barely glanced his way but instead headed for North Virginia Street on foot.

This perplexed Hobie. Why would the two thieves part ways? He would have to wait and see. It wasn't long before the other guy came out and started taking pictures of the building. Now Hobie knew his suspicions were correct. He was definitely casing the place. Now was the time for action. He started his cart and took a roundabout way to the building. He needed the element of surprise. He stashed it behind a large SUV and quietly approached the man.

"What the hell do you think you're doing?" he asked in his most imperious fashion. The criminal showed no fear or surprise but instead responded to the intrusion with a smarmy smile. This only confirmed to Hobie he was up against real pros.

"Architecture. I'm way into it. Just love anything out of the ordinary. I have a whole library of photos," said the evildoer.

A lame answer thought Hobie. Who could possibly believe anyone would be interested in such a boring building with little to no redeeming architectural qualities. He didn't want to tip him off though. He knew if he bided his time this might just be his golden opportunity. He was saved from having to say anything by the appearance of a black woman exiting the side door of the museum.

She ran over to this devil in front of him and he threw an arm around her. They waved to him and started for the guy's car. Now it all made sense. The reason the first guy had left was to leave the other, better-looking guy alone with this employee. His job would be to recruit her as an inside man for the job, or, if that failed, to gain valuable security information.

He watched them drive off, secure in his plan of action. He would be keeping a very close eye on this museum. A very close eye indeed.

THIRTEEN

"NOW OVER TO SCOTT FRENLEY." The news anchor smiled and Bones turned up the volume. The screen was filled with a picture of a floating strip of neon yellow police caution tape with CRIME WAVE printed on it.

"Just a second, kid. I love this guy! This is the funniest part of the news," said Bones.

He and Catfish stopped their pickpocketing lesson with Tek and focused on the television set hanging over the bar. "You should pay attention, Tek. You might learn something," Catfish said. Tek sighed and sat on a stool next to them. It was midday, still off-hours for the hall, and Tinman was practicing.

"Good afternoon ladies and gentlemen, Scott Frenley here. Yesterday afternoon during rush hour a man in a pickup truck was seen speeding on North McCarran Boulevard. The police officer who spotted him gave chase and the driver initially pulled to the side of the road. When the officer approached the car, however, the driver attempted to escape. The chase was short-lived as he promptly drove into a ditch and became stuck. Brilliant!"

Bones and Catfish cracked up.

"The driver was charged with speeding, attempting to flee a police officer, possession of an unregistered firearm, and a small amount of methamphetamine. I guess soon he's going to become very familiar with ditches. Digging them for the county that is!"

The two old guys choked with laughter. They slapped the bar and pounded the floor with their feet.

"What can I learn from that idiot?" asked Tek.

"Never do two crimes at the same time, buddy boy," explained Catfish. "The guy's packing bad heat and drugs and he's speeding? What a chowderhead."

"Next up, late last evening, a man jumped over a railing at The Nugget's Sports Bar and grabbed an undisclosed amount of cash. He then fled on foot. Police are searching for this man. Look closely, the photo is hard to make out," said Scott Frenley, sporting a sly grin as a very clear still shot from the video feed flashed onto the screen.

Bones howled. "He's practically smiling for the camera!"

"This numbnuts forgot a cardinal rule, Tek," cackled Catfish. "Never try and heist a casino. They're in the business of theft."

"Our final story, a man robbed the Prater Street Family Dollar Store yesterday afternoon, escaping with a small amount of money from one of the registers."

"For crying out loud," said Catfish. "Will these morons ever learn."

"An hour later, presumably the same man entered a Dollar General Store on Greenbrae Drive and pretended he was going to buy something. Clever!"

Catfish and Bones can barely contain themselves.

"He was not wearing a disguise but—wait for it folks, drum roll—he did have on dark clothing! Ooh. A man with a plan!"

"Now listen and learn, Tek. This is serious," said Catfish. "If you get busted robbing a place you're going to get the same stint in jail whether you're sticking up a lemonade stand or a high-end jewelry store. Remember you always have to balance risk with gain. Got it?"

Tek thought about this and slowly nodded.

"That's it for this issue of Crime Wave. This is Scott Frenley wishing all of you a safe and happy day. And remember people, come on now, if you're going to attempt a crime, show a little dignity!"

"See, I tell you this guy gets us," said Bones, switching off the TV.

"Okay, now can we get back to that thing about how the eye works?" asked Tek.

"One more time," Bones drawled. "If you're trying to distract a person's eyes while you fork the leather you can use your spare hand as a decoy. If I move that hand in an arc away from where it started, the mark's eyes are going to stay on the hand and the other hand is free to pick. Like if I were to point out a beautiful sky and keep moving my hand picking out pretty clouds. They stay distracted because the hand is moving in an arc. But if I move it in a straight line, their eyes are going to snap back to where it started and there's a good chance they'll see my other hand make the touch. Got it?"

Tek scrunched his eyes and concentrated. With his knuckles, he tried to rub the knowledge through his skull and into his brain. He dropped his hands and his shoulders sagged.

"No. I don't get it. Because once again, I'm not cut out for this," he said and kicked the front of the bar.

"Hey, hey, hey," said Bones, smoothing out Tek's hair. "That is no reflection on you. Why when you start going on about hacking it's like I am talking to an alien."

"Really?" asked Tek. "I guess it's just a knack."

"That's exactly what it is," said Catfish. "You just stick to what you know."

The front door swung open and Peach strolled in whistling. "How the hell did you get in here?" Tinman demanded. "I know I locked that door."

"That's your mistake," said Peach. "Too much of a temptation."

"What does that mean?!" demanded Tinman.

"We'll get to it. Sorry I disappeared on you," said Peach. Tinman just shrugged. "Hey, I wanted to thank you for the Peppermint tip."

"Worked for you, huh?" asked Tinman.

"Oh yeah. Course, after I got to know her over this past week I expanded on it. Now I call her Peppermint Twist."

Tinman hated to even ask but couldn't help himself. "Pray tell."

"Well when we're doing the dirty she does this little thing with her—"

"I don't want to know!"

"Suit yourself. You know this is the second time I've been in here and it's still a dump."

"Well it's the only dump around so here I am," said Tinman, and he went back to shooting.

"Doesn't have to be." Peach leaned over his shoulder as he took a shot. "Remember when we were kids and you always talked about having your own hall? I mean you wouldn't talk about anything else for a while. Don't you still wish you had your own?"

Tinman ignored him and tossed a few more balls out on the table. Peach said, "I take that as a resounding yes.

Well, if you had big bucks you could build your own. A real hall. Not this converted bar."

"And if I had big wings I could fly to the moon. Your point?" asked Tinman. When he didn't receive a response he stood up from the table and stared at his brother who grinned back.

"I was thinking we could follow Dez's suggestion."

"She was kidding."

"Well, I'm not. What do we have to lose?"

"Our freedom."

"Uh-uh. This isn't freedom, brother. You need money to be free."

There was no comeback to this thieves' truism so Tinman leaned back to the table. "I've forgotten all about those damn things. They're too well-protected. It's out of our league."

"Not necessarily. Let me show you something," said Peach.

"Forget it okay! I'm through with your little surprises!" Tinman smacked the cue ball and it careened off two rails and sunk a duck hanging on the far corner pocket.

Peach sighed and walked over to the bar. "Hey fellas, how's tricks?" Bones and Catfish shrugged. "How are you this fine day, Tek?"

Tek didn't answer at first. He eyed Peach closely and decided he was on safe ground. "What do you do?"

"Huh?"

"All these other guys have an angle. I figure you must have one."

Peach chuckled. "Let's just say I let myself into places."

Catfish caught Bones' eyes and lifted a brow. "What are you talking about?" Tek asked.

Peach looked back at Tinman hard at practice. "It's better if I show you. Got any money? Okay, I'll bet you twenty bucks I can get into this place with the door locked. I won't do anything to the actual lock though. I'll open it using the handle from the inside, but I'll be outside."

"So you're a magician?" asked Tek.

"Some people see it that way," said Peach. "Do we have a bet?"

"You're on," said Tek. "Bones, Catfish, you want a piece of this?"

"I'll lay a ten on it," said Bones. "Hell, yeah. I'm in," said Catfish. "Though I have a hunch we're getting hustled."

"Give me a few minutes, I need to get something out of my car," said Peach. "Lock up after I leave, top and bottom." He cocked his head toward Tinman and smiled as he stepped out of the hall.

Tek immediately locked the door and rushed over to Tinman. "How's he going to do it? You must know him better than anyone."

"What are you talking about?" asked Tinman, focusing on a tricky shot.

"He says he can get into this place without messing with the locks! He says he'll do it by just turning the inside handle."

Tinman snorted and dropped the ball in the pocket. Privately, however, he was wondering what new surprise his brother would drop that would probably cause him further grief.

A few minutes later, Bones, Catfish, and Tek were wondering if Peach was pulling a fast one when they saw a thin metal rod slide through the small gap at the bottom of the front door. The section of the visible rod was about three and a half feet long with a five by four-inch piece of rectangular mesh attached to the top end. A piece of string ran from the mesh down the rod and out the door. Where the bottom end of the rod met the bottom of the door it bent like an L with the other half of the rod outside.

The string went taut and the rod slowly lifted into the air. As it did, the bottom of it slid along the gap under the door and ended standing vertically. The mesh and string at the top were directly in front of the door handle and deadbolt.

The string slackened a little and the rod leaned in. With a little twist, the string draped over the deadbolt latch and it was pulled taut. Another little twist and the latch flipped open.

There was a gasp in the room. Bones, Catfish, and Tek snapped their gaping heads toward Tinman. Involuntarily, all four of them stood and zombielike walked to the door.

The string around the deadbolt latch slackened again and the rod leaned back and the string pulled away. The rod lowered a bit, enough for the piece of mesh to drape over the round handle of the door. The string was pulled taut and like a hand, the mesh grasped the handle. A little twist and the handle turned. The string went loose, the rod dropped to the ground and disappeared through the gap under the door.

Peach strolled in, holding the strange contraption. Tek spontaneously broke into applause. Bones and Catfish joined in the ovation. Tinman could only shake his head as he approached his brother, eyes wide.

Tek solemnly handed Peach the bet money. "What is that thing?!" he cried.

"This is called The Mule Tool. I picked it up in the early '90s from a guy who was trying to sell them to hotel security. His pitch was it would help when people locked their keys in their rooms."

Tek was leaning in closer. "This is the coolest thing ever!"

"Eh, I hardly ever use it. It's more like a toy, really. Check it out," said Peach, handing the tool to Tek. "I keep it around for sentimental purposes. It was one of the first tools I ever bought."

"One of the first?" asked Catfish. "You have others?"

"Christ, I got the set-up now. Took me ten years to put my kit together. Now I can pretty much let myself into anyplace. You want to take a look?"

Bones, Catfish, and Tek eagerly accepted the invite. Tinman, in a daze, followed them out the door and down the sidewalk to Peach's car.

As Peach unlocked the back gate of the wagon, Tek sidled up. "So you're a burglar," he whispered.

"Well, I know a little bit about it," said Peach. "Actually I know a lot."

He pulled the tarp aside to reveal a large metal case filling the wagon part of the car. It looked like it had been specially designed to perfectly fit the space. He pulled out a ring of keys and unlocked the case.

"In fact, some of the police reports have said my jobs were done by a master thief. I kind of like the sound of that. You'll have to take my word on it; I don't keep clippings. Too dangerous."

He pushed on the lid and it slid back toward the front of the car and like a roll top desk disappeared by wrapping around the far end. Inside was a tightly packed, well-organized selection of tools, some exotic, some recognizable. Peach's audience of four was too stunned to utter a word.

"I like to keep things tidy. You never know when you have to grab something in a hurry."

"You know how to use all these?" stuttered Tinman.

"Why would I have them," said Peach, giving him a perplexed look. "Anyway, over here are my picks. This is the diamond pick, rake pick, hook pick, double ball pick, half-round pick, and the wave shoot pick. All made from high-quality spring steel. This set is my favorite, from England. It's called the Fall Pick set and the tension wrenches are super sweet. Know what I mean?"

The four guys nodded dumbly. "In this section are the specialty picks. I've got the Snake Pick which is really only used for the Moores Lock."

"Why is it called a snake pick?" asked Tek.

"See how it has this funny bend at the end? Well, it's made this way so you can simply bypass the pins altogether. This hook grabs the cam at the back of the cylinder and you just turn it open. Babingbabang!"

Catfish and Bones met Tinman's eyes. They were all equally flabbergasted. Like good students they turned back to the presentation.

"The M-175 over here is a shim tool specifically designed to open most Master padlocks. This baby, the IT-1000 set me back a bundle but it's the only shim tool guaranteed to open the Presto 175 lock. I ran into one at a warehouse and had to buy this to finish the job. I also have a couple of electronic picks like this Cobra Pro, but I hardly use them anymore. Too loud."

"What's that?" asked Tek, pointing at a grouping of rods sitting on several manuals.

"That is the Master Z kit. I can open most cars with it. It comes with a series of pre-bent rods. The manuals show you exactly which rod has the right bend to open such and such a car. And of course the obligatory slap hammer for knocking out the ignition cylinder. I've got a key-making set in the back there for when I can get a good impression."

"Is this really Peach I'm looking at?" asked Bones.

"The new and improved, buddy."

"And I did lock the door to the hall, didn't I?" Tinman mumbled.

"Sure you did. But, hey, it's a residential Kwikset. Five seconds at most. Now, moving over to this side, this stuff is mostly for safes."

"You can open safes?!" squealed Tek.

"Most of them. Still looking for one that beats me. But it's kind of my specialty."

"Why's that?"

"Cause that's where the loot is little man," said Peach with a grin. "Also, there was a moment in my youth where I tried to get into a safe, and let's just say it was quite embarrassing. Remember the Ormsby House disaster Tinman?"

Tinman nodded slowly, still trying to comprehend what was happening.

"That experience inspired me to never let it happen again," said Peach. "Anyway, I've got your basic stuff like punches, drift pins, cold chisels, sectional jimmy, some high-end drills with diamond bits, an electric saw with carborundum blades, acetylene torch complete with hose and tank, thank you very much. Let's see, a 220-volt electric cutting torch and a burning bar. I do have electric blasting caps and some explosives buried somewhere in here. I don't like the noise, though. I also have Thermite to make a plasma arc but it really stinks bad. I've been experimenting with lithium but I haven't figured out how to contain the thermal runaway."

Catfish caught Tinman's eyes and jerked a thumb toward Peach as if to say, "Are you hearing what I'm hearing." Tinman was equally at a loss and could only shrug.

Peach unlocked a small black case and flipped open the lid. The interior was lined with foam surrounding three thin tubes with little wires coming out the tops. "I blew the wad on this baby. Even had to dig into my fall dough."

Bones let out a low whistle. "Always, dangerous. Touching your fall dough."

"True. But it was worth every penny," said Peach. "This is a cystoscope mostly used in the medical industry for, well, let's just say it's a delicate procedure, or one would hope so anyway given where they're sticking this thing. For my purposes, it has a light and a mini-camera on the end. I remove the dial, drill a hole in the casing, and insert this thing here. I can get a bird's eye view of the tumblers and security features inside the safe. Let's see, what else. Well, hell, I could go on for an hour."

He straightened up and looked at his pupils. Bones and Catfish were the first to react. They bent over with laughter and it took a while to get any words out of them.

"Holy mother of God, Peach, you're a bona fide peterman!" cried Bones.

"Peterman?" asked Tek.

"A jugger, boy! Hallelujah, we got a yegg in the family!" shouted Catfish, slapping Peach on the back.

Peach saw Tek was still confused. "It just means a safecracker. These guys are old. They talk funny."

Tek nodded gravely and went to give The Mule Tool back but Peach waved it away. "Borrow it for a while. See if you can figure out how to use it. But no breaking into some place for real. Not until I see if you've got the right stuff."

Tek's eyes sparkled. "Thanks, Peach! I'll take real good care of it!" Peach winked and Tek ran down the sidewalk and darted into the hall.

Peach had not yet met Tinman's eyes. He knew how he felt about what he used to be and wasn't sure how he would react to what he had become. As he locked up his tool case he felt a hand on his shoulder. He turned around and faced his brother. The look on Tinman's face was unreadable.

"What happened to you?" asked Tinman.

"I saw the light," said Peach. "After you and I split up I knew it was my fault. I knew I had to make something of my life. It was really your doing."

"But how did all of this happen?" asked Tinman waving his arms at the wagon.

"A couple months after we parted ways, I decided to dabble in a little burglary."

"And it went from there?"

"Actually, no. I got popped. First time out. I pulled a nickel."

"You did five years inside?" asked Tinman quietly, suddenly feeling very close to his brother. "Just a nudge under three. Got out for good behavior and overcrowding. But it was the best thing ever for me."

"Being in stir? Never heard that before," said Catfish.

"Well, my cellie was this old-time heavy. A real pro from the word go. He reminded me of you two. He even pulled some jobs around Reno, back when the fix was on. He said he knew Graham and McKay before they retired."

Bones said, "Would have been right around when we first blew into town, the early '50s."

"Hell, those two ran the action since the '20s, along with Abelman and Wingfield before they retired. The Big Four," said Catfish. "You got their approval, you could whiz, grift, heist, whatever. For a piece of the action, naturally. There were more bent guys in this town than straights."

"Heady times," said Bones with a wistful smile. "We were young, lean, and mean."

"And rolling in the green, brother," said Catfish. He held a palm out and Bones gave him five.

"Exactly," said Peach. "So he's like cut from the same coat, so to speak.

"Cloth," corrected Tinman.

"Even better. And brother, he sat on me hard, I tell you. Rattled my brain cells until I saw the light. By the time I got out, I knew pretty much what he knew about heisting and cracking peters. But he made me promise I'd continue my education. So I enrolled in locksmith school. I had to use a different name and naturally, I couldn't graduate and get licensed because of my status as a felon, which is a real shame since my teacher said I was the top guy in my class. From there it's been trial and error."

"No big errors?" asked Tinman.

"Nope. Not even a close call. I don't want to sound uppity-up but I feel I'm at the top of my game." He held his breath, waiting for his brother's reaction.

"No more guns?" asked Tinman.

"Ancient history."

"And you actually know how to use all this stuff?"

"You know, I'd really appreciate it if you'd stop asking me that!"

"Okay, okay. You're a pro now. From the sounds of it you could have the pick of the litter. Why are you wasting your time with these baskets?"

Peach spun away, jerking his head like he'd been slapped. He quickly recovered and stepped back to Tinman, their faces inches apart. "You really need to ask? We're brothers. We settle this score together."

Tinman blinked first. He could hear the distant beat of his heart as it picked up its pace. Peach was back.

"So what do you think?" asked Peach.

Tinman grinned. "I think we need to get our baskets back."

Peach smiled wide. "I was sure hoping you'd say that, seeing that I have the whole thing doped out."

"You've already got a plan?" asked Tinman.

"You don't think I was doing the twist this whole time, do you? Hell, this job is a cinch. To pull it off, we're going to need a couple more guys for the string. Mostly as jiggers." He looked over to Bones and Catfish who acted like they hadn't been eavesdropping. "You guys up for a little action? All you got to do is be lookouts. Maybe some diversionary action if needed."

"We'll split even. One basket each," said Tinman.

"Actually it will be two and a half baskets each," Peach corrected.

"How do you figure?" asked Tinman.

"Well, we might have originally taken four baskets but there are ten baskets in there now and given the grief we've gone through, I think it would only be fair if we take all of them as payback."

"That's like ten million dollars' worth of baskets," said Bones in awe.

"Well, the only fence I know who can handle this kind of thing is gonna beat us up pretty bad. Still, I figure we'll all make out very well indeed. What do you say?"

Bones and Catfish psychically exchanged notes. Both knew the whiz couldn't last forever, given Bones' bouts of arthritis. Neither of them had any experience in heisting, but they figured their expertise in other crimes would serve them well. Mostly, it was the thought of missing out on the action that made their decision. The gain outweighed the risk. Boom or bust.

Simultaneously, they turned back. "You got yourself two jiggers," said Catfish.

"When do we go?" asked Bones.

"Tonight," said Peach.

"Tonight!" cried Tinman. "Why so soon?"

"Don't you know?" asked Peach. "Tonight is Homecoming."

FOURTEEN

"OKAY PEOPLE, THIS IS NOT A LITTLE THING, this is humongous. This is Homecoming!" roared the Chief of Campus Security. "On top of that, this is the Battle for Nevada! It doesn't get bigger than that. Am I right?!"

"RIGHT CHIEF."

The thirty security guards dutifully responded with the required gusto. They were sitting in a meeting room lined with rows of uncomfortable chairs. There were a few token females. They all seemed to be taking their job way too seriously.

Hobie was in his normal seat closest to the back door at the far end of the last row of chairs. He rolled his eyes. What a bunch of simpletons he was surrounded by. Losers, all of them. In particular, he hated the retired cops. He had never considered joining the local force, even when he'd been shot down by the military. He would never sink to busting small-timers and rousting homeless people. He was made to take on the criminal elite. Tonight would be the beginning of his rise to glory.

"Now as you all know, the students get pretty fired up over this game. And who can blame them? Right?" asked the Chief.

"RIGHT CHIEF."

"This football game determines whether or not the Wolf Pack rules!"

"GRRRR."

"The Battle for Nevada is a tradition unlike any other! The Rebels from UNLV are going to attempt to steal the Fremont Cannon from us and they're going to try to do it on the gridiron. Meaning, we must not let any shenanigans occur off the field. I remember years ago when I just started working here and we were in possession of the trophy. A fraternity from Las Vegas tried to abscond with the cannon shortly before opening kickoff. That's why I've got my A-team down on the periphery of the field. Right?"

"RIGHT CHIEF."

"Okay, what are you waiting for? A-team dismissed. Remember, don't be shy about using those Tasers boys! That's why we got 'em!"

"YES SIR."

About a third of the guards leaped to attention, saluted the Chief, and departed to their stations. Under his breath, Hobie made a little "baaa" sound as they hustled out the door. Sheep.

"Okay, B-team you have been assigned to the bleachers and concession stands. I don't want to see any overly intoxicated students so you're in charge of flagging them if they act up. And watch out for hotdog thieves. It's become a serious problem."

"YES SIR."

Another third of the guards rose to attention, saluted, and marched out the door on their way to battle. Hobie could barely contain his disgust. He hated babysitting these rich, snotnose kids, conveniently forgetting he was of their same age.

"C-team, you have a most important assignment. Since much of our squad will be concentrated in the stadium, your job is to patrol the surrounding area. As you know, ever since 1999 when those idiot jocks tried to lift the cannon and dropped it, it cannot be fired after our touchdowns. Damn shame. If it were up to me the perpetrators would have been castrated. Right?"

"DAMN STRAIGHT."

"We've had reports that now when we score a touchdown, revelers in the parking lot are celebrating by shooting guns in the air as a replacement for the cannon. As much as I admire their team spirit, this is unacceptable and anyone seen doing it should be disarmed and held for the police. Most importantly, I want you to keep a close watch for cheapskates trying to sneak into the stadium without paying. They're a cancer!"

"RIGHT CHIEF."

Five other guards left the room. Only a handful was left, mostly women. All were anxious to receive their assignments, including Hobie. He had everything planned and there was only one thing that could go wrong. Ever since he'd seen the two crooks casing the museum, he'd been watching and preparing for the inevitable moment. He'd spotted the good looking one a couple of times since then, always roaming near the museum.

As the Homecoming game approached, he realized this was what the thieves were waiting for. It was a perfect cover. There would be so many people nobody would expect a heist to go down. Cretins. Hobie knew how the criminal mind worked and he was certain tonight was the night. He was so convinced he decided to bring a little helper to work.

Her pet name was Kelly. She was a Kel-Tec PMR 30 Handgun. She was a plaything compared to some of his other guns and the ones at Big Shot Shooting Gallery, but she was easy to conceal and packed a punch. She featured fiber optic sights and functioned through a unique, hybrid blowback system. She took a .22 Magnum, 30 round magazine that fit completely in the grip and weighed only 13.6 ounces. Svelte, to say the least.

He could feel her now, tucked deep into the front of his pants. He felt his loins stir and quickly put it out of his mind. Yes, he had everything planned. Now only one thing could go wrong, his assignment.

"D-Team, you have your normal assignments. No whining! With the rest of the squad tied up at the game, your jobs become even more crucial. You've got to make sure no bastards try and cheat us out of our parking fees!"

"RIGHT CHIEF."

He paused and sighed. He looked to the back of the room and noticed Hobie's rare grin. "No complaints, Hobie? That's a new one."

The remaining guards snickered. Hobie resisted the urge to pull out Kelly and blow them all away. "No sir," he said. "I'm just happy to be serving the wonderful University of Nevada Reno and keeping the future of our country safe."

The Chief narrowed his eyes. "Hm. Admirable notion. I'll take your word on it. But if I find you've set even one foot out of that parking garage it'll be your job. So no fantasies! Got that? I don't want any more disasters because of you. Don't start imagining some terrorist has taken over the Student's Union and decide to storm it. That's just in the movies."

The snickers got louder and Hobie had to chew on his tongue to keep from lashing out. "No sir. No fantasies. As you said, sir, this is a big deal."

"That's right! Now get out there and make this a night to remember!"

Hobie quickly slipped out the backdoor and headed for his electric cart. He couldn't be happier. He was assigned to the parking garage in between the Mackay Stadium and the Fleishmann Planetarium, a stone's throw from the Historical Society Museum. He would be in the perfect position to observe the thieves and make his move when the time came to strike.

The Chief was right. It was going to be a memorable evening.

FIFTEEN

TINMAN, BONES, AND CATFISH WERE IN LAWN CHAIRS on Tinman's rooftop deck. Behind them, a freight train chugged by gradually picking up speed for the mountains ahead. The sun was down and their faces were lit by a small table lamp, powered by an extension cord that ran along the deck and through the window of the apartment.

Bones and Catfish had their eyes closed. They were clad in silver and blue Wolf Pack sweatshirts and caps. Tinman was doing a crossword puzzle and was dressed in black denim pants, a black long-sleeved shirt, and white sneakers. He'd just bought the sneakers because they had gel insoles and he thought they would prevent him from feeling the malignancy with every step he took.

The look on his face showed he was perturbed. He flung the crossword book across the deck and it hung on the edge for a split second and disappeared.

"Why should I be required to know the name of some rapper?! It's called a crossword. That means the answers should be words, not the name of some fly-by-night thug who thinks he can rhyme."

Bones and Catfish opened their eyes but gave no insight into this vexing problem. Tinman exhaled loudly.

"Maybe he got a case of the nerves and skipped town. Maybe all his talk about being some big thief was just bluff."

"Maybe that's him," said Bones, jutting out his chin at a light, blue Buick Park Avenue Ultra sedan turning into the motel parking lot.

"Why would he be in that?" asked Tinman.

The car started around the back of the motel and he jumped to his feet. "Who the hell is that? Christ, they must see the place isn't open for business. I'm going to check it out."

On cue, Peach came strolling around from the back carrying two large garbage bags. He pounded up the stairs two at a time. He grabbed a chair and completed the circle.

"Where the hell you been?" asked Tinman.

"Borrowing our ride for tonight," said Peach. "Pretty sweet for a '92, don't you think? The owners swung for the Luxury Package. She's got a complete Bose stereo system with graphic equalizer, leather seats, Astro roof, and a 3.8 L V6 engine."

"You stole that," said Tinman.

"Well I'm not going to take my car to a heist, am I? First, we wouldn't all fit, second, having burglar tools near the scene of a heist is as good as having pulled off the job, even if you didn't."

"Makes perfect sense," said Catfish. "Where'd you pick it up?"

"Assisted living complex off North McCarran. I love those places. The owners rarely drive their cars and never at night. The carports block any view from the rooms and they never even know their car is missing. I'll drop it off tonight, none the worse for wear."

"You truly are some kind of pro," chuckled Catfish.

"And is the pro going to fill us in just a wee bit more than you did today?" Tinman grumbled. "I'm feeling a little naked here."

"Speaking of which, here's your disguise," said Peach. He opened one of the garbage bags and pulled out an oversized, grime-covered, polyester winter coat. He tossed it to Tinman who pulled his arms away in disgust and it fell to the ground.

"Where in the hell did you get that?"

Peach pulled out a second coat, equally nasty, and held it up for display. "Sweet, huh? I bought them off of a couple of homeless guys down by Rock Park. They thought I was nuts."

"Very perceptive," said Tinman.

"Hey, they need to be authentic. No time to distress new ones."

"Will you please explain what you're talking about!"

"I guess I didn't tell you everything, did I. Okay, let's go over this thing again. I'll fill in the details," said Peach. He pulled out a sheet of paper with some drawing on it and spread it out on the small table.

"Okay, you've all been on campus but we'll do a little refresher course. This is the museum and over here is Mackay Stadium. Down here is the planetarium. And in between is a three-story parking garage. That's going to be important for Bones and Catfish. Now, on the east side of the planetarium is a little hill with trees. I've stashed two grocery carts there. For obvious reasons, they're key to the operation."

He looked at the three guys who were completely dumbfounded. "Bear with me," said Peach. "Catfish, you drive. When we get about a half a block from these trees you're going to drop me and Tinman off. We'll already be in our disguises."

"As homeless guys," said Tinman weakly.

"Check," said Peach. "Now, Bones and Catfish, normally I'd have you park the car farther away from the heist, but with the game going on, parking on Virginia is going to be at a premium. And that means city cops. I don't want to chance them spotting our borrowed car."

"Good thinking," said Bones.

"So we'll put the car in the parking garage. It'll be safe there for the short time the heist will take. But I don't want you just hanging around in their too long and draw suspicion. After you drop us off, wait ten minutes to give us a chance to get on campus, scope it out, and get into position.

Now you drive the car up Virginia, turn in here, and go right into the parking garage. The other reason I got this particular car is it has handicap plates so you'll be able to park on the north side of the garage in this section here or here. This railing on the second floor will give you a perfect view of the museum and surrounding area. You shouldn't have to leave the garage unless you spot trouble down below and need to divert."

"Got it," said Catfish.

Peach pulled out a thin black square about two by two inches. It had a small screen on the front under which were three buttons. "Bones, you take this. It's a call button system, sort of like the old pagers. If there is any trouble you push this center button and it will send a message to me, letting us know we need to skedaddle. I've already preprogrammed the message. All you have to do is push the button."

"What's the message say? Quick, run for cover," said Tinman snidely.

"Girl," said Peach.

"Huh?"

"Well you said 'Quick run for cover' and I said 'Girl,' so now you have 'Quick run for Cover Girl,' got it?"

"Hey, you still doing those things?" asked Bones with a grin.

"Show's still on? Why wouldn't I?" said Peach.

"Let's get on with it!" Tinman demanded.

"What's with the homeless guys?" asked Catfish.

"I'm kind of proud of that myself. First, after you drop Tinman and I off, we get our carts and wheel them up the sidewalk, and enter the campus. We'll continue past the museum and the parking garage until we know everything is clear. To sell the cover, there are some dumpsters here and there we can scrounge around in."

"Forget it," said Tinman.

"When it's clear we backtrack and approach the museum from the north. We stash the carts here, directly behind the museum's back wall."

Catfish clapped his hands a few times. "Very clever using the homeless guys. People don't even like looking at them."

"Exactamundo," said Peach. "By the way, I've been meaning to thank you for all the grift sense you taught us when we were younger. When I was a stick-up guy I didn't really get it. The most I'd do is put on a ski mask. But when I moved into my new line I found it quite useful. In fact, my very last job was a residential heist at a golf community. I used the grift to set up my cover by acting like I was this golf equipment salesman, see."

"Can we please stay focused!" said Tinman gruffly.

"Sure, sure thing. Remind me to tell you about it later Catfish."

"Thanks, I will. And you're welcome," said Catfish, glowing like a proud father.

"Why do we need two carts?" asked Tinman. "Wouldn't one be less cumbersome?"

"Well, I thought about it, but I figured we'll have ten baskets. We divide them up into two garbage bags with one bag per cart. This way, if there's trouble and we have to ditch one we'll still get half the baskets."

Tinman thought hard for a way to discount this idea but it was too good and he just shrugged. "And you don't think anyone's going to be suspicious about two homeless guys so far away from downtown?"

"Well, this goes to the heart of why we're going tonight. Wherever there's a crowd, especially a beer drinking crowd, the can collectors congregate. With Homecoming and the Battle for the Cannon, this is a big game. It's natural the scavengers would be on hand."

Tinman was certain his tenant, Rudy, would confirm this, but he was still in the mood to be difficult. "I still don't get it. I thought burglars liked doing heists when no one was around," said Tinman.

"Actually, the old guys will tell you there's nothing like hustle and bustle to hide a crime. Nobody's expecting it for the very reason you stated."

Everyone waited for Tinman to argue the point, but he knew he was out of his league and waved his hand impatiently, prompting Peach to continue.

"Okay. When we have the baskets we put them in the cart and wheel them onto Virginia Street. That's your cue to leave the garage and drive down to the gas station right around here. It's the one with the sign that says 'Unleaded: An arm. Premium Unleaded: A leg.'"

"I know the place," said Bones, chuckling.

"Now I've got this timed out pretty good fellas. When you see us move into position, you can figure five minutes to get into the museum. Twenty seconds each for the locks on the cases with ten cases, so call it another three. A minute to get the baskets in the bags and two to get back outside. Another minute to get back into our disguises and two more to get out onto Virginia Street."

"Got it. Twelve minutes give or take from the time you hit the joint," said Catfish.

"Right. That's when you leave. It'll take us about three minutes to get to the gas station and away we go."

"You seem pretty confident about the timing," said Tinman.

"Absolutely. Piece of cake."

"And what fancy tools have you picked out for this job?" asked Bones.

"A ladder," said Peach. "And what a honey. I picked it up at Harbor Freight for a song. I love that place. They were having one of those parking lot tent sales. You wouldn't believe how cool this thing is. It's called the MT-16 Multifunction Telescoping ladder and it folds down to just about four feet! You can use it as a twin step ladder, a stairway step ladder, a scaffold base, or, for our purposes, an extension ladder."

Bones, Catfish, and Tinman stared at his beaming face with dismay. Their magician was a fake. The plan was crumbling in front of their eyes.

"You mean to tell me all you're taking is a ladder?" blurted Tinman.

"Well, I'm not bringing it with us. Who would believe a homeless guy had one of those. I already have it stashed behind the museum."

"But what about getting into the doors and the cases?" asked Bones.

"Well, I have this. He held out his right hand, showing off a large ring. "It's called the Rogue's Ring. There's a tiny pick and tension ring hidden in here. I also have another model that has a hidden shim for getting out of handcuffs. Anyway, this'll do the trick for the locks on the cases. But we won't be going through the doors. We're going in the roof."

Tinman gave a little snort. "Door locks too tricky for you?"

"Hell no, maybe two minutes to break. But both the side and front door are too exposed. No trees or bushes or anything. Now those things sticking out on the side of the building—"

"Buttresses," said Tinman.

"Right, those things are perfect blinds for a ladder."

"And what, we're going to cut a hole in the roof?" asked Tinman.

"Let me read you something," said Peach. He pulled out a folded sheet of paper, opened it, and started reading. "The building's security system is limited and outdated and does not meet normal requirements. There are a few security cameras and alarmed doors, but this is not sufficient to protect the people, priceless artifacts, manuscripts, photographs, and library collections in the building. The roof hatch is original to the building and has reached the end of its useful life. The compression spring operators do not function properly, the latches and handles are worn and the seals and flashing have deteriorated. A faulty roof hatch is a safety hazard to anyone accessing the roof."

Peach looked up and smiled. Tinman's head began to hurt. "No lasers?" he asked.

"I told you that was a bluff," said Peach. "Those little boxes on the ceiling are video cameras and they're not monitored. By the time they check the tapes we'll be long gone. By the way, in the pocket of your coat is a ski mask. We'll put those on when we go inside."

Tinman nodded knowingly. "I suppose you got all this info from Peppermint."

"No way," said Peach. "Rookie move. When the cops start investigating they're going to interview everyone working in there. If I pumped Peppermint she'd be sure to put things together and point the finger my way. All we did is play doctor. Oh, and she finally remembered where she'd seen you. It was the video from Virginia City. She saw it on YouTube and showed it to me."

Tinman's head dropped. Peach continued, "By the way, despite the comments a few people left, I for one think you held your own. I particularly liked the thing you did with its tail. Truth is, most of the people who saw the video were rooting for you. Some were even calling for a rematch."

"I told you there was a future in this," said Catfish.

Bones started tittering but quickly clammed up when Tinman shot him a look. "Where did you get this stuff about the museum?"

"I also found it online when she was busy doing her grad research. It's a pdf of a Facility Condition Analysis Report for the museum from last year. They were asking for money to upgrade their security systems."

Catfish said, "I can't believe they put that kind of stuff online. How stupid can you get?"

"Don't knock it," said Peach. "Stupidity is my best resource. Anyway, I later found the budget breakdown for that year and the museum had their requests shot down. Money was too tight. The roof hatch has never been fixed. I did a preliminary run just to make sure and the only thing between us and those baskets is a padlock. Which is really shameful in my opinion."

"You were already up on the roof?" asked Tinman.

"Planning is everything brother," said Peach. "The only thing more important is sticking to the plan. Oops, almost forgot. This is for you." He handed Tinman a small black flashlight.

"I thought we didn't want anyone to see us," said Tinman. "Why would we use one of these."

"It's not for us to see," said Peach. "And let's hope we don't have to use it. See I don't carry guns anymore so this is my protection in case I come face to face with some snoop during a job."

Tinman scrunched his face and stared at the little flashlight. "You hit 'em with this?"

"Yep. Right in the eyes. It's the Shadowhawk X800 military-grade tactical flashlight. It's like 40 times brighter than a normal one. It's set on strobe. If you get into trouble just turn it on here and focus it right at their eyes. You'll temporarily blind them enough to get away. Guaranteed, it's your best friend on a heist."

Tinman eyed the little light with newfound respect. He nodded thanks to his brother and carefully tucked it into a pants pocket.

"Anything else we need to know?" asked Bones.

"I think that's it," said Peach. "Oh, I found out the campus guards are only allowed to carry Tasers so whatever happens, we won't have to worry about being shot."

"How reassuring," said Tinman.

"Right!" said Peach. He turned to Bones and Catfish. "By the way, I love the getups guys. You'll blend right in. I did find this in the car. Thought it might be useful." He held up a portable folding walker.

Bones grinned. "Yes, we'll make use of that."

"Aw, geez, brother, you're gonna have to lose the shoes," said Peach.

"Why?" asked Tinman.

"Well, first thing is, they're white."

Tinman stared sheepishly at his gleaming new sneakers. "Right. But I just bought them with the last of my dough."

"Second they leave tread marks the cops can match up. Unless you want to throw your new shoes away right after the heist you'll put these on." He tossed Tinman a pair of soft, dark, crepe shoes he always wore on jobs.

Tinman stared at them. He saw the thin soles and knew with every other step he'd be conscious of the ballooning growth on his foot. He slowly began untying his sneakers, praying the nasty thing wouldn't explode and spawn.

"You sure have come a long way, Peach," Bones drawled. "From the way you planned this out, I take it you've been mobbed up before."

"Actually, no," said Peach. "I worked with one string for a while but they were amateurs. Carried guns. Always trying to double-cross. Sometimes I've used a guy as a wheelman or to help me with a jug that required special tools. But mostly I've been a lone wolf. And you know, it's held me back some. Limited the kind of heists I could pull. With a good string, you can go after the big hauls, the stuff you can't do when you're solo. Problem was, I just never felt I could trust anybody."

"And now you got us," said Catfish. "If you can't trust the Posse who can you trust."

Peach, Tinman, and Bones all looked at Catfish, grins breaking out. Peach cried, "I forgot all about that! It's what we called ourselves when we first went out on the road together."

Catfish smiled and nodded. Peach said, "Hey if this goes well, we can move on to bigger jobs! The kind of stuff I've been dreaming about."

"If this goes well," said Tinman, "we're all going to retire."

Peach grinned. "Sure. Sure thing, brother."

Peach did a quick study of each face in his string. It was mandatory. He had to know they were all of one mind, the only thing keeping them from taking a fall. Satisfied, he nodded. "Alright boys. Let's do this. The Posse rides again!"

SIXTEEN

HOBIE PEERED THROUGH THE GUN SIGHTS and sighed. He was on the second floor of the parking garage, tucked into the northeast corner. From here he had a perfect vantage point to see the museum and surrounding area but he could not be seen from below. He'd borrowed the sights from one of his rifles and was using it to scope out the situation. It was less obtrusive than binoculars and just as efficient. Kelly was now hidden in the small of his back.

He had watched as the crowds funneled in for the big game. He had done his best to seek out anyone who seemed out of place. Nothing was out of the ordinary and his sixth sense had not set off any alarm.

Now, opening kickoff had come and gone and he was starting to doubt himself. He knew this must be the night the crooks had chosen for the heist. It made perfect sense. But they weren't here. It made him so mad he wanted to spit, and he did.

He leaned back on the low concrete wall and stared out at the road between the museum and the Transportation Services Building. It was a moonless evening and the high-pressure sodium bulbs in the light towers cast an orange glow.

He saw a couple of bums, looking like radioactive ghouls, pushing grocery carts. They turned off the sidewalk bordering the east side of campus. He wasn't at all surprised to see them. Despite the long hike up the hill from downtown, a game like this with tailgating and beer drinking always brought them out in droves. These two were a couple of early birds, the rest would come closer to the end of the game when more garbage had accumulated. Vermin. Living off the discards of others.

Part of his job was to chase them off but this was another order he refused to obey. He didn't even want to get near them. Probably had lice. He noticed their carts were empty. They were expecting a big haul of cans. As they passed the parking garage on their way to the stadium, he saw one do a quick dive of the dumpster out front. Disgusting pigs. He looked away. The very sight made him sick.

Where could they be? He couldn't even bring himself to think about what would happen if he were wrong. It would mean his sixth sense had failed him and that would be the end of his world. He held fast to his vigil, panning the sights back and forth, sniffing out evil. It was out there. He just knew it.

A large Buick sedan pulled in off North Virginia and his heart skipped a beat. Could this be it? He didn't think they would be dumb enough to bring the getaway car with them. That should be parked somewhere away from the heist. Still.

He focused his sights and saw two old guys in the front of the car, both wearing Wolf Pack caps. A handicap tag swung back and forth from the rearview mirror. He groaned. Alumni. The worst. They always acted like they owned the place.

They turned into the entrance ramp of the garage. Hobie prayed there was an open handicap spot on the first floor. His hopes were dashed when he saw the car appear at the entrance to the second floor. There was no chance for him to hide now. His cart was right beside him. He could only hope they had cataracts and wouldn't see him. Just to be on the safe side, he crouched next to his cart and acted like he was fixing something.

The car pulled into the northwest section of the parking level where the handicap spots were. The two old guys slowly got out. One of them was taller and had a little Hitler-like mustache. They had on fan sweatshirts and were holding dowels with miniature Wolf Pack pennants attached. They looked his way and he ducked.

He heard honking and saw the fascist leaning into the car, beeping the horn. He groaned. He couldn't leave his station. He knew that would be the very moment the thieves would strike. And if that happened he'd have to kill these old guys. Fair punishment for preventing him from stopping evil.

The shorter one started walking his way—if you could call it that. He had a gimp and looked like he might go face down into the cement any second. Hobie slammed his fist into the seat cushion on his cart. No use breaking a hand by punching the metal siding. He stood and put on his sternest no-nonsense look. He knew how to handle these geezers.

"Game's that way," he said and thrust a finger in the general direction of the stadium.

"We know that you stupid little shit," said the short one.

Hobie had to work very hard indeed to keep from throttling him on the spot. "No need to be rude, sir."

"No need to be dumb either," said the gimpy guy. "You don't think we know where our team plays. We were roaming these grounds long before your daddy knew how to beat off, much less make babies."

The tall one stopped the incessant honking and approached. "We're late for the game! You need to give us a ride."

"Do I now?" said Hobie, crossing his arms. He could feel Kelly stirring, just itching to even the odds.

"Yeah, you do," said the Nazi. "My friend here has trouble walking distances. I checked with your chief before we left home and he guaranteed you'd be more than happy to give us a lift."

The invalid gave him a smarmy smile and Hobie's left cheek started twitching like it always did when he was ready to explode, or cry. "Is that right?"

He knew right away it was a dumb thing to say. It was passive. He must remain aggressive. He hated when the wrong thing came out. He could tell from the looks on these two farts they knew they had him.

The tall guy looked down at him. "You want to give him a ring and check it out? Be my guest."

Defeat left a bad taste in Hobie's mouth. He swished it around with his tongue and cocked his head. "Get in."

"Gotta lock up first." And he plodded back to his car. The short one shoved Hobie out of the way, hobbled to the cart, and half-rolled his way into the back seat.

Hobie spit the foul taste from his mouth. He waited impatiently as the tall one lumbered back from his car and plopped down next to him. He started the cart and it lurched forward.

"Take it easy, piss ant! You want to give me a coronary?" screeched the guy in the back.

Hobie couldn't think of a thing he wanted more. He veered toward the exit ramp and tore down it. As he pulled away from the garage he was intent on delivering these invalids to the stadium as quickly as he could and return to his lookout.

He was so focused he didn't see the two homeless guys with their carts slip down the little access road behind the museum. He also didn't see the old guy in the back of his cart see the same thing and quickly pat his friend on the shoulder.

It took Hobie quite a bit longer than he expected because of the crowded parking lots surrounding the stadium. There were limited tickets for such a big game and the unlucky fans who were shut out had set up camp outside. Most of them were watching the game on battery-powered television sets. Others were getting live feeds on their phones from friends inside the stadium.

Hobie had to inch his way around makeshift camps complete with lawn chairs, beer coolers, Wolf Pack banners, and fools too loaded to care how stupid they looked. As the minutes ticked by he felt a bubbling rage brewing in his gut. Every second counted. The kind of pros he was up against would work fast and be in and out of the museum in no time.

He tramped on the gas pedal. Up ahead a shirtless man was twirling a Hula Hoop, his gyrations causing the wolf's head painted on his chest to look like it was growling. Hobie growled back and nearly ran him over. The inebriated fan called for a fight. Hobie was more than game but the Arian next to him punched his arm and tapped his watch. Hobie hated him. Even more when he stuck a finger in his ear and twisted it like he was clearing out wax. Old people are so gross.

They approached the main entrance to the stadium where the ticket takers awaited. Hobie slid the cart to a stop in front of the gate.

"Damn it to hell," the old guy croaked. "We gotta go back to the car. I forgot my walker. Come on jack off, turn this stagecoach around. We're missing the game!"

Hobie knew if he took his hands off the steering wheel he'd spend the rest of his life in prison. The urge to rip these two guys apart and stomp the bloody shreds into the ground was all-encompassing. Still, did he have a choice? He couldn't allow them to ruin his plans. One hand came off the wheel. He slowly turned to the old men, his other hand clutching onto the wheel like a drowning man grasping the edge of a sinking lifeboat.

"HOBIE!" A familiar voice roared.

Hobie turned back and saw the looming figure of his Chief, quickly approaching. "What the hell are you doing away from your assigned post?"

Hobie wasn't sure he could talk. He was quite sure if he tried, the words that would come out would not be welcome. He was unexpectedly saved by the tall guy.

"Your boy here is helping us out Chief," he said. "My friend has trouble walking and he offered to give us a ride down here. Just like you promised."

The Chief was taken aback. "I promised?" He quickly recovered. "Of course! We aim to please! Nothing is too good for our alumni. After all, you're the ones that make all this happen." He beamed. This was tricky ground. Silver-haired, wrinkled skinned landmines everywhere.

He looked at Hobie and managed to say without choking, "Good job, Hobie."

"Problem is, I forgot my walker. We're going to have to go all the way back to the garage. I hate to take up your boy's valuable time."

"Nonsense. He'll be happy to run you to your car and back. And don't worry fellas, no score yet so you haven't missed much. Well, Hobie, what are you waiting for? Get a move on kid!"

Hobie's left cheek was dancing the rumba. But he knew the only safe thing was to obey orders and get rid of these codgers as quickly as possible. It was the only way to complete his mission and fulfill his destiny. He saluted the Chief, spun the cart away, and sped into the melee.

On the way back, he tried to block his mind from the fury threatening to overtake him. He concentrated on the feel of Kelly nestled in the small of his back. He fantasized about offing these two fogeys and stuffing their bodies into the trunk of their car. The thought calmed him considerably and his chin stopped twitching.

Once through the parking lot party, the going was smooth. As they approached the garage, he scanned the periphery of the museum. Nothing seemed out of the ordinary. He was just about to hang a left onto the entrance ramp when he spotted the two bums with the grocery carts. They were pushing them through the parking lot bordering the museum, seemingly on their way to Virginia Street. It struck him as funny but he couldn't figure out why.

His passengers followed his stare and immediately started yammering. "Come on douche bag!" "We're missing the game, you dork!"

In a haze, Hobie drove into the garage. Something was wrong, out of kilter, but he couldn't place it. He could care less about those bums. So why were they stuck in his mind? It must be his nerves from having to deal with these insulting, foul-mouthed fogies. He relaxed. He was certain he hadn't missed the heist.

As he climbed up the ramp to the second floor, he reassured himself there was nothing wrong. After all, two homeless guys come to a game, get their cans, and leave. Probably just avoiding the traffic rush at the end of the game. He pulled the cart behind the Buick and the old men piled out.

"Give us a hand with this kid."

Hobie sighed. He could argue but the fastest way to get rid of them was just do as they ask. Besides, they had saved him from the Chief. He heaved himself out of the cart and walked to the car. The fascist unlocked the doors and said, "It's in the back seat."

Hobie looked inside and saw a portable walker. No big deal. Why couldn't they get it themselves? He leaned in and the short guy pressed in behind, offering needless instructions.

Hobie grabbed the walker and was lifting it out of the car when the alarm went off in his head. Two guys coming to collect cans with empty carts. Two guys leaving with empty carts.

"EMPTY CARTS!" he blurted.

"You losing your shit, boy?"

Hobie pushed back from the car, practically sending the short guy to the ground. He tossed the walker away and raced to his cart. He expected the old guys to be yelling at him but they must have been too shocked. He could care less. He started the cart and whipped it around, heading for the exit ramp, his mind rapidly unraveling the mystery.

The homeless guys had empty carts meaning they weren't collecting cans and they weren't bums. They were the thieves undercover. They were coming from the museum. The loot was stashed under the big puffy coats.

He smiled at his keens sense of deduction. This was D-Day. The moment of truth. He careened out the garage and veered to the left. He saw the evil ones in front of the Transportation Building. Soon they would be on Virginia Street and out of his realm.

As he approached, he saw one of them reach inside his coat. He was trying to get the draw on him! These two banditos were looking for a showdown.

One hand stayed on the steering wheel. The other pulled out Kelly. Even on a moving cart, Hobie knew from this distance he could take them out. But he wanted them alive. He wanted to see their faces when he told the law how clever he'd been, predicting their plan, foiling it at the last moment. He did, however, need to let them know he meant business.

Forty yards and closing. The two guys snapped their heads toward him like they'd just seen him. A clever ruse. He raised Kelly into the air and fired two shots.

SEVENTEEN

"THIS THING ITCHES. AND IT STINKS."

"We'll take them off before we go in," said Peach.

"And we'll have to put them on again when we come out," said Tinman. "And they'll still itch and stink."

"Stop bitching. It takes a little sacrifice to be a millionaire."

Tinman thought about this as he pushed his cart. He realized it was a valid point and stopped whining.

Up until now, everything had gone according to plan. After Bones and Catfish dropped them off, they retrieved their carts and pushed them onto campus. They scoped out the area and saw the security guards concentrated in and around the stadium. They made their way north and east around some outlying buildings.

Now they were ready to make their move. When they were sure everything was clear they pushed the carts down a little hill and approached the museum from behind. They stashed them against the building and shook off the heavy coats. Peach pulled on his ski mask and covered his hands with nitrile gloves. Tinman followed suit.

A couple of sheets of plywood were leaning on the back wall. Peach reached behind them and found the ladder was right where he'd left it. He pulled it out, waved for Tinman to follow, and slid into the shadows on the side of the building. When he reached the first buttress, he unfolded the ladder. Slowly and silently he slid the top section up until it extended to the roof. He turned to Tinman with a grin.

"This is serious," said Tinman. "What's with the happy face?"

"I always smile when I'm working."

"Why?"

"I love my job," said Peach, the grin widening. "Okay, I'll go first. When you hit the top, stay low."

It had been a long time since Tinman had done anything like this. He wasn't exactly nervous. It was more like petrified. He was determined not to show it to his brother. He shrugged and curled his mouth as if to say, "You don't think I know that? I do this every day."

Peach turned and before Tinman could say, "Be careful" he was on the roof. Tinman started up. The first rung landed right on top of his growth and he winced a little. He adjusted his foot and made a mental note not to do it again. As he climbed, he grudgingly had to admit Peach was right. They were completely in shadow with the buttress hiding them from any probing eyes.

He made it to the roof and immediately went prone. "Okay, what's next?"

When there was no response, he carefully lifted his head and saw a hand sticking out of a hole in the roof. It was waving at him. He shimmied over, hugging the roof like he was in boot camp and some sadistic lieutenant had decided to use live ammo for this particular training.

When he got to the hatch opening he peered down, hoping the drop wouldn't be too far. There was Peach, beaming and pointing at a table he'd placed under the hole. He looked like a new mother who wants to show off what just popped out of her.

Tinman lowered himself, his body fully extended with hands clasping the edge of the hatch opening. Peach guided his feet to the tabletop and he landed safely. He hopped off and his brother slapped him on the back and they took off for the display area.

Peach was holding a little penlight with black tape covering the lens. A small hole cut in the tape allowed just enough light to see. They scooted past the gift shop and the director's office and stepped into the museum.

Peach held up a hand to stop Tinman. He reached up on the wall and removed the front of the video box. He fiddled with something. The little red light on the front went out. He waved his arm with a flourish and Tinman stepped inside.

Directly in front was the Dat So La Lee display, the green cases with the Lucite tops stood in a row. All ten of them empty.

Tinman never thought of himself as someone who gasps a lot. But lately, he seemed to be doing it often. Peach almost never gasped, but he joined him. After they'd caught their breath, their eyes met briefly and they looked back at the display cases, hoping it had been a mirage or trick of the eye. It wasn't. They gasped again. It was becoming a bad habit.

"Are we in the right place?" asked Tinman, realizing the minute it came out it was probably the dumbest thing he'd ever said.

"It can't be," said Peach, his grin long gone.

Tinman said, "They must have been onto us."

"If they were onto us, this place would be full of cops right now."

"So where are the damn baskets?"

Peach could only shake his head in utter disbelief. Tinman's utter disbelief had faded and now he was angry. He impulsively slapped the nearest case and Peach grabbed his hand. "We gotta get out of here. We'll figure this out later."

Tinman was oblivious. He kept shutting and opening his eyes, hoping the baskets would magically reappear

Peach tried shaking him out of his trance. "Come on."

"There has to be something in here to steal!" Tinman bellowed

* * *

When Catfish and Bones had first pulled into the garage and seen a security guard scoping out the grounds, they were gobsmacked. He was positioned perfectly to spot Peach and Tinman. Like he knew ahead of time what was going down.

They had jumped into action and successfully diverted the guard. On their way to the stadium, Catfish had given Bones the office that, according to the timeline Peach had given, the heist was over and they should head for the meeting place. The security guard never suspected so much could be silently transmitted with a finger in the ear.

They were feeling pretty good about themselves on the way back from the stadium until the guard had frozen at the sight of Peach and Tinman in their disguises. The two old guys were equally stunned to see them as they were supposed to have been long gone. They did their best to delay the guard but as they now stood watching him tear through the garage, they were nervous.

"What the hell got into him?" asked Catfish.

"I don't know, but that guard is on to something," said Bones. "Worse yet, when he was getting the walker and I forked his leather I felt something else."

"Like what?"

"He's packing," said Bones.

"Well for God's sake send them a message!"

"Huh?"

"The pager thingy!"

"Right!" Bones reached in his pocket and pulled out the little black box. His nervous fingers fumbled and he nearly dropped it. He tried to hold it steady but it kept bobbling around in his hand.

"You can riff a poke with your eyes closed but you can't push a little button! Give me that thing!" Catfish grabbed the pager and pushed the send button. They both smiled with relief.

Two gunshots rang out. They looked at each other, eyes wide. "Christ! We gotta get to the meeting place! Come on!" cried Catfish, and they leaped into the car.

* * *

Nothing Peach did could stop Tinman from his mad treasure hunt. He was running helter-skelter through the museum looking for something, anything, of value. He'd already discounted an 1870's copper bathtub used by miners, a penny-farthing bicycle, a miniature replica of a twenty-mule freight train, and a marble tombstone with the name John Bell etched in it. He was sweating profusely and his eyes were glazed.

"We have to stick to the plan!" cried Peach. "We're already three minutes behind!"

Tinman didn't hear. He was staring at a beautiful display showing off no more than a dirty flour sack. "Why would they have this? What's so damn important about a flour sack?!"

"We'll come back sometime. Learn all about it. I promise."

His face drooping, Tinman asked, "Why is this happening?"

"I don't know, brother. But we need to figure it out somewhere else. You understand?"

The words sunk in and Tinman nodded. Peach hooked an arm around him and half-pulled, half-shoved him into the hall and over to the table under the hole. He helped Tinman up and egged him on as he scrambled out. After he was safely gone, Peach shoved the table back against the wall. With a running start, he jumped for the hatch and caught the edge. He pulled himself up and soon was lying next to Tinman on the roof.

After Peach closed the hatch and snapped on the padlock, they shimmied over to the ladder and Tinman went down first. When they were both on the ground, Peach folded up the ladder and put it back behind the plywood.

"Don't you want to keep your cool ladder?" asked Tinman, still in a daze.

"Better it stays here. We may need it again. Besides, I'm not going to be seen carrying it off this campus. Somebody may think I stole it."

Tinman found this hysterical and broke into a giggle fit. Peach shook him hard. "Trey! Wake up. We have to keep going. Bones and Catfish are going to wonder where we are."

Sanity slowly seeped back into Tinman's mind. He shook his head to clear away the fog and nodded. The two yanked off their ski masks and gloves. Peach made sure to stuff them deep into the dumpster behind the museum.

After they pulled on their coats and retrieved their carts, they were ready to move.

Peach looked at Tinman, all business. "Not too fast, no nervous movements. We've got nothing on us so no need to act as if we do."

Tinman understood. He laid a hand on his brother's shoulder and nodded once. Peach grinned and they pushed their carts around from the back of the building and into the museum's parking lot.

There was no one in sight. They both privately sighed relief. With heads down, they slowly wheeled their carts through the parking lot on the way to the little road in front of the Transportation Services Building. A hundred yards and they'd be on Virginia Street.

Out of the side of his eye, Peach saw a guard in a security cart stop at the entrance to the parking garage. Bones and Catfish were with him. Tinman followed his stare.

"Christ, what do we do now?" he asked.

"Nothing. Bones and Catfish'll take care of it," said Peach.

The cart remained motionless as they neared the entrance to the road. Finally, it turned into the garage and disappeared.

"What did I tell you," said Peach.

They continued onto the road and headed for Virginia Street. When they were about halfway there, Peach felt a little vibration in his coat pocket.

"Hold on a second. Bones is paging me," said Peach.

As he reached into his coat pocket, he froze at the sight of the security guard in his cart racing toward them. Tinman was ready to bolt. Peach said, "Don't panic. He's probably just trying to roust us for dumpster diving."

"What if he knows something?" asked Tinman.

"What can he know? He can't know anything." They both watched as the guard raised a handgun and fired two warning shots.

"Tell him that!" screamed Tinman.

"Come on! We have to get off the road!" cried Peach.

They veered onto the gravel alongside the Transportation Building, the carts bouncing wildly. The gravel ended at the yard in front of the planetarium.

Peach yelled, "Lose the carts!"

Tinman shoved his hard and it rolled partway down the hill on the east side of the planetarium and slammed into a tree. Peach's cart only went a few feet before toppling over. Tinman saw the guard jump off his cart and start toward them. He was running low with his gun out in front like he was in a war zone.

When Tinman looked back he saw Peach leaning in front of a service entrance door to the Fleischmann Planetarium. Even though the building was erected in 1963, it still seemed futuristic. Max Fleischmann made a lot of money in gin and yeast and a fair amount of his fortune had been donated for buildings on the UNR campus.

The structure was in the design of a hyperbolic paraboloid in which form follows function. The roof is unique with large wing-like sides that jut up to the sky and taper down in the center. The back slopes down until it's only ten feet from the ground, while the front soars upwards creating a sort of sliding board in the middle.

Tinman could care less about architectural design. As he ran over to Peach it came to him that the roof looked exactly like the Giant Lunar Moth from the original Doctor Doolittle movie. Funny why that would come to his mind at such a point, but, hey, that's what he thought.

Peach had his ring pick in the lock of the door and was working calmly but quickly. Tinman looked back and saw the guard kneel and take aim. He heard a click and the cylinder in the lock turned. The two ducked inside just as a bullet twanged off the closing metal door.

Tinman and Peach leaned against the inside of the door, panting heavily. "Man, the guy sure has a hard-on for dumpster divers," said Peach.

"I'll say," said Tinman. "I thought they weren't supposed to carry guns."

"He must have not got the memo."

"What did the message say from Bones?" asked Tinman.

"Trouble."

"Now he tells us."

"Let's go. We have to find a back way out of here," said Peach, and they stepped away from the door. They surveyed their surroundings and found they were in some sort of intergalactic, interactive space gallery. The curved room was filled with glowing replicas of planets and stars. There appeared to be no other people. Peach led the way through the eerie, dimly lit room. They arced around past a giant moon complete with craters and stopped short when faced with two lifelike astronauts in spacesuits.

"Maybe we could hide in those," suggested Peach.

"I'm claustrophobic."

"I never knew that!"

"It just dawned on me. Keep going."

After weaving their way through the displays they found what appeared to be an exit. It actually looked more like one of those airlocks on spaceships, right out of Star Wars. Peach motioned to Tinman to lose the disguise. They both shed their coats and tossed them in a corner. Tinman was relieved. He'd been itching like crazy and this was no time for distraction.

They gingerly stepped through the neon-glowing chamber and exited into the main area of the planetarium. Directly in front was a giant orange sphere housing the Dome Theater.

Which, if anyone's wondering, housed the first atmospherium-planetarium in the world with the ability to simulate both day and night conditions and a full range of atmospheric phenomena, including cloud formations, thunderstorms, and rainbows with an optical device to project images of atmospheric phenomena inside the dome. It was also the first planetarium in the country featuring a 360-degree projector capable of providing horizon-to-horizon images and through time-lapse photography showing an entire day's weather in a few minutes. So there.

A couple of feet to their right was a display case showing a large rock hanging from a chain. The write-up said it was a thirty-pound meteorite. Peach made a quick mental note. He'd read meteorites were wildly expensive and from the looks of it, it would be an easy job for a rainy day.

Past the meteorite was a half-circular staircase leading to the theater entrance on the bottom floor. To their left, about thirty feet away was a small gift shop and another stairway going down to the other side of the theater. In front of the gift shop was a college student, half-asleep at the ticket counter.

Directly past him and outside the glass front doors was the maniacal security guard peering at them. He yanked on the door handle. Locked. It was kept that way after dark. He began pounding on the door and the college kid stirred.

Peach dashed to his right and down the far stairway. Tinman loped after him. When they got to the bottom floor they found a little corridor wrapping around the base of the orange globe. Not sure which way to go, they went to their left and ended up in front of the entrance to the theater.

Neither of them was in the mood to see a show so they continued around and spotted an emergency exit. To get to it, they would have to go under the other stairway. As they started, they looked up and saw the boots of the guard tromping down. They backtracked and quickly reconsidered the notion of taking in a show.

The sign above the entrance said, "No Entry. Program Now In Progress." This had never stopped them when they were kids. They quietly opened the door and slipped in.

* * *

Julius Payne had never taken LSD before. He'd smoked a little bit of pot and felt this sufficient preparation. He was wrong. This was like nothing he'd ever experienced. It was like his brain was making love to his body.

He looked around in the dark to see how his friends were handling it. He and his little gang were sophomores at the university. They still lived on campus in dormitories. All were highly intelligent with very few social skills. Outcasts. No frat would dare have them and all but a few parties were off-limits.

There were seven in his clique. They had two computer whizzes, a mathematics genius, a linguistics specialist, and the other three were into science but had yet to declare their majors, Julius being one of them.

His roommate, a stoner and soon-to-be dropout, had turned Julius on to pot at the beginning of the semester and Julius had turned his friends on. Everyone enjoyed it immensely. That's why when his roommate presented him with the offer to buy a teeny little square of hardened, purple gel, Julius jumped on it.

The small square was evenly divided into sixteen mini-squares. He said it was called Purple Window Pane. It suddenly dawned on Julius his last name was the same as the name of the LSD. How wild is that?!

The thought rushed through him like laughing gas and he burst into hysterical giggles. His buddies scattered throughout the otherwise empty theater cracked up as well. Could they read his mind? Was telepathy one of the symptoms of this exotic drug? Did they agree it was the funniest thing ever in the history of man? What was? What was so funny? He couldn't remember. It had something to do with his name. What had something to do with his name? What just happened? Where did it go? Where did what go?

The music lured him back into some semblance of reality. The planetarium was having a special showing of Pink Floyd's, Dark Side of the Moon, with a mind-blowing, three-dimensional star show as the backdrop. When his friends heard about it, they decided this must be the place for their maiden trip.

None had any interest in football, Homecoming, or some dumb cannon that didn't fire anymore. This was the place to be. And, they had it all to themselves.

They'd dropped the acid about an hour before showtime. At first, they all agreed it was no big deal. Now, it was really kicking in and it was a very big deal. The 360-degree projector was tossing out asteroids that began as little dots on the far horizon and grew to fiery balls that exploded in your mind.

Beginning with a heartbeat, Pink Floyd was carrying them through time and space, from birth to death, a continuous exploration of human frailties. Greed. Inner conflict. The futility of it all. And now, madness.

The music slipped into "Brain Damage," the next to last track, and it was really freaking Julius out. His eyes were fixed on the dome screen as a surreal image of our moon spun and weaved around the room. He was getting dizzy just watching it and wondered if he was going to fall down. Then he realized he was sitting and this was the funniest thing ever in the history of the world, besides the other thing that was so funny . . . that he couldn't remember.

The words were haunting and terrifying and satisfying all at once. He wondered if he was the lunatic they were singing about.

He felt a giant rush as the LSD peaked. His head tingled. The space show took on a new dimension and he began to see stars that weren't on the screen. Now he saw two men in black clothes slithering down the aisle toward him. Were these his inner demons coming out to make their case for insanity? Or was it performance art?

He watched, fascinated, as they drew nearer. He lifted his legs to let them pass and as they did, they both glanced up. They had identical faces! It was twin demons. They slipped by and he decided to follow. Perhaps they would show him the way through the secret portal to Hades. Why would he want to go there! Go where? Why was he on the floor?

He watched the black demons disappear down the main aisle and he crawled onto a seat. His eyes scanned the pitch-black room, above, the moon turned slowly until its dark side filled the sky. A new figure loomed. It was the silhouette of another demon but it was erect and appeared to be looking for something. Was this the King of Demons looking for his subordinates who had just crawled past?

He thought about telling the King where to look but decided it was none of his business. The moon continued to spin, becoming larger and larger, until its bright side appeared showing the craters and mountains and valleys.

"I know you're in here! Now come out and fight you cowards!" cried the King. He raised one arm and it looked like he was holding a scepter.

The scepter erupted with flame and there was a loud boom that blended perfectly with the crescendo of the music. A hole appeared directly in the middle of the man in the moon's forehead. What a show! What a drug! He and his nerdy buddies applauded in appreciation.

A crack of light appeared in the front wall of the theater. He saw the two crawling demons slip outside. The King must have seen them too because he dashed after them. Unfortunately, he dashed a little too quickly and ran shin first into a row of seats. He howled in pain. Julius never knew demons could feel pain and he roared with laughter. His buddies must have read his mind because they joined in.

The King cursed and waved his scepter around as he stumbled through the seats. He made it to the portal of hell and another crack of light appeared in the wall.

As the music eased into the finale, Julius felt like the singer was inside his body and the words were oozing out his pores. The sensation made him warm and fuzzy.

For some odd reason, he thought about his major. He had been leaning towards biology but now it seemed so dry, lifeless. Perhaps chemistry.

* * *

When Peach and Tinman snuck out the handicapped entrance, they were in the narrow hall that curved around the giant orange globe. Directly in front was a sign in red paint with an arrow pointing to the emergency exit they'd seen before going into the theater. Peach led the way.

"Man, what a show!" he said over his shoulder. "Too bad we had to miss the end."

Funny how different twins can be, thought Tinman. He was never so happy to be away from outer space. His eyes were still lolling around in his head trying to adjust to the new light. His equilibrium was shot and now he was following one lunatic while trying to get away from another with a gun.

"The shot he fired is gonna bring more heat. Gotta move," said Peach. They reached the emergency exit and saw it was alarmed. "No time to disarm it. And when we go through here, all hell is going to break out. You ready?"

Tinman nodded weakly. Peach said, "Okay, here we go. Hit the ground running and head straight for Virginia Street."

He shoved the door open and the alarm started wailing. He took one glance ahead and veered sharply to the left.

"Where you going?!" cried Tinman. "Virginia's that way!"

"And so is a hundred yards of open space. No trees, nothing. We'll be sitting ducks. We'll double back. He'll never expect it."

They ran around the round building and were met by a ten-foot-high chain-link fence. Peach didn't hesitate. He leaped high, clasped onto the links, and scrambled up. Tinman was no cat burglar, but the moment seemed apt to emulate his brother. He threw himself into the fence with a vengeance and managed to catch up to him at the top.

Peach was about to flip over to the other side when he realized the lip of the roof was reachable. He stretched out and grabbed it. "Give me a shove!"

Tinman had no idea what he was doing, but having no better ideas himself, he did as requested. Peach pulled himself up and egged Tinman on. Tinman with much longer arms was able to wrangle up without help. The two were perched on the top of the front of the roof. Behind them, the wings spread out to either side. In the middle was the slope leading to the bottom, just over the maintenance door they'd broken into.

Now Tinman felt exactly like Doctor Doolittle on the Giant Lunar Moth. A crescent moon had risen and he wished there was some way they could bring this slab of cement to life and fly off into space.

They looked down and saw the security guard burst through the emergency door. He started running across the open space leading to Virginia Street. Abruptly, he stopped and scanned the surroundings. He seemed to be thinking, trying to read their minds. Which way would they go? He must have had a knack for ESP because he spun around and his eyes quickly spied them atop the roof. He aimed and fired.

Peach yanked Tinman down just in time and the bullet whistled over their heads. "New plan!" cried Peach. "He's coming around the front. We have to go now!"

He dropped to his butt, pushed with his arms, and slid down the slope in the center of the roof like he was snow sledding. Tinman watched in horror as he reached the bottom, flew into the air, and landed on the lawn in front of the planetarium.

He started breathing again when he saw Peach pop to his feet. He stopped breathing again when he saw the security guard race around the building and get the drop on his brother. Peach threw up his arms. Despite the grief his brother brought him, there was no way he was going to let him take this rap.

He plopped down, gave a shove, and shot down the roof. His steering was not as good as Peach's because he veered off to one side and slid partway up one of the wings. This only served to give him more speed as gravity took over and forced him back to the bottom tip of the roof. When he reached it he was completely on his back with no idea where he was aiming. He left the roof like a torpedo, arms held tightly to his side.

He hit something hard and landed on top of whatever it was he hit. He felt hands pulling him up and saw it was Peach. Once on his feet, he realized the hard thing he'd hit was the security guard who was lying on his back, his eyes doing little circles in his head.

"Thanks, brother," said Peach. "Is he dead?"

"Does it matter?"

As they turned to go, the security guard snatched Tinman's ankle. At first, he thought it might simply be a cadaveric spasm. He saw the guard's open eyes and hissed, "Well, he's definitely not dead!"

Peach swung around and saw the situation. "Blast him!" said Peach.

"Blast him?!" said Tinman, furiously trying to yank his ankle free.

Peach flicked on his tactical flashlight and aimed the high-powered strobe at the guard. Tinman caught on quickly and the two closed in with their beams. The guard was instantly blinded and his hand fell away from Tinman's ankle.

"Now can we please stop messing around and get out of here!" said Peach.

They started down the hill, weaving around trees. "I have a feeling the nutcase isn't done yet," said Tinman. "And he's way faster than us."

"Right!" Peach swerved and headed for Tinman's cart. He grabbed the handle and yanked it away from the tree it had rammed into. "Like when we were kids."

Tinman remembered how they used to have grocery cart races with other young delinquents. He half-shoved Peach away and said, "Fine. But I get to steer."

"Why you?"

"Remember, we found we needed the most weight in the back for balance."

Peach wrinkled his mouth and nodded. It was true. "Damn, I never get to steer."

They shoved the cart the last few yards to the sidewalk. Peach climbed on the front, his heels hanging over the bottom metal frame. He pulled his shoulders back and grabbed onto the top front of the basket. Tinman held the handle and had one foot on the bottom frame while the other pushed.

* * *

The sky was white and very bright. He was sure it was night, but it looked like day. His eyes were incapable of blinking. The sky began flickering from pitch black to bright white, over and over.

He heard wailing and it was the planetarium alarm that pulled him out of his strobe-induced hallucination. As the sky slowly returned to its normal nighttime shade, details of the chase flooded his brain. The memories of his actions caused blood to rush into his face and it felt hot. Perhaps, just maybe, he'd gone a little overboard.

Shooting the gun in the theater was a teensy bit over-the-top. He knew he could forgive himself such zealousness but he was fairly certain others wouldn't. This was confirmed when his walkie-talkie started squawking angrily. The Chief was ordering all guards to the planetarium. Reports of an armed madman. Police on their way. Approach with extreme caution. Tasers at the ready.

He rolled to a crouch and saw two police cruisers fly onto campus. They would never understand. They didn't see it took people like him to combat pure evil. Their reality was different than his. They were blind.

He stared at Kelly and for a split second thought about going out in a blaze of glory. But where would the world be then? Would it be a better place without his protection? He thought not.

He tucked Kelly away and scooted toward the trees. He spotted one of the carts used by the thieves, lying on its side. He always loved riding them when he was a kid. The decision made, he upended it and raced it down the wooded slope.

* * *

Even though Tinman always got to steer, he wasn't very good at it. He had managed to maneuver the cart off the sidewalk and onto the road. He even had it pointed in the general direction of the gas station on the opposite side and down a little bit. But that's as good as it got.

As they neared the gas station, the cart quickly picked up speed on the steep grade. He and Peach saw the Buick with Bones and Catfish in it. Unfortunately, being in the back of the cart came with another important duty— braking.

When Tinman placed a foot on the macadam, the thin crepe sole immediately shredded, exposing his growth. He briefly thought this might be a good thing. He could grind the evil nastiness off! There was little time to mull over the wisdom of this action because a truck loomed in front.

He yanked on the handle and passed on the right. As they sped past the gas station, they saw Bones and Catfish staring out, slack-jawed. Tinman resisted the urge to wave.

The cart was now well over the speed limit and gaining. Fortunately, due to the game, traffic was light around the university. The traffic lights were still working, however, Tinman was reminded as he blew through a red light at 15th street, nearly barreling over two coeds in the crosswalk.

Fourteenth Street came and went as did the School of Arts. Tinman realized that one good thing out of this was there was no way the security guard could catch them now. At the bus stop near College Drive, some people saw them and starting pointing and egging them on. Tinman watched as their attention was drawn to something behind. They started pointing at whatever it was. He risked a peek and saw the crazy security guard on their other cart racing toward them, quickly closing in.

His thoughts of slowing down were replaced with the need for more speed. He hunkered down closer to the cart, trying to cut the wind. It worked. The cart leapt forward and bore down on the crossing at Eleventh. Ahead, he could see where the road crossed over Interstate 80, with downtown just beyond—where traffic was heavy.

* * *

Rudy had requested his entire army be present for tonight's momentous can collecting rally. The Battle for Nevada was the most anticipated event of the year for aluminum scroungers and he wanted to make sure he got the lion's share.

Rudy looked the part of a general, sort of a cross between Napoleon and a tree stump with limbs. Short, with thick, sinewy arms and legs, an abnormally large but rock-solid torso. The prematurely balding head still had a patch of dark hair that artfully swooped in an arc over his forehead.

His soldiers were armed with empty carts and were halfway between Eighth and Ninth. There was a long climb ahead and he rallied his troops.

"Come on, boys! Keep dreaming about all those wonderful ripe dumpsters just waiting to be harvested."

"RIGHT CHIEF!"

"Hey Rudy," said his trusted lieutenant. "Look at the crazies. Must be some frat boys had too much to drink."

Rudy followed his look and saw a grocery cart trundling toward them. The guy on the front reminded him of one of those carved figureheads on the prow of old ships. Except this one was not a buxom lady with flowing hair, and he didn't look like a frat boy. He looked at the guy in the back doing a bad job of steering.

"Hey! That's my landlord!" cried Rudy.

He saw Tinman glance over as he neared, "Terror" stamped on his face. Rudy started barking orders. "Alright, men! You know what to do! We've got to stop that runaway cart!"

"RIGHT CHIEF."

His lieutenant yelled, "Rudy, look, there's another one!"

Rudy quickly spotted the second cart. "Eh, it's just a campus guard. Let him go." He hopped on the back of his cart and with a push took up the chase with his army right behind.

Rudy and his squad were much more adept at riding grocery carts than the average person, such as Tinman. They were also better equipped as they all wore heavy boots, perfect for braking and finite steering. They quickly cut the distance between themselves and Tinman's runaway cart.

By the time they passed Eighth Street, they were pulling alongside. As they crossed over Interstate 80, Rudy and his lieutenant grabbed ahold of the basket and began braking. Other soldiers pulled in front. Like stopping a runaway stagecoach in an old western movie, they corralled the cart and brought it to a halt just at the crossing of Seventh and Virginia. The neon lights atop the entrance to Circus Circus Casino were just a block ahead.

Peach collapsed into the waiting arms of several of Rudy's gang. Rudy looked at Tinman's ashy face. "You out for a joy ride or something, Tinman? There are better ways to get your kicks you know."

Tinman peeled his fingers from the handle of the cart and threw his arms around Rudy. "I owe you for this. Big time. Anything you want."

"Oh yeah?" said Rudy. "Well, you know what I want."

Tinman lifted his head from Rudy's chest and nodded. "You got it, Rudy."

The other cart zipped by, heading for the heart of downtown. Cars honked angrily as it avoided crash after crash. "You know that guy?" asked Rudy.

"Not intimately," said Tinman.

"Oh good. Because from the looks of it, he's in for a rude awakening."

* * *

This was definitely not as fun as it was when he was a kid, thought Hobie as he hurtled into downtown. Too many cars. Too many obstacles. Too much of a chance he could die. And what a way to die. So unflattering. What do you put in the obituary? Murdered by shopping cart?

There was no time to figure it out. A large group of people was crossing the street at Sixth and Virginia. He waved for them to get out of the way, but they were too drunk or too unhelpful to listen. He was already in enough trouble without killing a group of tourists. He leaned to his left and pulled hard on the handle of the cart. That's where he went wrong. Had he leaned to his right, he may have been able to avoid slamming headlong into the giant glass doors at the front of Circus Circus.

The cart smacked dead center into the middle of the right door and came to an abrupt stop. Hobie took two deep breaths and a loud wrenching noise drew his attention. A crack formed in the bottom of the door and quickly extended to the top. He held his breath, hoping for the best. Which was not what happened. The glass collapsed, shards raining down on top of him.

Inside the casino, he saw several burly security guards coming his way. What to do. Run. If he could just get around the corner he could hail a cab and escape.

He wrenched his hands from the destroyed cart and bolted down the street. As he careened around the corner of North Sierra he saw a cab. He reached for his wallet and found it was gone!

He must have lost it during the chase. With no other option, he jumped into the cab and pulled out Kelly. "Get me out of here!" he barked at the Middle Eastern driver.

The cabbie smiled into the rearview mirror and turned around. In his hand was a gun. Hobie recognized it as a

Ruger GP 100, six-shot, double-action revolver, chambered for a .357 magnum. Kelly was a cork gun compared to this.

Hobie nodded his appreciation and jumped out of the cab. As he sped into the parking garage for the casino he wondered why people like him, put here to save the planet, always got the short end of the stick.

EIGHTEEN

"OW!"

"Sorry, Tinman, but it's the only surefire way to get rid of them," said Rudy. "This is the voice of experience talking."

Tinman was sitting on one of his metal chairs, his hair damp. Bones was in the ratty recliner, Catfish on the edge of the bed, and Peach in the other metal chair. The small television set was on and they were idly watching a rerun of Hogan's Heroes in anticipation of the late news.

Rudy leaned over Tinman using a specialized lice-picking comb to hunt out the parasites scampering around in his hair.

"It's okay, Rudy," said Tinman. "I'm just happy you had one of those combs."

"Goes with the territory," said Rudy. "Hold still, I think there's just a few more. You're lucky. They weren't in here long enough to lay eggs."

"Technically, they're called nits," said Tinman, giving Peach a harrowing look, who responded with a deeply apologetic shrug.

On the television, Newkirk was confronting Hogan. "Of course I can open that safe, Colonel. But it's not about that, is it? The place is guarded like the Bank of England. How are we supposed to get by the bleedin' guards?" Hogan gave one of his smarmy looks and Newkirk rolled his eyes.

"I'm sorry you had to miss the game, Rudy," said Tinman.

"No biggie. I still get my cut whether I'm there or not. The perks of being in power. Now about this favor you owe me."

Tinman had once made the mistake of telling Rudy about Dez's prowess at the poker table. Ever since he'd been badgering him for an introduction.

"Next game, right? I get the invite," said Rudy.

"Sure, sure, but it's not going to be until her Christmas party," said Tinman.

"I can wait."

"And you're going to need a stake. This isn't penny ante."

"Well I thought that was part of the favor, staking me," said Rudy.

There was a long pause broken by Rudy chuckling. "Just kidding. Don't you worry. I'll have a stake. I won't need much though."

Bones looked at Catfish and they rolled their eyes. "Okay, that should do it," said Rudy. "Now remember, you'll need to wash your hair again, like three times. If you have any more problems, get a tub of mayonnaise and goop up your hair, then cover it in a bath cap for five hours. After that, rinse it out and dry it with a blow dryer. It'll definitely take care of any survivors."

Tinman studied Rudy and realized he wasn't joking. He prayed all of the little buggers had been found. He was a mustard guy and there was no mayonnaise at hand, so he'd have to venture out and buy some with money he could ill afford to spend. Especially now.

The opening credits for the news came on. "Rudy, I hate to ask this, but I need to talk to these guys in private," said Tinman.

"No biggie. I gotta run anyway. Big game under the highway tonight. Everybody's flush with cans from the Homecoming game. I believe I'll make out very well indeed." Rudy snickered as he packed up his comb and pulled on his heavy parka. "By the way, what was that security guard doing chasing you anyway? I find it hard to believe a guy like you would be caught publicly urinating."

Tinman averted his eyes. Rudy scanned the room and received similar reactions. "Hey, let's all say we just forget I asked. I learned a long time ago not to stick my noodle where it isn't wanted. What I don't know, doesn't hurt you, right? Pleasant dreams, gentlemen. And nice meeting you, Tinman's brother."

"Peach. And thanks a lot, Rudy. You're a good man to have around."

Rudy glowed. "It's what I keep telling myself. Ta ta." He opened the door and swaggered out.

"You gotta forgive me, brother," said Peach. "I swear I didn't know."

Tinman didn't answer. Instead, he pointed a finger at the TV. Peach got up and turned the volume louder. Crime Wave was just getting underway.

"Good evening, ladies and gentlemen, this is Scott Frenley, and do we have an entertaining report for you tonight. It all starts on the UNR campus where apparently a security guard lost his marbles and began shooting up the place. Shots were first heard around eight thirty near Mackay Stadium."

"Yessir, that's when he took those first two shots at you," Bones drawled.

"Yeah, thanks for the late heads up," growled Tinman. Bones hung his head and looked sheepishly at Tinman.

"It was originally believed they were coming from people in the parking lot, however, it was determined the Wolf Pack had yet to score a touchdown and there was no cause for celebration. A short time later, the attendant at the Fleischmann Planetarium reported a gun being fired in the Dome Theater."

"My ears are still ringing," said Tinman.

"Interestingly enough, when the police arrived, the theatergoers were still enjoying the presentation! Apparently they thought a psychotic security guard shooting off a gun was all part of the show!"

"It was kind of weird, huh? I mean those kids were so relaxed during the whole thing," said Peach. "They even let us crawl by and not one wondering what we were doing there."

"Tonight's showing was, however, Pink Floyd's, Dark Side of the Moon. Police, therefore, determined the cause of the unusual reaction may have been due to consumption of an unknown illegal substance."

"They were tripping!" cried Peach. "I thought the show was incredible and I was straight! Imagine how cool it would be—" Tinman shot him an incredulous look and Peach clammed up.

"Witnesses of the shootings say they could see no reason why the security guard had flipped his lid. There were no reported thefts and the police found no evidence of wrongdoing anywhere on campus. Maybe somebody forgot to put change in one of the meters!"

"See! I told you there was nothing to worry about. Nobody knows nothing about the break-in," said Peach.

"Well he must have known," said Tinman, pointing at a picture of Hobie on the screen.

"The security guard is now wanted by the police for discharging a firearm in a restricted area and public endangerment. The Chief of Security has stated the security guard has been relieved of his duties, saying, and I quote: "He never fit in with my troops. I'm happy to be rid of the putz." End of quote. Well, no love lost there, hey folks!"

"It's just too strange. What the hell got into the kid," said Catfish.

"Damn it! I tell you, he was onto us," said Tinman.

"Our last story also took place near the UNR campus. In what is being described by police as a fraternity prank, two grocery carts were seen racing each other down North Virginia Street. We only have video of one of the carts which we'll roll now."

"Please don't let it be ours," said Tinman.

A video plays showing Peach and Tinman zooming down the hill. Tinman's head dropped.

"Great. All my life I stay under the radar and now in less than a month, I'm famous."

"You can't really see your face," offered Peach. "Not like with the ostrich video."

"Golly, gee, don't I feel a whole lot better now!" Tinman snapped.

"Just saying."

Scott Frenley said, "The cart you see here came to a stop shortly before downtown, aided in part by a gang of homeless people! Nothing like having friends in low places!"

"I ought to knock that guy out. That's no way to talk about Rudy," said Peach.

"The other cart, however, did not fare as well. Reportedly it and its driver ran headlong into the front door of the Circus Circus Casino causing extensive damage. We're not sure, however, if that meant to the door or to the driver, as he fled the scene and has not been identified."

"At least the nutcase got his," said Catfish.

"Turn it off," said Tinman.

Peach got up and clicked off the TV and said, "There it is, boys! We're in the clear. Nothing to worry about."

Bones and Catfish wanted to agree and end it there, but the look on Tinman's face told them this discussion was not over. Tinman leaned back in his chair and focused on Peach.

"You screwed up," he said.

"At least admit I got us in and out clean," argued Peach.

"Yeah? Well, I imagine you know far better than me it's not about getting in and out clean, it's about getting away clean."

Peach had absolutely nothing to say in response. He'd been thinking like thoughts ever since they reached the motel. He shrugged into his chair, waiting for the onslaught.

"How long did you case the joint, Peach? About a week, isn't that right?" asked Tinman, not looking for a response. "All by yourself, huh? Now back when we were kids, what did we learn?"

Peach hesitated, feeling the bear trap around his ankle. "Never case a joint by yourself, in case you're recognized."

"Bingo! You get the booby prize," said Tinman. "But you were in such a hurry to show off to us just how good you were, you didn't involve us in that part of the scheme, did you? No, you didn't. First mistake. The kid must have seen you. From what Bones and Catfish said on the way back. Tell us again."

Catfish cleared his throat. He didn't want any parts of this inquisition and ensuing crucifixion, but Tinman's glare forced his hand. "It was mighty strange. When we hit the parking garage, that guy was on the alert, like he was waiting for you two."

"Ah hah! We can therefore assume he knew something was in the air," said Tinman. "Agreed?"

The other three guys grudgingly nodded. "We can also assume your intel regarding guards only using Tasers was incorrect," continued Tinman.

"Now I think that's a little unfair," said Bones. "The kid was one donut short of a dozen. Look what he had in his wallet. A lifetime membership to the Big Shot Shooting Range. And instead of pictures of girls or his kids, he's got snapshots of guns. He's just a loose wire. Peach could not have accounted for that."

"Uh-huh. What do you think?" asked Tinman, his laser eyes locating their target.

Peach mumbled, "Always plan for the unexpected."

"And you guys," Tinman continued. "What's the idea of coming back to the garage so soon?"

"Wait a minute, we were right on schedule," Catfish argued. "You guys were late."

"Which brings us to our final point," said Tinman. "Tell me about another adage master thieves live by."

Peach got up slowly and wandered over to the kitchen, his back to Tinman. "Never go in unless you know the loot is there." He spun around. "But how was I to know they were going to move them?"

"Gee. Maybe when you were doing the twist with Peppermint, you might have popped the question?"

"I told you that's a rookie move!"

"More rookie than breaking into a joint and walking away with nothing?" asked Tinman.

"You know," started Bones, "if the baskets had been there, you would have been nabbed for sure, now we know the kid was onto us."

"There's a point! Hadn't thought of that," said Peach, desperately grabbing for straws, even if it was the short one.

"I still wonder what happened to those damn baskets," said Catfish. "Obviously the kid kept whatever he knew to himself. The museum didn't move them because of us. So where did they go?"

"Frankly, I don't care. In fact, I hope I never even think about them again. Tonight, I've fallen off a roof, been shot at several times by a psychopath, and nearly died in a runaway grocery cart."

"Don't forget the lice," said Peach, choking on his words as he tried to stuff them back down his throat. To toss blame elsewhere he said, "Speaking of the grocery cart, why didn't you try braking?"

"Because you gave me those little bedroom slippers to wear!" Tinman bellowed. "If I'd had my new sneakers on, I could have done that!"

There was a tense silence as everyone licked their wounds. Peach was the first to recover. "I don't know what we're worrying about. There's no record of the burglary. All we have to do is wait until the baskets come back from wherever they are and we hit the place again."

Bones and Catfish saw the validity in Peach's argument. Tinman, however, did not. He snorted and clapped his hands. "Brilliant! Yeah, you go right ahead and work on that, Troy. Best of luck."

Peach smiled brightly. "Okay, I think I will. But first things first, I've got to return the Buick."

"Sure you do! Have to tie up all those loose ends! Right? The trademark of a master thief!"

Peach headed for the door, his back to Tinman. "You can think what you want, brother, but I'm gonna make this right." And he was gone.

Tinman flicked his hand at the door in dismissal. "Let's call it a night, guys. I've got to take a shower."

"I believe you do," said Bones, slowly rising. "Hopefully it will clean out your brain."

"What are you talking about?" Tinman asked.

Catfish rose and leaned into his face. "Peach is a yegg. That's his job. An important part of the string but not the only part. Seems a little too easy to dump this all on him. You want a better plan, next time you do it. That's what you claim to be good at, right? Figuring how to run the balls?" He cocked his head at Bones. "Let's get out of here. Before we catch whatever he's got."

Tinman started to say something in his defense but the door clicked shut and he was left talking to himself.

NINETEEN

THE LADIES GATHERED IN THE CLUBHOUSE of the Lucky Charms Retirement Community were in quite the tizzy. As members of the Events Committee, it was their job to make sure the annual Thanksgiving celebration went off without a hitch. The problem was, to seat all the expected partygoers in the clubhouse, they needed fifty-two tables.

They spent a good part of their meeting scribbling out floor plans in an attempt to squeeze all the tables in. They were meeting with little success. They figured out how they could move the large sofas in front of the giant screen TV into the storage room, but there still wasn't enough space. They needed to fit another two tables and the problem had become quite vexing.

This development located off North McCarran Street was very upscale. All the women had originally lived in houses far too large for the size of their families. Therefore, a lack of space was a foreign concept.

As their allotted time for the meeting wound down, the ladies fell silent. All were now looking across the room at their bane. The pool table. They could care less it was a regulation size, top-of-the-line, Gold Crown V Brunswick, with Simonis 860 felt.

They were old school and believed what was so aptly sung about in The Music Man: Where there's pool, 'ya got trouble. The pool table was not only causing a problem for this event. There had been many occasions when some of the men in the community chose to play the childish game while they were having a meeting or tea party.

The hideous clacking and clashing of the balls made it nearly impossible to concentrate on their idle pleasures. The problem had become so taxing that not two weeks ago they put out a petition to have it permanently removed. They posted them throughout the community, even putting them on windshields of cars, despite the fact this was technically against the rules.

The response was positive, mostly women siding with their noble cause. After receiving what they believed an ample amount of names to win the day they presented it to the Governing Board. The problem was the Board was comprised mostly of men and when the women didn't receive a prompt response, they felt certain their husbands were conveniently shelving their request.

As they stared at the pool table in angry repose the door of the clubhouse swung open and a handsome man with a breezy air strolled in. Some of the women eyed him salaciously, seeing him more as a cream-filled bonbon they might nibble on someday when their husbands were on the links. Yummy.

The man smiled sweetly and waved in two more men. Or rather man-monsters. They were huge with caps pulled low. One was as white as most of the women's hair and the other had a permanent tan. Each held two square dollies.

The dreamboat floated over to their conference table. "We'll only be a few minutes lovely ladies. Don't want to be disturbing your important business any more than we have to." He motioned to the two gorillas and they galumphed over to the pool table.

The chairwoman rose. She was the youngest of the bunch and still retained some of her looks and figure from younger days. "May I ask what it is you're doing?"

The studmuffin looked surprised. "Didn't you hear? Your petition to remove the pool table has been granted."

There was a collective gasp. The bad habit was spreading. The chairwoman impulsively grabbed the man's hands in hers. "You're serious? The Board has officially approved it?"

"Just got the call! We've got the truck waiting right out there. In no time, your problem will be solved and you can enjoy the quality of life you deserve."

The women watched as the large workers hefted each leg of the table onto a dolly. They were too stunned to speak, but in their minds, each one kept thinking the same thing: "Our husbands listened to us!"

More than one decided perhaps, as a sort of thank you gift, tonight might be a good time to give their hubbies a little treat. After all, it had been quite a while, years for some. Yes, that was the ticket. Positive reinforcement. You do something nice and you receive a treat.

The table was now perched on the four dollies, one under each leg, and the large men were pushing it toward the front door. The horrible thing seemed dwarfed next to the godsent giants.

The chairwoman, still grasping the handsome man's hands, looked deeply into his eyes. Perhaps this young man deserved some sort of treat. It was worth a try. "Is there some way, any way I can repay you?"

"The look of happiness on your lovely face is payment enough, ma'am." Then he winked. A sly wink. The chairwoman was not so old she didn't recognize it. She felt a warmness below which she hadn't felt in oh so long. So the other women would not know what she was up to and muscle in, she silently mouthed her personal cell number. The babe magnet made a small nod, only perceptible to her. The warm spot suddenly felt moist.

"Well, we'll leave you to your important doings, ladies. And I guarantee you peace and tranquility from this moment on."

"You promise?" asked the chairwoman.

"Scouts honor," said the heartthrob. As he turned and walked to the front door, the ladies spontaneously leapt to their feet and the applause thundered throughout the clubhouse. Now there would be fifty-two tables and not one covered in green felt.

TWENTY

EVERYTHING WAS WRONG. The hall was deader than usual. Amber was acting strangely, constantly looking at the clock, though closing time was a long way off. He hadn't seen Bones and Catfish since the aborted heist. Even Tek had deserted him, though he could know nothing about what a jerk he'd been to Peach. And from what he could tell, his brother was in the wind, maybe forever.

Scariest of all, however, his game was off.

Only by five percent or so, but it was troublesome. It wasn't his shotmaking. It was his position play. It had been off ever since the debacle at the Historical Society. When he wanted to put the cue ball four inches to the left of his next object ball, it would land an inch shy. To most, this would not seem to be much of a big deal, to Tinman it was disastrous. Being one inch short of his position threw the balance of the run off and he was forced to ad-lib.

He was right to be concerned. There's nothing worse than a pool player losing his touch and feel for position. Winning depended on it. It's why he was meticulously marking the position of the balls for every shot and placing a paper marker where he wanted the cue ball to land after the shot. If he wasn't exact, he set up the shot again and did it until it was perfect.

It wasn't working. The energy was wrong, inside him and in the hall. He'd never liked McCue's but recently he'd come to despise it. Tonight it had come to a head, in no small part due to Amber's strange attitude.

"Don't you ever do anything else," she asked, suddenly appearing right behind the pocket he was shooting at.

Tinman sighed and looked up. "You're in my light."

"Why don't you go home early for once," said Amber, committing a cardinal sin by placing both hands on the table in front of his shot path. "There's no action here."

"You got your period?" asked Tinman, straightening up.

"It's none of your business!" said Amber. "And no I don't."

"So why are you haranguing me?"

Amber huffed and spun away. She wandered around the tables, looking like she was deep in thought. When she seemed to have come to some sort of conclusion, she marched back. "You have to go. The owner's coming tonight."

"And?"

"Dammit! He told me to shut down early and make sure the place was empty by the time he got here."

Tinman raised an eyebrow. So that was it. He knew Amber's history with the owner and why she was now in charge of the hall. He thought, however, any amorous involvement was long over.

"Just promise me you two won't use my table," said Tinman.

"Don't worry. I'll make sure to cover it first," said Amber.

He nodded and began to unscrew his cue. Amber physically relaxed and even managed the first smile of the evening. "Good for you!" she said. "You can go home, watch a little TV and get a good night's sleep. Maybe whatever's bugging you will go away."

Tinman stopped putting his cue in its case and stared at her. "I never said anything was bugging me."

Amber answered by placing her fists on her hips and staring him down. Defeated, Tinman shrugged and stowed his cue. He decided he'd take it home and give it a good cleaning. Maybe a new tip. That might help.

Without another word, he pulled on his light jacket, grabbed his case, and headed for the door. He raised a hand in farewell without looking back and stepped outside. Amber immediately rushed to the door, locked it, and ran behind the bar to collect her things.

Tinman meandered down the sidewalk. Not sure if he was really going to his room or not. No one was going to tell him where he should go. After a block, he decided there was no other place to go. He pulled out his cheap toss away cellphone he bought from Seven Eleven and called Garshasp.

He only had to wait ten minutes before he saw the familiar cab pull down the road. It stopped, and he climbed in.

Normally he and Garshasp's conversation went like this, "Heya, Garshasp." And Garshasp would grunt. It was an ideal relationship. Tonight, however, for some reason Tinman felt the need to talk. He knew he was on safe ground and could say anything he wanted because in all the years he had known his driver, he'd never heard him speak more than a few words of English.

He began, "You know how it is when things just don't seem to be clicking?"

"Umh,"

"It's like the world is off-kilter. Like someone forgot to put all the screws back in the right place and now the washing machine is making some sort of funny noise. It's just not working like it used to."

"Umh,"

"The worst thing is, I don't know if it's just me or if the whole world is out of alignment."

"No worry it pal. Couple weeks go, some crazy get in my car and pulling gun on me. But I learning him, okay. I showing him this."

Garshasp lifted an ugly-looking handgun with a very long barrel. Tinman barely glanced at it. His eyes locked on Garshasp. "But . . . wait, I though you didn't—"

"No! Yes I loving guns! America land of the free guns," said Garshasp, smiling into the rearview mirror.

"Not that, I mean, I thought you didn't . . ." said Tinman staring at Garshasp's mirror reflection. "Never mind." He settled back into his seat and zipped his lips. Life never gets easier.

Back at his apartment, he sat in his easy chair and pulled out his cue. He examined the tip with a small magnifying glass and determined it was in perfect condition. He sighed. The problem was him.

With that cheery thought, he decided to take up Amber on her suggestion and turn in early. He desperately wanted a smoke before bed but hadn't had the money to buy any in an eternity. In the last two weeks, he cleared a little under six hundred dollars at the hall.

As he brushed his teeth he thought about the growth, which, to his eyes, now took up half of his foot. In reality, it was only about an inch across. He undressed down to his boxers and fell into his little bed.

At first, sleep didn't come. Like every night for the last two weeks, the only thing his brain could think about was how to get the baskets. Those damned baskets. He should just forget about them, but it wasn't possible. Whether he liked it or not, it was thieves' blood coursing through his veins. He was consumed with the need to devise a plan to get those baskets. The problem was, every plan he came up with needed Peach's expertise. And Peach was gone. Because of him.

This was his last thought before drifting off to sleep about half an hour after arriving home. It was a restless sleep and in it, he heard the crashing of pool balls. This didn't surprise his subconscious mind. Pool was the only thing he ever dreamed of. In his dreams, he would run balls. Sometimes he would wake up and the run would be so vivid he would go to the pool hall and recreate it.

What surprised his subconscious was how realistic the sound of the balls had been. There it went again. His eyes popped open not ten minutes after drifting off. He listened. Nothing. He closed his eyes and focused on his breathing.

He heard a little click and knew this was no dream. Something was in his room. With one eye he scanned the apartment. What was that at the door? It looked like some kind of fishing rod. Familiar, but he couldn't place it.

He shook his head to make sure he was actually awake. Slowly, he reached over and clicked on the bedside lamp. There it was! The fishing rod was weaving around in front of his door, like an emaciated cobra ready to strike. He swung his legs over the bed. Before he could move, the door handle turned, the fishing rod dropped to the ground and his door swung open.

"I did it!" cried Tek, as he plowed inside.

"What in the hell are you doing here?"

"Did you see? I did it!" squealed Tek. "Come on, hurry up! They sent me to get you. The surprise is waiting."

The very word sent shivers down Tinman's spine. He despised surprises. They were rarely good and when they were bad they were very bad. He had a strong urge to boot the kid out of his room, lock his door, and wait until the world became sane again.

Still, the look on Tek's face piqued his curiosity. He grumbled to himself as he pulled on his pants. Tek busied himself with wrapping up The Mule Tool.

"Think you might give me a little hint?" asked Tinman, working on his shirt.

"No way! They said they'd beat my ass if I did."

"Who's they?"

"I'm not telling you that either," said Tek, oblivious to Tinman's glare.

"Where are we going?"

Tek laughed. "They warned me you'd be like this. Will you just come on! It's not far."

"How did you get here?"

"I can't hear you," sang Tek.

Fully dressed, Tinman walked to the door. He glanced at the Mule Tool. "I thought you were supposed to give that back to Peach."

"That's between him and me," Tek snarled. "Mind your own business."

Tinman shook his head. "Lead the way, you little creep."

As Tinman followed him out the door he thought he might have guessed the surprise. It must be Peach was back. It wouldn't make sense for him to leave for good and not get one of his tools back. If it was true, he had mixed emotions. He desperately needed his brother but wasn't sure what further chaos he would cause in his life. Either way, he was fairly certain this must be the surprise.

As he reached the bottom of the stairs he discovered his guess was wrong. Out of the door of the old motel office and convenience store stepped the two walking monoliths he'd met at Dez'.

His first thought was she'd sent these two apes to shake him down for the tax money. He couldn't really believe she would do such a thing, but how else to explain their presence. And what were they doing inside a boarded up part of the motel?

They spotted him and headed his way, fierce looks on their faces. Tinman reached out to push Tek out of the way. This was his fight and he didn't want the kid hurt by these beasts. Tek, however, shrugged him off and jogged over.

The albino put his fists on his hips and stared menacingly at him. "You didn't spill the frijoles, did you chico?"

"Hell no!" cried Tek. "You think I'm dumb enough to mess with you guys?"

Malice elbowed Angel and they both grinned. Angel tousled Tek's hair. "We're sorry to run off, Tinman. We wanted to wait until the surprise but Kutchy and Koo are probably starving."

"And they might have to go pee-pee," said Malice.

Tinman was in a state of shock and could find no sane reply. Angel slapped him on the shoulder nearly knocking him to the ground. "You're a lucky guy, Tinman. As they say, friendship is a rainbow between two hearts, right? If you ever need our help again, don't hesitate to ask."

A cab pulled into the parking lot. Malice and Angel waved and hopped inside and drove off.

Tinman felt the need to sit down. He was not given the opportunity because Tek started pushing him from behind. In no position to fight back, he allowed himself to be shoved and dragged to the front door of the old office.

"Well, go in why don't you!" said Tek.

Tinman was quite sure this was the strangest dream he'd ever encountered. Up until now, it had been disturbing but not permanently scarring. He wasn't sure, however, if he wanted to go through that door.

He had no choice in the matter as Tek impatiently flung it open and shoved him in. The office section was now arranged like a lounge/bar using tables from the motel rooms. There were a few liquor bottles and a cooler of beer on the office counter. A red velour curtain hung in the entrance to the old mini-mart. Seated, were Catfish, Bones, Peach, and Rudy, all wearing shit-eating grins as they nodded in greeting. Everyone looked so real, thought Tinman.

"Drumroll, please," said Catfish. They all beat on the tables and the rumble built to a crescendo. "And curtain!"

It parted with a flourish and there was Amber, also sporting a shit-eating grin. Behind her sat the most beautiful sight in the world. A pool table. And not just any table, discovered Tinman as he floated into the room, instinctively examining it with his expert eye.

It was a regulation nine-foot Brunswick in mahogany with nickel trim. He felt the tightness of the pockets and noted the longer rails, engineered to strict World Pool-Billiard Association specifications. This was a Brunswick Tournament Edition. And not just any Brunswick.

"It's a Gold Crown V," he whispered in awe.

The others had moved in around him. "Nothing but the best for the best," said Peach.

Tinman stuttered, "But how? Who?"

215

Catfish threw an arm around Peach. "The master thief here is the one responsible."

"Surprise, surprise," said Bones with a little smirk.

Tinman turned to his brother. "This is no dream?"

"It's yours," said Peach.

Tinman closed the distance between them. "But why?"

"I know how much you hate practicing in public, worried you might give away your speed and all. Now you can hone up here and seek out the action in the hall."

"No. I mean, why, after what I—"

"Did? Well, that's exactly why. After all you've done for me, the least I can do is start paying back. Let's just call it a down payment and leave it at that."

He held out his hand to shake. Tinman stared at it, pushed it away, and grabbed him in a bear hug. Everybody clapped and the party started.

Tek was sent to Tinman's room to retrieve his cue. While he was gone, beers were passed around and Peach recounted the stealing of the table.

"The night I returned the Buick," he said. "I saw these petitions on everybody's car. The ladies were fed up with the table. It's when I hatched the plan. Took me a little while to line up the truck and recruit Angel and Malice."

"That's why they were here?" cried Tinman.

"Of course," said Peach. "Why, what did you think?"

"It's not important," said Tinman. "I just can't believe you asked for help from those two creeps."

"Hey, don't be too quick to judge from their looks. Actually, they're really nice guys. When I told them about your predicament, they volunteered. They didn't even want any money."

"Huh," said Tinman. "Dez doesn't know about this?"

"None of her business. I swore Angel and Malice to secrecy."

"And you just strolled right in there, during a meeting, and wheeled it out of there," confirmed Catfish.

"And get this," said Peach. "When we were leaving, they gave us a standing O."

Everyone whooped it up. Rudy slapped Peach on the back. "Forget me. Looks like you're the good guy to have around."

"You got that right," said Tinman.

Tek ran in with the cue and everyone called for a demonstration. Tinman happily proceeded to put on a trick shot exhibition. He started with "the butterfly" where six balls grouped in the center of the table are all sunk with one shot, each dropping in a separate pocket.

He moved on to "the snake shot" where all fifteen balls are placed in a winding chain from one end of the table to the other. The cue ball hits the one ball which hits the two and so on, ultimately dropping the last ball in a corner pocket in a fifteen-ball combination shot.

"Christ Almighty!" cried Rudy. "I knew you shot pool. I didn't know you were a pool god!"

Tinman started setting up a triple-kiss shot when Tek wandered over to the corner where Peach was sitting. "Tell me something."

"If I can," said Peach.

"When did he get his nickname?"

Peach grinned and leaned back. "Well, let's see. He was younger than you. I'd say maybe twelve."

"Who gave it to him, you?"

"Oh no. It was an old hustler, they called him Titanic. He was in the Silver Cue one day, just killing everybody. My brother watched all day, waiting for his move. That night, when everyone else was running scared he challenged him to a game. The Titanic started laughing cause he was so young. I thought Tinman was going to break a cue over his head. Instead, he called him a coward. Oh boy, did that get to him. It also got to his game. By midnight, my brother had cleaned him out. On the way out the door, he dubbed him Tinman."

"I don't get it. Why Tinman?"

"Because he's got heart."

"But the Tinman doesn't have a heart!" argued Tek.

"Pool talk. When you say a hustler's got heart it really means you got no heart. See?"

Tek scrunched up his face and looked like he wanted to spit. "What are you talking about, man?"

Tinman made the kiss shot and everyone applauded. He bowed and started setting up "the machine gun" where several balls are sunk rapid-fire into the same pocket after each hits three rails.

"Let me explain. Like nobody I've ever seen, Tinman can peg exactly how much a mark has in his pocket and how much he can stand to lose. And he will not let the guy off the hook until he has every last cent, no matter what. If he's playing him one way, for greed, and that peters out, he'll go the other. Either way, it doesn't matter if the guy's whining or getting mean, he will not unscrew his cue until the job's done. So to have heart as a hustler means you can't have any heart. Now you see?"

Eyes wide, Tek glanced at Tinman. "He's dangerous."

Peach laughed. "Only on the table, little man."

By 2 AM, the party was winding down. Rudy had already left for his room. Tinman called his driver to take Bones, Catfish, Amber, and Tek home. Peach offered to cover the tab for the rides. Garshasp showed up ten minutes later and knocked on the office door. Tek let him in.

"Hey Garshasp!" said Tinman, still shooting. "Lookie what I got."

Garshasp frowned. "No more driving with Garshasp to the hall?"

Tinman laughed. "Don't you worry, friend, I'll still be needing you."

"Umh."

Tek turned to Peach and handed him The Mule Tool. Peach said, "You can keep it for a while longer if you want."

"Thanks anyway. I'm working on a prototype for a modern version. It's a macro-robotic design based on the origami folding principle."

Peach looked to the others, all equally in the dark. He said, "Well, good for you. I look forward to seeing it."

Tek called, "Hey, Tinman. Think maybe I could get a key to the clubhouse?"

Mid-stroke, Tinman stopped. Clubhouse? He said, "I thought you didn't need keys anymore."

"You deserve more respect."

Tinman looked at the kid differently than he ever had before. "Sure thing, Tek. You got it."

"Well, hell, I want one too," said Bones.

"Check," said Catfish.

"Are girl members allowed?" asked Amber.

"Relax, I'm on it," said Peach.

"Cool. By the way," said Tek, "my sixteenth birthday is coming up, and either you or Tinman need to teach me to drive."

Peach raised his brows and looked to Tinman who shrugged indifferently. Tek, seeing his request falling on deaf ears, continued. "I'll be getting my learner's permit and I have my mom's car to practice in. All I need is a responsible adult."

Amber found this hysterical and it soon spread around the room. Tinman laid his cue down and walked to the door. "Well Tek, Garshasp here is the best driver I know. I bet he'd be happy to give you some lessons for a fair price. Right Garshasp?"

Garshasp smiled wide. "You got it boss."

"Alright, let's get out of here," said Amber, stepping outside. "Don't be a stranger, Tinman!"

Bones, Catfish, and Tek followed and soon Peach and Tinman were left alone. "Up for a quick game of nine ball?" asked Tinman.

"Sure thing."

Tinman racked the balls, but before removing the diamond rack he looked to Peach at the other end of the table. "I'm sorry. About the way I treated you."

"When was that?"

Tinman grinned and shook his head. "This is really something else. All these years and I never had my own."

For a second, Peach thought Tinman was going to cry, but he shook it off and beckoned him to break. Peach slammed the cue ball into the rack and nothing dropped.

Tinman stalked the table, looking for the best run. He chose his leadoff ball and leaned down. "I can't get them out of my head. It's throwing off my game. We have to do something."

Peach smiled. "We do indeed. In fact I never stopped working on it."

The game forgotten, Tinman closed in on him. "You know where they are?"

Peach said, "You remember the chairwoman I told you about tonight? At the retirement place? Well, I forgot to mention she had a little thing for me."

"Shocking."

"That's what I'm thinking, being somewhat older and all. But still a looker, believe me. Anyway, after I got the pool table and stashed it over here, I gave her a shout."

"Are you crazy? By then, she must have known the whole petition thing was a ruse!"

"Of course she knew. But she didn't care. She thought it was a hoot. Apparently our little heist really pissed off the hubbies. She insisted on showing me her gratitude and it nearly killed me. Insatiable, if you know what I mean. Even after my first visit, Sage insisted she still had more gratitude so we arranged for a meet at a motel downtown."

"Sage. I don't even want to know what her pet name is."

"Sagebush. Get it?"

Tinman was in such a good mood, he howled for a solid minute. "No kidding," said Peach. "And she loves it! Can you believe it? Highfalutin lady and all."

"Hey. Who was it once told me, high or low, they all got the same itch."

"Uh, I guess that would be me. Anyway, after our meet in this motel, she says she wants to show me a little culture. Maybe she's trying to dress me up a little, like all the girls do. I'm game, so off we go to the Nevada Museum of Art. Did you know the place is the only accredited art museum in the state? I don't know why but it was surprising to me. I mean, it's in Reno."

"Huh. That is surprising."

"See! Anyhoo, we're wandering around in there looking at all the pretty pictures, and wham there they are."

"The baskets?!"

"All ten. Sitting there just as pretty as could be. They must have been on loan or something when we hit the Historical Society."

"Damn. What rotten luck."

"Right! That's what I'm thinking. Now naturally, with Sage along I can't really case the joint so I don't know nothing from nothing about the security. Therefore, I was thinking the two of us could go on a little field trip tomorrow."

"Get a little culture in our lives, huh?"

"Never hurts to improve oneself."

"I can think of millions of ways."

TWENTY-ONE

THE HISTORICAL SOCIETY MUSEUM is to the Nevada Museum of Art as Baby Bear is to Papa Bear. The latter was at least four times the size of the former and was an imposing figure located just west of midtown on Liberty Street. The building was designed by an internationally renowned architect who was inspired by the geological formations of the Black Rock Desert. It stood four stories and it's 68 ft. high by 250 ft. long torqued exterior walls were sided by giant black sheets of a zinc material wrapped vertically around the building. The sheets were purposely creased to simulate the rock textures found in the Black Rock Desert. At the rear, the fourth floor and outdoor viewing plaza were recessed and jutted above the rest of the building.

Tinman knew nothing of the architect's vision. As he stood on the corner of Liberty and Hill waiting for Peach to enter the museum first, he thought the building looked like an oil tanker run aground. The Exxon Valdez immediately came to mind. The jutting fourth floor in the stern reminded him of a control tower. The way the two exterior walls curved in, nearly meeting at the front, made a perfect prow.

Whatever it was meant to look like, it was nothing if not imposing. Strangely, he was not nervous at all. The mess at the first museum they'd broken into, had flushed him of all negative thoughts. He was playing for keeps now and anxiously awaited his chance to case the inside.

To keep a low profile, he and Peach decided to enter at different times. A couple was always easier to remember than an individual. The plan was to act like tourists while they methodically researched the security systems and located the most likely way to break in. Peach had entered a few minutes earlier, his camera swinging from his neck. After a few more minutes of pacing, Tinman crossed the street and approached the museum.

On the front patio, he passed a series of two-foot-high cement blocks carved into letters that could only be read by being in front and over the sculpture. The inspirational message read, "Inhale Exhale." Tinman made a mental note to practice the preaching.

To the left of the entrance was a sculpture made out of bent metal rods, the cavity filled with fist-sized river rocks. The figure was of a man crouching on one knee, his head and back bent over the sidewalk, arms tucked inward. Tinman thought he looked like he'd had one too many and was about ready to hurl. He was fairly certain, however, the artist had something else in mind.

A gigantic, oblong, copper column stood to the right of the three entrance doors. Tinman pushed through and found himself at a long counter with a pleasant young lady demanding ten dollars. He sighed and shelled it out. She gave a brief rundown of what to expect and sent him on his merry way.

The first floor seemed to be mostly reserved for a gift shop to the left of the entrance, a book store to the right of the front counter, and a long section of dining tables stretching nearly to the aft of the ship, filling the vast majority of the ship's hold. A small café at the rear of this expanse served light lunches and snacks. Purportedly, all the tables were used for diners and patrons of the café, but it was well past lunch and they were empty. Just to the left of the café was an elevator. Next to it was a short hallway that ran to the back of the museum. At the end of the hallway was an emergency door opening out to the east side of the building.

In the center of the room was a broad staircase that doubled back on itself after reaching each floor's landing, zigzagging its way to the upper floor. To the right of the bottom stairs was a tall metal sculpture made to look like a totem pole, the top narrowing to the width of a spike.

Tinman's confidence was high as he marched to the stairs. As he started up to the second floor he noticed a woman staring at him from above. She was tall, only a couple of inches shorter than he, had painfully short hair, a ruddy complexion, and her clothes bulged from powerful muscles hidden underneath.

She had the air of a security guard but was not dressed like one. Instead, she was in casually formal attire with pants, a button-up shirt, and a jacket you might see on a theater usher. At first, Tinman thought she might be a patron. It came as quite a surprise to find he was aroused. He never thought he'd be turned on by a woman who looked like Jack Lalanne, but, hey, that's amore.

He pushed the feelings away. This was no time to hit on some chick. Maybe after he was a millionaire. He looked at his feet as he climbed and fully expected she would be gone when he looked back. When he reached the first landing, however, she was still there, staring at him. He now saw she was wearing an official name badge and had an earbud connected to a small two-way radio. Definitely security.

"Hello," she said, in a deep, husky voice.

Tinman nearly fell backward down the stairs. He grunted and sidled by. He scooted to his left and into the first gallery. All of the galleries on each floor were to the left of the stairs with nothing but air to the right and a view of the dining area below.

The first gallery held only a handful of visitors who were admiring what appeared to be brightly-colored abstract art. Upon further examination, Tinman discovered it was a display of Australian Aboriginal art from someplace called Tjuntjuntjara. All of the pictures were supposed to have originated from dreams and visions and represented some aspect of the culture. Tinman was thankful he didn't have such dreams. To him, they would be nightmares.

He was about to move to the next gallery when he spotted the security guard eyeballing him from the hall like she was waiting for his next move. Preparing to pounce. He leaned into the next picture in line and found it was made by a man from the Pitjantjatjara tribe. Being a wordsmith, he couldn't help but wonder why these people would work so hard at making words that were barely able to be pronounced, much less spelled.

When he looked up the security guard had vanished. He sighed. It was just a coincidence. There was no way she could know what he was up to. He stepped into the hall and headed for the prow. Along the way, he passed a display of art depicting the American work ethic. Now, this was something he could sink his teeth in. He had always been very disciplined and admired the pictures of early Americans toiling away with plows and axes.

The hallway opened into a small room with an exhibition of photographs exploring the altered landscape of the modern age. As he perused the photos it made him depressed. He hated it when good things changed. Just like his city, no one knew when to leave well enough alone.

He began to see elements of the security system. Everywhere he looked were small, black, half-domes concealing what must be video cameras. Now a seasoned pro he knew they weren't killer lasers.

Moving out of this room he reached the front of the ship which housed the largest room he'd been in. It held all the really big paintings and some murals. The room was only accessed from the second floor, but looking up he could see the third floor had a balcony overlooking this room.

As he studied this feature, the security guard appeared like the phantom of the opera in drag. Despite at least a dozen other visitors in the room, her gaze locked on him. He found it impossible to look away. What could she possibly know? She said something, presumably into her two-way radio. A little smirk spread across her face and she nodded at him. It was a look that said, "I know exactly what you're up to."

He shot out of the room and loped down the hall. Past the first gallery he'd been in, was a small nook dedicated to the Seven Magic Mountains, a public art display south of Las Vegas. It was comprised of seven thirty-foot high fluorescent totems made from limestone boulders. The panoramic photo showed the precariously stacked neon slabs forming psychedelic castles in the sand.

He acted like he was fascinated when actually he was peeking around the corner waiting to see if the guard would come in search of him. Sure enough, within a couple of minutes, he saw her clacking down the stairs. He ducked behind a corner and waited until she moved down the hall, heading for the prow.

When she was out of sight, he started for the stairs. His instincts told him to get out of there as quickly as possible. But when he reached the landing and looked down he decided he couldn't let paranoia drive him from his job. He wanted to see where the baskets were and determined he was not leaving until he found them.

Halfway up the first flight was a landing where the stairs doubled back and headed for the third floor. As he pivoted, a shiny object caught his eyes. He turned back and was amazed to see a massive Mylar balloon suspended by a thin cable attached to the ceiling high above. The top of the balloon was at eye-level with the remainder floating above the dining area. He was surprised he hadn't seen it when he first entered the museum.

He couldn't take his eyes off it. It was magnificent. Perfectly symmetrical. A giant silver pool ball. The shiny round surface reflected everything in its view. His distorted face stared back at him as if he was in a house of mirrors at the carnival. He had an overwhelming urge to reach out and touch it, but it was at least six feet away.

He shook his head to break the spell and took the last stairs to the third floor. Peach told him the baskets were up here but wasn't specific. He turned left and started down the hall, planning to search prow to aft.

He didn't bother to look at the displays on the walls of the hallway but instead moved right into the gallery at the end, currently dedicated to artists specializing in depicting UFO's and aliens. The pictures were freakish and disturbing. Life with humans was weird enough without mixing in visitors from other planets.

He stepped to the balcony perched over the large mural room. He was standing exactly where the guard was when she had looked down at him. And down below, there she was staring up at him. His eyes popped. She raised a hand and gave a little wave. He made a silent yelp and took off through the alien gallery and down the hall.

Across from the third-floor landing was an entrance to another gallery. He slipped in and found himself in a large maze-like space divided by white, L-shaped partitions. The outer walls were bright yellow and arced from corner to corner. The ceiling was formed with many angles like a piece of origami paper unfolded. The gallery displayed many artists' works, each getting a section of wall or partition.

Tinman moved swiftly, his eyes barely scanning the artwork. He was looking only for baskets and having little luck. As he twisted his way through the labyrinth he spotted another guard and held his breath. This one, however, had little interest in him, merely acknowledging his presence with a little nod and moving on.

Tinman breathed a little easier. If the female guard did know what he was up to surely she would have informed the rest of the team. He almost laughed at how silly he'd been.

Then he saw her out of the side of his eye, obviously looking for him, and moving in his general direction. He pulled back quickly and hid in the corner of a partition. As he waited for her to leave, he looked at the display. It was made up of pencil drawings of nude females. They were quite realistic and he felt like he was a kid again at the local drugstore, sneaking a peek at a Penthouse.

He risked a glance and the guard had disappeared. He dashed to the doorway leading to the hall. Before stepping out, he looked to see if it was clear. As he moved he caught a glimpse of the guard at the far end, her back to him. To his left was an entrance to a gallery dedicated to touring exhibits. He ducked inside and there were his baskets.

An elderly couple shared the room, but they were busy oohing and aahing. The display cases were slightly more impressive than the ones at the Historical Society but didn't seem to present any major problems. There was one small, half-dome in the corner of the ceiling, no doubt holding a video camera. As he studied the room he made a mental note of its relation to the stairs just down the hall a few paces.

Now that he saw the baskets again he was even more determined to return them to the rightful owners. Satisfied with his research he decided there was no point in going to the fourth floor where the Sky Plaza was located. During a heist, he and the Posse would have no reason to venture farther up.

He decided there was nothing more to do here, especially while being tailed. It was Peach's job to find out about the alarm systems and the locks and they would meet up later. Time to skedaddle. He bolted out the door and collided headlong into Peach.

"There you are," said Peach. "Nice museum, huh? Did you see the cool display on aliens?"

"I've seen all I need," said Tinman. "Time to go."

"What's the rush?"

"I'm being stalked."

Peach giggled. "Come on, who would want to stalk you?"

The female guard appeared at the end of the hall, spotted them, and moved quickly in their direction like she had a purpose in mind.

"Her," said Tinman.

He didn't wait for a response, scurrying to the stairs and heading down, two steps at a time. Glancing back he saw the guard talking to Peach. She must be onto both of them! It didn't matter. If he could figure out the perfect plan, there was nothing anyone could do to stop them.

TWENTY-TWO

PLAN F. OR WAS IT G? He'd lost track. The perfect plan was proving to be elusive.

Part of the problem was he didn't have all the necessary information. It was nearly two hours since he left the museum and no sign of Peach. He was, therefore, having to assume certain facts. He knew instinctively this was not the way to go about finding the perfect plan, but there was nothing else to do for the time being.

The process had taken his steel trap of a mind and turned it into mush. It was a case of paralysis through analysis. He was in the clubhouse, nervously pacing around his pool table where several balls were spread around. Each one represented a part of the puzzle.

The ten ball was the baskets. Other balls were placed where exit doors were located and so on. As he started working on a new plan he would move the balls around the table, which represented the museum as a whole.

His early plans started simply enough and were quickly ruled out. Now he was becoming more and more elaborate, making the plans more and more ludicrous. He knew the answer was there, he just had to figure out how the balls moved.

Plan F involved stealing a helicopter, landing it on the roof, injecting sleeping gas in the ventilators to knock out the guards . . . you get the point. He swept his arm across the table, scattering the balls.

Plan G. The door swung open and in strolled Amber carrying a wooden crate.

"Hey Tinman," she said, breezily, placing the crate on the counter.

"How did you get in here?" asked Tinman.

"Peach gave me a key this morning before you two went on your field trip."

Tinman marched over. "He told you about the field trip?! How much do you know?"

"That you were going on one. So how did it go?"

"Fine." He spun around and went back to the table

Amber started pulling various odds and ends from the crate. A cocktail shaker. A jar of olives. A bottle of Worcestershire sauce. Cherries. Stirrers. Different size glasses. "I think it's so special two brothers can spend quality time together."

"Umh."

"I used to love field trips when I was in school."

Tinman had no experience with schools or field trips so he couldn't relate and consequently had nothing further to add to this scintillating conversation. Amber continued, "I remember once in junior high we went to this museum in Carson City. The one with the big coin press from the old mint. I'll never forget it. It was the first time somebody got to first base with me. His name was Danny. Danny Southerland. He cornered me in the basement where they have the mine display. God his hands were cold."

"What are you doing here?"

"Hey, Peach said you said girl members were allowed in the clubhouse!"

"If that's what I said, fine, but what are you doing here now?"

"The place has to have a proper bar, right? Being the designated bartender, I need a properly equipped bar. So I picked up a few things from the hall. They were in the storeroom. The owner will never know."

"Umh."

Amber finished emptying the crate and walked to the table. "What are you doing?"

He looked at her with a look designed to silence but it didn't work. Amber said, "Is this some new kind of game where you don't use a cue?"

Tinman slumped to the table and laid his head down. Amber said, "Are you feeling alright? You look like you're constipated."

Tinman tried the look again, this time with a little more oomph and a trace of snarl. Amber said, "Definitely constipated. I can see it written all over you. What you need are some olive oil and lemon juice. Try a tablespoon of that first. If it doesn't work, try rocking back and forth when you're on the can. That always helps me. Well, gotta go. Cabbie's waiting. See you around!"

She waved and headed out the door. Tinman sighed. Now he'd lost his train of thought. Right. Plan G. Maybe a daytime heist.

Twenty minutes later he was tied up into knots. The idea was to hire some kids to create a diversion in the prow of the ship that would draw in all the security guards. Meanwhile, the Posse would grab the baskets, scatter, and leave through different emergency exits. In all the commotion, they might just be able to make it if they had getaway cars waiting. The problem was after the heist when the kids would surely be questioned. Even if they hadn't been told about the heist when they were hired, they'd put two and two together and rat them out for the reward.

Plan H. He hadn't a germ of an idea. The door opened and there was Peach. Tinman said, "About time."

"I got carried away by the culture. What's cooking?"

"I'm working on a plan."

"Pray tell."

"It's a work in progress."

"May I shed a little light?" Peach asked, leaning over the table. "I found out a few things that might help."

"I don't know. I've been over this and I'm wondering if you were right all along. We should just wait until the baskets go back to the Historical Society and hit it again."

"Well, you see—"

"I know, I know. We're both a little superstitious over that place but compared to this Museum of Art, it's a lead-pipe cinch."

"I know, but—"

"Okay, I understand you don't want to go back there. What if we wait until they're moving the baskets and hijack the truck. We switch places with the drivers, no rough stuff or anything, we use chloroform to knock them out, and once the baskets are loaded we roll on out of there. Huh. Come to think of it, it's the best idea I've had so far. What do you think?"

"The baskets aren't going back to the Historical Society," said Peach, hoping it wouldn't come as too much of a shock. It did. Tinman angrily swept the balls across the table and they ricocheted off each other and fled.

"See, they're going on tour. Kind of like a rock band. After this museum, they go straight to D.C., where they have a special display set up at one of the Smithsonian buildings. After that, they start crisscrossing the country. They'll be out of play for at least a year."

"How do you know all this?!"

"The Director of Special Projects told me. Helluva nice guy."

"You talked to someone in there! Are you crazy? It's so rookie."

"Not at all. He actually approached me. It's different. See?" Tinman shrugged, still privately trying to get his brain wrapped around the dos and don'ts of proper casing.

"After you left, I was admiring the baskets and this guy comes in with a clipboard, so I figure he's in the know. He happens to see I'm in love with these baskets and he tells me to enjoy it while I can. Like anybody would, I ask what he's talking about, and off he goes. Those types love to tell you how important their jobs are so I just let him keep talking."

As he listened, Tinman absentmindedly shoved the balls around the table. Peach continued. "Anyway, the baskets are there for another eight days. Then off they go. And though I like your idea about changing places with the drivers, the only way that's going to fly is if we come packing. Like with a bazooka. Apparently, the people in charge of security during the tour are a group of elite guards provided by some wing of the government. The baskets are considered cultural icons and they really get the white glove treatment."

Tinman paced around the table and eventually accepted the news. "Okay, back to the drawing board. We'll have to hit the museum. I'm using the balls to represent things. The ten ball is the baskets. The one, two, three, four, and five are all the exits, at least from what I saw. What did you find out about the locks and alarms?"

"Let's put it this way, now I know what it means to be the only accredited art museum in the state."

"What's that?"

"As much money as you want for security."

"Swell."

"Yeah. You saw all the video cameras. And these aren't just regular cameras, these are PTZ's, like they use in the casinos, capable of panning, tilting, and zooming, all controlled by a remote operator. One camera essentially scopes out an entire room or gallery and gets a full 360-degree view."

"We'll be in masks. Like you said, who cares what they see after the heist is done."

"I'm pretty certain these cameras are monitored twenty-four seven. I'm not sure, however, if it's done onsite or not. That's why I want to get to this other bit of news."

"Stay focused. What about the locks and alarms."

"Well, the bolts on the doors can be remotely opened by a controller somewhere else in the building. Like the ones in prison."

"Watch your language."

"Sorry. Anyway, I can get in one of those doors, but it'll take time. It's not like a normal lock. Besides picking it, I'll have to short circuit the electrics, and meanwhile, someone is probably watching me at work through the exterior cameras and will be there to greet us once I get it open. As far as alarms, no motion sensors which again leads me to believe the eye in the sky never sleeps. The windows are wired so a door is our best bet. You got the normal fire and smoke alarms and there's probably some kind of sensor alarm for vibrations and excessive sound but it's more for earthquakes, and we don't plan on making a ruckus, do we?"

"Anything else?"

"Well, the display cases are a little trickier than the ones at the Historical Society. But if we can get to them, I'd say a few minutes each."

Tinman stopped his pacing. Now that he had all the information he looked at the table in a new light. He slowly started shifting the balls around. "Let's say the fifteen ball is you and me. And the fourteen ball is Bones and Catfish. What's the best door to try?"

Peach pointed to the three ball on the west rear end of the building. Tinman nodded. "Okay, what if the fourteen ball creates a diversion over here in front of the building. This draws the attention of whoever is monitoring the cameras. Now, assuming they're not monitored in-house, but by some remote security company, it should give us a window of time to get inside, undetected."

"That's a big assumption. It's usually cheaper and more efficient to monitor in-house. Especially with such a big operation."

"Well, we don't know that's what they're doing, do we!"

"Exactly, like I've been trying to tell you, I have this other—"

"Will you wait a minute!" Tinman wandered around the table, looking at every angle, hoping an epiphany would come. It didn't.

"Mind if I add a new ball to the mix?" asked Peach in a very deferential manner. Tinman flung out his hands in exasperation, giving Peach the floor.

Peach grabbed the eight ball from a pocket. "The way I see it is we need an inside tipster to find out how those videos are monitored."

"I don't see that happening."

Peach grinned and plopped the eight ball in the center of the table. "The security guard you thought was stalking you. Turns out you were right."

"Aha! I knew it. Well, hell, that sinks it doesn't it? We're already dead in the water before we start."

"Not quite. She's got the major hots for you."

"Huh?"

"That's why she was hounding you. She was trying to make a hookup."

"Why would she be hot for me?"

"Funny you ask. I was so taken aback I asked the same thing. Turns out you have what you call, 'those arms.' "

"Those arms?"

"Sure. It's a primal thing. Going way back. Women are attracted to the guy with the kind of arms that can protect and support, see? They want a man who can slay the mastodon and triumphantly drag the beast back to the cave where she can make up a nice celebratory stew. Anyway, apparently, you got 'em. Lucky dog."

"She told you all that?"

"Nah, I just know stuff. Like you with words."

"Did she know we were together?" asked Tinman.

"Not exactly. After you crashed into me, I guess she saw us talking. When you took off, she came over and asked if we were friends. I told her no, but we share a love of culture and often run into each other at museums and the like."

Tinman shook his head. "And she bought that crock?"

Peach shrugged. "Anyway, she really wanted to talk to you but she said you were being standoffish."

"She was stalking me!"

"I told her you were just shy. I could tell she liked that. Maybe she's got the maternal instinct or something. Like she wants to be your mother. Either way, she'd definitely like to see you again. In my opinion, it's a no-brainer. She's just what we're looking for."

"What, I'm supposed to go back there? Start flirting with her in one of the galleries? Come on."

"It's better if you see her outside the museum. Here's her number. She asked me to pass it on." Peach pulled out a slip of paper and balanced it on top of the eight ball.

Tinman stared at it as if it might bite. "Kind of forward of her."

Peach shrugged. "You got those arms, big guy."

Tinman circled the table, eyeing the slip of paper like he was a prairie dog outmaneuvering a rattlesnake. "It just doesn't feel right. Like I'm behind the eight ball."

"Of fire."

"What?"

"Before and after."

"Knock it off."

"Sorry. Just habit."

Tinman sighed and continued his circling. "Anyway, if I milk her for information and this heist comes down, I'm going to be the first one she suspects."

"Maybe," said Peach. "But I don't think it's a problem. First of all, she's the initiator. Just like that guy was with me. There's no way she can think you planned it so she would make a pass. Second, I have a hunch she may not be too happy in her job. And a disgruntled employee is the best kind of tipster. They're always looking for ways to put one over on the man."

"What makes you think that?"

"Well, while we were talking, I heard her getting some grief over her radio, like someone yelling at her. She got real pissed and turned it off. A minute later, some guy I took to be her boss shows up and somewhat rudely broke up our little chat. She went off with him and boy she looked like she wanted to rip his larynx out."

Tinman knew he was running out of reasons he shouldn't do this, but he couldn't bring himself to give up. "What's she like?"

Peach let out a belly laugh. "Does it matter? Jeez Louise, brother, you want these baskets or not?"

"I just want to get your take on her! Is that too much?"

Peach scrunched his mouth, thinking how much of his take on the guard he should pass on. He had to be careful. His brother could sometimes be gun shy around women. "I'd say she is not the type to make passes on guys very often. So you must have impressed her. It's obvious, though, she's no shrinking violet. Given her looks and figure I would also guess she doesn't have a lot of beaus fighting over her."

Tinman frowned like he'd picked the runt of the litter and now had to defend his choice. "What's wrong with her looks and figure?"

Peach forced down a grin. "Nothing at all! I'm just saying some guys might be turned off by a girl who could probably knock 'em out with one blow."

Tinman waggled his head. "A firm body doesn't bother me. I think I can handle myself."

"That's the old moxie I know! Give her a call."

"Right now?" yelped Tinman, his bravado fading as fast as he could get the words out. "I have to think. I need some air."

Peach sighed heavily. Tinman ignored him as he walked to the door. He opened it, stepped out, shut the door, and two seconds later dashed back in.

"It's Dez!" he cried.

"What? You think I'm blind?" Dez yelled from outside as she pounded on the door. "What are you doing in there? Let me in!"

Tinman looked to Peach who shrugged and nodded. Tinman opened the door and Dez bustled in. She took one look at the pool table and twirled to Tinman.

"Look who's doing so well they can buy themselves a little toy! Must have cut into a fat mark, huh? About time." Dez barked. "Guess you forgot all about those taxes, though," Tinman was speechless so she continued her tirade. "Well the city hasn't forgotten and I'm sick of dealing with it. We're going to take care of this debt right now. Give me a buck."

She stuck her hand out and Tinman stared at it. She snapped her fingers to move him along. He fumbled in his pocket, pulled out a crumpled dollar, and dropped it in her hand. She opened her purse, stuffed it inside, and pulled out a folded sheet of paper and pen. She walked to the pool table and without unfolding the paper laid it down.

"Sign on the bottom," she demanded. Tinman was unsure what all this meant but he started to believe she might be letting him off the hook. After all, she did have a heart buried somewhere deep inside. He leaned down and without examining the paper, signed on the bottom line.

Dez snatched it up and fluttered it in front of his nose. "You are now officially free of any debt to me."

Tinman couldn't believe his luck. He felt like hugging her and may have if she hadn't continued talking.

"You are, however, now in major hock to the city."

"Huh?"

"This place is all yours, buster. Now the man can start harassing you. And if you don't pay up real soon, they're going to confiscate this dump and you'll be sleeping on the streets."

"Huh?"

Peach plucked the paper from her fingers. He examined it and leaned into Tinman. "It's the deed to this place. You're now the owner. Congratulations."

"You can't do this," said Tinman.

"I just did," said Dez. "Ever since my party I can't draw a good hand to save my soul. It's getting tight. Really tight. And the city is demanding their money. I'd float it for you if I had the scratch but I'm tapped out. Now it's your problem. Besides, with the Dynamic Duo back together again I figured you guys to skip town like before and leave me with the tab."

Tinman was desperate to change her mind. "Not like you to toss money away."

"This fleabag isn't worth squat or believe you me I'd sell it in a heartbeat. That is if I could even find some chump dumb enough to take it off my hands. This is the perfect solution. For me, anyway."

Tinman's desire to hug was replaced by the urge to throttle and bury the body by the railroad tracks. He felt Peach's arm around him. "Don't fret it, brother. Dez here is actually doing you a favor."

"I am?"

"Sure, Dez, sure," said Peach taking her by the shoulders and guiding her to the door.

"I wasn't trying to do him a favor," sputtered Dez, trying to catch up.

"Well, I've been reading about how the city is working to develop this whole area on East Fourth. Could be, someday soon, this land will be worth big bucks to a developer. Maybe a couple hundred thousand giving the way property values are going up."

"Where'd you read that? Are you serious?" asked Dez, quickly regretting her rashness.

"Have I ever been untruthful to you?" asked Peach with an angelic smile.

Dez narrowed her eyes. "You're so full of crap. Anyway, the deed is done. Hey, that's a play on words, isn't it?" She looked to Tinman who grudgingly nodded.

She said, "Well, I have to go, cab's waiting." Before she left she glanced again at the pool table. "You really need a better light for that. You're not getting any younger. You need to take care of the peepers." She gave Tinman a little peck on the cheek, Peach a rap on the head, and sashayed out.

Tinman stared at the door until gravity took over and he sagged into a chair. "Did you really read that stuff?"

"Nah," said Peach. "I just couldn't stand watching her getting the best of you."

"Thanks."

"Don't mention it."

"I need money."

"What are you going to do about it?" asked Peach.

Tinman looked at him, his face hardening like cooling steel. "Give me the phone number."

Peach moved quickly to the table, not wanting Tinman to have an extra second to change his mind. He grabbed the slip of paper and slapped it into Tinman's waiting hand.

Tinman looked at it. "Cassandra?"

Peach thought for a moment. "Mama Cass?"

Tinman nodded. "Works for me." He pulled out his phone and dialed.

TWENTY-THREE

REASONABLY SATED, SHE TURNED OFF HER ASSISTANT and placed it in the bedside table. She made a mental note to get new batteries. She sniffed the air. Mmm. Musky. The lingering scent on her body was exactly what she needed to lure in her prey. She giggled at herself. It had been a while since she'd been on the hunt and she was really looking forward to it.

She went to her closet and pulled out the hanger holding the outfit she'd chosen for her lunch date. The closet did not possess one dress because she loathed them. They never showed off her muscles in the right way. Her body was a finely tuned instrument of destruction and she wanted everyone to know it.

Usually. Today, however, she knew she had to be careful or she would flush the quail before it was time to fire. As she thought about this, she slipped on her burgundy pair of vintage high waist buckle palazzo pants which made her look even taller and more imposing than usual. Her retro top was a white Lolita blouse in chiffon with long sleeves, stand collar, fancy ruffles on the cuffs, shoulders, and chest area, and a large, flat bow around the neck.

She drifted into the bathroom and stared at her face. She rarely if ever used any makeup, but she was shooting for the feminine look so she'd picked up some glitter cream which she unartfully smeared on her eyelids and upper cheeks. To complete the presentation she managed to tie a little silver ribbon in her short-cropped hair. The result was a cross between Minnie Mouse and Jimi Hendrix. She was pleased.

It was important she hook this man. What was his name? It didn't matter. All that mattered was she needed him if The Plan was to succeed. She knew she was not long for the Museum of Art and she wanted to go out with a bang. She laughed at the choice of words. How fitting.

She'd become a security guard because there were few other jobs you could beat the crap out of someone and not get in trouble. All you had to do was catch someone doing something bad and indeed it became your job to beat the crap out of them. She didn't care about what bad guys did, that was their business. She was in this for herself. She lived to beat people up.

The problem was, she had yet had the chance, at least at her regular job. Her first position was at a bank. She started there right after high school and in six years not once did someone try to rob it. It was a huge disappointment. She left for a job guarding a factory that produced dental supplies. It proved to be a lapse in judgment. Who's going to steal dental supplies?

When she was thirty, she tried a job at a casino but there was an unfortunate situation where she got to beat the crap out of someone who was manhandling a gambler. It turned out to be a pit boss who had caught a cheat and was escorting them out. The pit boss didn't press charges, but she was let go on the spot.

On a whim, she applied and got the job at the Museum of Art. She figured they must have a lot of valuable items that would attract bad guys. In the two years working there, it had not been the case. Not only that but when she accepted the job she had no idea they were trying to pervert the very essence of what it meant to be a security guard.

In her opinion, a security guard should appear threatening, someone you don't want to mess with. When she first started, she spent hours in front of a mirror perfecting her snarl, sneer, and icy stare. In the opinion of the Captain of Security at the museum, however, her definition was outdated and needed to be brought into the modern, more enlightened age.

This belief led to the development of the VSO, short for Visitor's Service Officer. What did that mean? It was all so weird. The idea was to have the guards interact with the visitors. Ridiculous! To excel in this position she must strive to be approachable. Inconceivable! The main directive was toward friendliness and customer service. Outrageous! She'd been forced to learn all about the museum building and its collections so she could—wait for it—answer questions! On top of it, there was mandatory training in how to smile, say hello, and make eye-contact. Pshaw! The final insult: they were no longer able to wear traditional, badass uniforms. What's up with that?!

Needless to say, she sucked at it. So much, that for two years she'd been in constant jeopardy of losing her job. Tough. They could have it. And soon they would. The other day, when she saw this man come into the museum, she knew she had to have him. He was perfect. He had those arms, abnormally long and powerful. Her gift of prophecy assured her if there was any man alive who could match up to her, it was him.

At first, it was pure lust, The Plan had only come later after she was switched to graveyard for apparently harassing him. What did they want? She made eye contact, she said hello, she even managed a smile. But the Captain thought she was overbearing. He was monitoring the cameras throughout and saw the man leave the museum prematurely. He blamed it on her. He lectured her about how it takes four times the amount of money to get a new customer than to keep a regular one. She snorted at him and he stuck her on graveyard.

And this was unacceptable. She simply could not give up her nighttime hours to stare at a bunch of video monitors. This was when her real life happened. This was when she indulged in her passion, the very meaning of her existence. For two days she had endured the night shift, and decided, if all went well with this man, she would make Friday her last day at the museum.

She checked the clock and it was soon time to go. She stared at the vivid illustration of her namesake hanging above her bed. Cassandra, daughter of King Priam and Queen Hecuba of Troy.

According to legend, she gained her gift of prophecy when she fell asleep in a temple and snakes whispered in her ears allowing her to hear the future. Most contemporaries thought she was insane and failed to believe her prophecies. Fools. Might have wanted to listen when she told you about that Trojan Horse. Don't you think?

Cassandra worshipped her namesake like the most ardent religious believer. Her ring name, The Snake, was even chosen in her honor. Her dream was to become the top-rated MMA woman fighter in the world. For now, however, she was honing her skills in the underground, illegal world of cage fighting.

It was an age-old sport, originating in ancient Greece and called pankration. The only real difference in today's sanctioned sport of mixed martial arts is now they have a few rules. It's why she gravitated to the illegal version held in abandoned warehouses and other secret locations. No rules. No doctors. No safety net.

She figured if she could succeed in the no holds barred environment, she could make it in the legitimate scene. And she was not going to let some dumb job get in the way. Underground cage fighting happened at night, late at night, so it was simply not possible for her to stay on the graveyard shift. Her destiny lay in the ring, or cage, if you prefer.

She already missed two bouts because of her late shift and had gotten wind her opponents thought she was losing her nerve. She gritted her teeth. Nothing was further from the truth. The thought made her angry. And when she got angry it made her want to fight. And when she wanted to fight she usually got a little assistance from a well-placed shot in a muscle or two.

Juice, arnolds, gym candy, pumpers, stackers, roids. Call it what you will, anabolic steroids was the nectar of the fighting gods. She resisted the urge to have a little taste. That could wait until later. She didn't want to have one of her little episodes at lunch, now did she. It was important she be on her best behavior. After all, she needed this man to like her.

* * *

There was absolutely nothing to worry about. He kept telling himself this so it would sink in. It was essential for the task at hand. A bit of "heavy lifting" as they call it in the trade. Locate a tipster and milk them for information without them knowing. He and Peach had utilized this process when they were younger. They had once robbed a business lady of a bank deposit and the idea came from a disgruntled employee.

Tinman used to play pool with the guy and he was always complaining about his boss. One night he laid out the perfect plan to rob her, but he was all talk. Peach and Tinman adopted the plan exactly as it was laid out and successfully pulled off the heist.

So why was he so nervous? Because that was then and this was now. Back then he was Mr. Cool. Smooth. Cutthroat. The consummate pool hustler. Always one step ahead of everyone else. He lived by his personal motto that everyone is born naked; no one has an edge unless they convince the other guy they do. All you had to do was be the guy who convinces the other guy, and you win.

Ever since his action fizzled, he felt he'd lost the killer instinct. He was uncomfortable in his body. Since Peach had returned, the feeling was more pronounced.

His brother now had bona fide skills. He could call his own shots. He didn't need him anymore. The fact he was hanging around trying to help him out made Tinman feel like he was accepting charity. Peach would be horrified to know he felt that way, but it's the way it was.

Just like the original metal man came to a crossroads with Dorothy, Toto, and the others, Tinman was at a juncture. In the movie, they took the wrong way, got stoned in a poppy field, and ultimately fell into the clutches of the Wicked Witch of the West. Tinman knew he couldn't afford to make the same error in judgment. He had to accept his present situation and discover a new way to thrive.

It was beginning to look like the most likely path to follow was the one his brother took. He knew he had the nerves to pull off a major heist, he just wondered if he had the skill set to be successful. Peach was convinced his talent was in planning. If true, the Art Museum would be his first big test. Now he just needed the right information to come up with the perfect plan. He swallowed hard and looked out the window of Garshasp's cab.

There was absolutely nothing to worry about. Mama Cass seemed very nice over the phone. Hungry was perhaps more apt. She had been so excited he called, and had readily agreed to meet for lunch. He offered to let her pick the spot and she immediately chose a little Greek joint on West Fifth Street. She claimed she had some connection to the Greeks. It made little difference to him. He disliked restaurants and seldom ate out. One was as bad as the other.

Peach offered to give him fifty bucks to cover the tab and it irked him he had to accept. Catfish loaned him a nice shirt and some pants, and he certainly looked the part. So why was he feeling like he was on the way to the prom with a face full of acne?

Perhaps it was his long hiatus from mingling with the opposite sex. His desire for such activity had waned along with his swagger. Also, this girl seemed so eager. It bothered him. He was afraid she would want to turn this little tryst into something more serious. What with her infatuation with those damn arms of his. He wasn't sure what to do if she went in that direction.

With one notable exception in his past—where to his knowledge he had dodged a bullet—he only went to women who were absolutely proven to be infertile or past child-bearing age. This made the inevitable parting of ways free of the risk of having a little walking, talking reminder of his indiscretions.

There was absolutely nothing to worry about! This was merely a fact-finding expedition. No more, no less. He forced himself from his fretting and concentrated on the rules for the task at hand.

Let the mark do the talking. This was easier since it was a woman. Only if necessary should he subtly maneuver the conversation where he wanted it to go. Once the information is obtained, don't end the talk too abruptly. To avert any suspicion, when parting, make it clear you would be more than happy to meet again. If you don't get the information, make sure you do a clean job of killing yourself.

They were only two blocks away. Even though it was a crisp autumn day, he wiped the thick sweat from his brow. Garshasp eyed him through the rearview mirror.

"Hot date, eh?" he asked with a wide grin.

"Umh."

"No be worry, Tinman. You gots what it takes baby."

"Let's hope."

For some reason, Garshasp thought this was the funniest thing since the Iran-Contra Affair. He was so engulfed in laughter he almost missed the restaurant and was still gulping for breath when he dropped Tinman off.

Tinman looked across the block at the white, clapboard, two-story house, converted into a café. On the wraparound porch, a few small tables were set up for dining. Despite the nip in the air, there she was at a table at the corner of the porch.

She rose and beckoned him. As he crossed the street, she came into better view. At first blush, she was a mythological goddess sprung from Mt. Olympus: statuesque, ethereal, eminently powerful. On closer inspection, she morphed into David Bowie doing a Prince impersonation, or maybe it was the other way around. Against all reason, he was smitten.

It wasn't as if she was his type. In fact, he couldn't remember ever being with, or interested in, a woman who fit her description. But there it was. He felt the same stirrings as before. This immediately complicated the situation.

She sprung from the porch, grabbed his arm, and thrust herself into him. The ensuing hug produced several snaps, crackles, and pops. Despite his concerns over permanent damage, he was pleased to find a pesky kink in his back had been obliterated in the onslaught.

She pulled away and studied his eyes which really freaked him out. She smiled and leaned into his ear. In that tantalizing, husky voice she said, "I can hear the future. And it tells me you and I are going to make magic. Do you believe my prophecy?"

She pulled back and appraised him with a sly, seductive smirk. He stumbled. He remembered the task. He regained his footing. "Who am I to doubt such a beautiful woman."

Hey. What else was he going to say? After all, he needed this woman to like him.

* * *

Two hours later, Tinman reeled into the clubhouse. Bones and Catfish were playing gin and Peach was pouring himself one. They watched as he plopped into a chair like he'd just finished his first half-marathon and hadn't realized he was supposed to train beforehand.

Nobody spoke for what seemed like a very long time. Peach shot some office at Catfish and he nodded.

"How was the food?" asked Catfish.

"Huh?" asked Tinman like a D student in an ESL class.

"What did you eat?" asked Bones, drawing out his words.

"Some things that start with an S," answered Tinman.

"Could be spanakopita," said Catfish.

"Or possibly souvlaki," added Bones.

Peach piped in, "Don't forget saganaki."

"True," said Catfish. "Was it chunks of meat on a skewer, or a square slab of fried cheese, or little turnover pastry things stuffed with spinach and feta?"

Tinman nodded and pointed a finger at him.

"Hah! Score," crowed Catfish. "I love those things. Especially when the filo is cooked just right and it's nice and flaky."

"No. All of the above," said Tinman.

"Yikes. You had every one of those things that start with an S?" asked Peach.

Tinman nodded and closed his eyes. They figured he was taking a well-deserved post-lunch siesta when he lifted a hand and pointed in Peach's direction.

"Pour me one of those."

Peach looked to Bones and Catfish in surprise. Tinman did not usually drink, and none of them had ever seen him drink gin. Nevertheless, Peach sloshed some of the clear liquid in a small glass and placed it in his waiting hand. He downed it in one gulp.

His eyes shot open. Now he realized why he never drank gin. He shook his head, rose to his feet, and wandered around the room.

"Um, when you come to, suppose you could tell us what you found out?" asked Peach.

Tinman, still pacing, said, "The videos are monitored in-house."

Everyone sighed. "Damn," said Peach. "How many guards involved?"

"Just one. Person on graveyard. They have a room on the third floor with all the monitors. The guard locks themselves in until the morning shift."

"We got troubles," said Peach.

Tinman spontaneously broke into hysterical giggles. This was also so out of character, the guys involuntarily rose out of their seats. Tinman was so consumed he bent over and clutched his gut.

Peach placed a hand on his back. Tinman peeked up. "She's the one working graveyard."

"Mama Cass?!"

Tinman brought himself under control and eased into a chair. "Her boss stuck her there after he thought she was harassing me. She says it was the last straw. She's quitting on Friday."

"I figured her for an unhappy camper," said Peach. "Friday, huh? Four days away. Maybe there's some way we can use this. So you guys really hit it off huh?"

Tinman looked at him with a silly look and broke up again. The guys had to wait a few minutes before he could talk without spitting all over them. Finally, he blurted, "You might say that! Yeah! That's one way to put it!"

Peach grabbed him and shook hard. "Get ahold of yourself, brother."

Tinman grabbed him back, still giggling insanely. "She has it in her brain to get one over on the museum before she leaves."

"Oh yeah?"

"Yeah. You know how? She wants to go out with a bang!" Tinman squealed. "Get it? I mean literally! She asked me to go in there Friday night and have sex with her in the museum! It's payback time. They've been shitting all over her so she wants to fornicate all over their precious museum!"

Tinman abruptly stopped his laughing. He looked Peach deep in the eyes. "I'm screwed."

Peach's face was glowing. "Screwed? Are you crazy? This is the gift we've been looking for! It couldn't get any better!"

Tinman walked toward his pool table. Peach, his eyes narrowing, followed. "You did say yes, didn't you? Please tell me you accepted the lady's generous offer. Hey!"

"I told her I had to think about it."

"What's there to think about? She's our ticket inside that place!"

Tinman couldn't meet his eyes. "I think she's into the kinky stuff. She didn't actually say so, but she was hinting all around. Feeling me out, seeing what I was game for. I don't know what she's got in mind."

Peach guffawed. "I'm sure you can handle whatever curveball she throws. Now, please, just get on the phone and tell her you'd be honored to help her go out with a bang."

"No," said Tinman retreating to the far side of the table.

"For the love of Pete! How kinky could it be?" demanded Peach.

Tinman mumbled something under his breath. Peach scooted closer. "What was that?"

"What if she has a foot fetish?"

Peach froze. He looked to Bones and Catfish for help but they were in the same fog. "So she sucks on your toes? No big deal."

"Oh yeah! Well, I'll show you, Mr. No Big Deal," said Tinman, marching back to the lounge. He sat down and ripped off his left shoe and sock. Peach sat next to him and raised his eyes in question. Tinman stuck his foot in his face. "Bet that'll really turn her on!"

"What?"

"That, that thing!" screeched Tinman.

"Wart?"

"What?"

"The planter's wart you got," said Peach. "Say, we really are twins. I've had a couple of them over the years but mine are always on the right foot. We'll just pick up some quick-freeze stuff. Be gone by Friday, no sweat."

He looked at Tinman's quickly reddening face and said, "Don't tell me that's what you been worrying about."

Bones and Catfish started tittering but with a wave behind Tinman's back Peach silenced them. Tinman's foot lowered in sync with his eyes.

"It's been a long time," he said. "I'm worried I may not be able to, um, entertain her long enough to do the job."

Peach massaged his shoulders like a trainer egging on his boxer. "You'll knock her socks off. Hell, you're a lady killer. She'll be begging you to quit. But don't keep her waiting too long on this. She may find some other guy with those arms of yours, and we'll be left flapping in the wind."

Tinman nodded and pulled out his phone. Peach started giggling.

"Are you laughing at me?!"

"Perish the thought! But you gotta admit, it's funny. At the first museum, Peppermint has the hotties for me, and I get lucky. Now at this museum, Kinky Cassie's craving you. So you're gonna get lucky. Who woulda thought museums would be so lucky for us?"

Tinman exhaled deeply and looked up from his phone. "You never quit, do you?"

"What? What did I say?"

"And what's with Kinkie Cassie?"

"Well, she sure as hell doesn't want to be your mother."

TWENTY-FOUR

"I'M NOT GOING THROUGH WITH THIS!" cried Tinman.

"Sure you are," said Peach. "Don't be such a baby. What's the worst could happen?"

Tinman thought about this and decided there was nothing worse than having to live with himself if he didn't go through with it. He gritted his teeth and plopped his foot into Peach's waiting hands.

Peach cradled it on his knees and grabbed the little foam applicator holder. He inserted it into the opening of the small aerosol can and pressed down. There was a hissing sound. Tinman's eyes widened.

"Close your eyes," said Peach.

"Why?"

"You're freaking me out."

Tinman obeyed the order and Peach removed the foam applicator which was now saturated in an icy cold liquid. "Here goes nothing." He held the foam on the wart for several seconds.

"It aches!" said Tinman.

"That's normal," said Peach.

"You didn't tell me that! Now it stings!"

Peach said, "Still normal," as he read the rest of the instructions. "Any second now, it'll probably start itching."

"You're right, it does itch."

He went to scratch his foot and Peach swatted his hand away. "The itch means this stuff is working. You want that thing to spread?"

Tinman wrapped his arms around his chest and tucked his hands in his armpits. He stared at his brother as he disposed of the applicator and placed everything else back in its box.

"Thanks," said Tinman.

"My pleasure. Well, so to speak."

"When we get these baskets, where do we have to go to fence them?"

"Nowhere. This fence I use is mobile. He drives around the country in an RV. Hardly ever leaves it. He has a driver who really looks the part. They move from one RV park to the other. Wherever the action is. Pretty clever. Tough for the law to get a handle on him since he's always on the move. Claims he's the only mobile fence in the country. He told me one time he's thinking of franchising the idea."

"And he can handle this sort of thing?" asked Tinman.

"Oh yeah. He's an Arab. Here illegally. From Saudi Arabia or some such. A real horse trader. Claims he's from a royal family and has all these connections with people who are too rich for their own good. They just love snatching up stuff from this country. Particularly if it has any historical significance. I've done quite a bit of business with him over the years. He drives a hard bargain, but he's the best there is for this kind of thing. All I gotta do is give him a buzz and he'll blow on into town. Might take him a few days depending on where he is."

Peach grabbed two beers from the refrigerator and handed one to Tinman. They clinked their bottles and drank deeply. Peach flopped onto the easy chair, a relaxed grin plastered on his face.

Tinman studied him. "There's something different about you. I can't put my finger on it. You always were pretty cocky, even when you were screwing up. But this is something else. Like you have a secret."

Peach met him eye to eye and waited. Tinman said, "At first I thought it was because you learned a trade. But there's something else going on."

"I never could hide anything from you," said Peach, leaning back with his hands cupping his head. "Okay, you're right. I do have a secret. I've got someone watching my back. Keeping me safe."

"They must keep a low profile."

"Well, you can't really see him."

"Uh, huh. You're saying you have an invisible guardian angel."

"Exactly. But this is the fallen one," said Peach. "You know, Old Nick, Beelzebub, Lucifer."

"The devil is your guardian angel," said Tinman. "And may I ask how you arranged this."

"I sold him my soul," said Peach. "Helluva good deal. Best decision I ever made."

For some time, Tinman was too stunned to speak. He kept waiting for Peach to laugh and say it was all a joke. The longer he studied him, however, the more he became convinced he was telling the truth.

He leaned in. "Are you insane?"

"It was put to me by my cellmate in stir. One day we're talking about the oddities of life and he says when we were kids everyone was telling us about heaven and hell. Both unknowns, right? But, as the story goes, if you believe in heaven the only way to get there is to be really good. Now, hell, you go there if you're really bad and spend your whole life having fun. You with me so far? Okay. Now, I don't believe in either of them. But what if I'm wrong? So, I figure if I sell my soul to the devil, I'm hedging my bet. Right? Because whether or not either of these places is real, I still get to have fun while I'm living, see?"

"No."

"Okay, let me try again. As far as I can tell, life is all about keeping your shit together until you die. Can't argue with that. And when you die, you don't know what's going to happen, right? Maybe we all go to heaven no matter what you do in life. So I go and sell my soul to the devil not knowing this and in the end, it turns out to be a crock. There is no devil and no hell. We all get to go to heaven. So all along, I got to have a good time and still get to the pearly gates. Point in case, hedging my bet."

"You are insane."

"Hear me out. So now you have another popular option. Nothing happens when you die. We don't go anywhere except into the ground—unless you prefer cremation. No heaven, no hell. Then my deal with the devil works as well. I get to have a lot of fun and convince myself I'm invincible. Law can't catch me because the devil's got my back. I win either way, right?"

"And what if there is a hell?"

"All the better. I'm already tight with the man."

"Friend of the devil, huh?"

"The Grateful Dead! That's my theme song!"

"Naturally."

"Stick with me, brother. As far as I make it, my deal covers you as long as we're together. Sweet, huh? Two for one."

Tinman couldn't take his eyes off him. Now he clearly saw what he'd been missing. There was an aura, no, a force field around Peach. It was odd. Instead of being frightened for him, he was envious.

"You figure out the plan yet?" asked Peach.

Tinman smiled. "I'm working on it. The devil's in the details."

TWENTY-FIVE

IT WAS EXACTLY 1:00 A.M. and they'd all fallen asleep in their chairs—the plan still unfinished. Twenty-four hours from now, Cassie would be letting Tinman into the museum. The thought stirred him awake. His brain was churning away like it refused to join his body in sleep.

For the last few days, he and the Posse furthered their research. Bones and Catfish monitored the police and found they should not be any problem. They rarely passed the museum on their nighttime rounds and when they did, they barely gave it any notice.

Peach broke into a store two blocks from the museum, stealing nothing, but purposely setting off the alarm. The response time was nearly six minutes. Enough to get away if Cassandra caught onto what they were doing and threw an alarm.

They found that, despite the windows surrounding the lower floor of the museum, there was little chance of being seen outside, as they were heavily tinted and only a few cursory lights left on at night.

The problem was Tinman had two criminal enterprises which he had to overlap. Cassandra's plan was certainly key to their success but it didn't provide all the solutions to their particular plan. She told Tinman that on the night of their rendezvous she would be located on the third floor in the security command room. They agreed he would be at the chosen door at the side of the building at the designated time. When she saw him on the exterior camera, she would stop all video recording and buzz him in remotely.

But she would still be able to see what the cameras saw, so it wasn't as easy as just having the rest of the Posse scoot in along with Tinman. It meant Peach and the others would have to come in another way. They settled on the rearmost door, near the loading dock. This door had a keypad and Peach said he could figure out the code using some contraption that ran through all the possible number combinations until it found the right one. It could take up to thirty minutes, which was twenty-seven minutes too long.

There was another way to open it without the right passcode, but he said it would most likely trigger an alarm. Trigger an alarm. Alarm. He was missing something.

Then it hit him. He knew immediately he had figured out the run.

He jumped from his chair and went to the pool table. He placed the balls in various positions and grabbed his cue. As he shot, he quietly talked to himself.

"Ten minutes to one, Bones and Catfish come into camera view, here." He hit the cue ball and it shoved the one and the two ball to the far end of the table, the prow of the ship.

"They play drunk. Get into a little shouting match. This draws Cassie's attention from other exterior cameras. She'll also be looking for me to come in that direction. She'll be frustrated at these two guys. She knows she can't buzz me in with them there. She'll be watching to see what happens. A few minutes into their play, I enter here." He hit the cue ball into the three ball which joined the one and two ball cluster.

"Now, she's definitely watching. I send a page to Peach. He gets into position at the aft-most door. He'll only be in view of the rear camera for say four seconds if he crosses from the cluster of trees here to the door here." He sailed the cue ball to the other side of the table and it ricocheted off a rail, hit the four ball, and sent it rolling near the left corner pocket, the rear door.

"From what he says, once he crosses that field of vision he can't be seen right up against the door. Bad camera placement on the wall. Camera can't tilt down far enough. There's a slim chance she'll see him make the cross, but if she does we'll know it soon enough and nix the job."

"I could also go down there tomorrow after closing hour and pop out the pesky street lamp that sits back there," said Peach, standing next to the curtain separating the two rooms. Bones and Catfish peaked over his shoulders. "If she happens to be looking, it'll make it a lot harder for her to see anything, and I get to use my slingshot to boot."

"Good idea," said Tinman.

"All this sounds good, so far. Keep going. I don't want to break your roll."

"Okay. How long do you think it will take once you're in position to get the front plate off the keypad and make your splices—without throwing the bolt yet."

Peach didn't hesitate. "Four minutes, give or take a few seconds."

"Good enough. It means we three are going to have to keep up our play for that long."

"Cake," said Catfish.

"When you're ready, Peach, you send me a page. Those things vibrate don't they? I mean they're not only text messages."

"I can set them to do that."

"Okay, once I get your signal, I shoo away Bones and Catfish. You two hightail it to here."

He hit the cue ball and it knocked both the one and two ball around the table landing just shy of the left corner pocket. "Your job, for the time being, will be to keep a lookout on that side street. Make sure nobody sees Peach by the door."

Bones and Catfish nodded. Tinman continued. "After I'm sure you two are at least partway around, I move into position here. About midship."

His cue ball knocked the three ball and it sailed near a side pocket, the door Cassie would buzz him in.

"Now here's the linchpin. What I couldn't figure out until I remembered something you said yesterday, Peach. When she buzzes my door open, you told me the alarm system for all the exterior doors is temporarily disabled until that door shuts again."

"I see where you're going," said Peach, with a grin.

"When I hear the buzz and the bolt go on my door, I send you a page. We open our doors at exactly the same time." He hit the cue ball and it slammed into the seven and eight balls sandwiched together, they split and simultaneously pocketed in the left side and corner pockets.

"No alarm. Don't open the door yet. There's sure to be an interior camera, and there's still a chance Cassie might see. Wait until I'm inside and get her into view. She said that once I'm in she'll come out of the control room and lead me up. I'll be here on the first floor at the base of the staircase."

He sent the three ball to the center of the table. "I imagine she'll be here on the third-floor landing." He rolled the five ball into position.

"Now we're sure she can't be watching the monitors because I'll be with her. I send you a page, you signal Bones and Catfish and the three of you go in through the rear door and down through the stern."

He rolled the one, two, and four balls and they landed several inches off the bottom rail toward the center of the table. "It'll put you at the elevator with the stairs in front. I'll be able to see you, but you won't be able to be seen from above and that's where she'll be. Waiting for me.

"After that, it's pretty straightforward. We shouldn't need to have any more communication. You see me go upstairs, wait five minutes for us to get to whatever room she's chosen for the soiree. Then you go up the stairs to the third floor and start working on the display cases."

Peach, Bones, and Catfish studied the table and let the plan sink in. They all nodded.

Tinman went on. "Since we don't have a designated wheelman, we're going to need Catfish to leave early. Peach, when you first go in, can you rig the back door to stay unlocked and not set off any alarm if it's used again?"

"Done. Take an extra two minutes once I'm in."

"Nice. So when you have, say, two or three baskets out of the cases, get them in a garbage bag and Catfish splits, down the stairs and out the same door you came in." He sank the two ball in the left corner pocket. "Just like taking the trash out, you stroll over to where the car's parked. This way, if the rest of us get caught, we still have a few baskets. If we have to, you turn them into fall dough and get us a damn good lawyer."

There was a heavy silence. All of them knew this possibility existed and Tinman was right to plan for it, they just didn't like talking about it. Catfish gravely nodded. He would have a serious responsibility if the thing turned sour.

"Now you wait until you get a signal from Peach saying he's ready with the rest of the baskets. Move the car here, just off the loading dock. Peach and Bones come out the way they came in and away you go." Rapid-fire, he sank the one and four balls in the corner pocket.

"After my little romp with Cassie, I'll make my own way home." He fired at the three ball and it zoomed around the table, caroming off three rails and dropping into a pocket.

"I think that covers it. If Cassie somehow gets wind of what's going down, I'll take care of her before she can trigger any alarms."

Catfish grinned. "What if she puts up a tussle? I wouldn't want you to get hurt."

"Thanks for your heartfelt concern. I'm sure I can handle one woman on my own. Just nobody panic and go out any of these other doors. They're all alarmed and we'll have the fire department and police screaming down at us, instead of just a pissed off chick. And if we have to make a run for it, whatever you do, no one head into the prow. It's a dead end. No way out but back the way you came."

He studied the table, retracing his steps. Satisfied he'd covered everything, he looked to the others. "What do you think?"

"Well, damn, Tinman, that's as beautiful as a summer Alabama sunset," drawled Bones.

Tinman looked hopefully to his brother, the opinion that really mattered. Peach smiled. "It'll work. Nice job."

"Aren't you forgetting one thing?" asked Catfish. "What if this moll is a prankster and leaves those cameras running."

"No way," said Tinman. "I told her if she wanted me in on this I was not going to have my face showing up on some video. Hell, she couldn't have agreed more. Even though she's quitting this job, she knows if there's any proof of what she's doing she could get into serious trouble with the law. Her goal is strictly to get her private kicks by getting one over on the museum."

"I think Tinman's reading her right. It wouldn't make sense otherwise," said Peach.

"Well, if we pull this off, she's going to have a lot of explaining to do, proof or no proof," said Catfish. "Where does that leave you, Tinman?"

He'd been thinking the same thought since he started planning the heist. His skill was in reading people and their weaknesses. He felt confident he'd worked it out.

"Since I'll be with her the whole time, she'll know it wasn't me," he said. "She can think I was in on it all she wants. She won't even be able to prove I was there. No video recordings. She doesn't even know my real name. And in her position after a heist would you even want the law to know you let some stranger into the museum?"

The others quickly agreed with the logic. Peach wandered around the table and ended up shoulder to shoulder with Tinman and said, "I hate to bring it up, but this whole thing is riding on one little detail."

"Opening the doors at the same time?" asked Tinman, wondering what he'd missed.

"No. That'll work fine. It involves you."

"Me?"

"Well, you're the one who first brought up your, uh, staying power. I mean, it's going to take me at least three minutes for each of those display cases. That's thirty minutes if we want all ten. So don't jump her right away. Give us five minutes to get to the basket gallery and get started before you make your move."

"Hell, that's no problem. It'll take me that long to get my clothes off," said Tinman.

"Well then don't pop your cookies too soon. Every three minutes you hold out is another million bucks."

All the guys appraised him. Up till now, he'd been feeling pretty good about himself. It had been a while though. For each of them to get a million bucks he would have to last at least twelve minutes. It seemed like a stretch. Especially given he was going to be doing it with the female version of Adonis.

Maybe during the act, he could imagine she was Mother Teresa, or Eleanor Roosevelt, or maybe an ostrich. Yes! That would do it. He grinned, feeling the old confidence flooding back. The plan was complete.

"Just worry about your job. I'll keep my end up."

The choice of words sent the other three into hysterics. "You do that, Tinman! Keep it way, way up there!" Bones shrieked.

"Yeah! No slacking!" cried Catfish. "You wouldn't want to go soft on us!"

Tinman looked to Peach who shrugged. "Come on, fellas, I think you're being premature."

TWENTY-SIX

THE ONLY THING SHE WAS WORRIED ABOUT was whether or not this man could go the distance. She hoped so. She was so amped up! Of course, the 600 mg. of steroids she injected earlier had a little bit to do with it. Still, she predicted this would be a night neither of them would ever forget.

The clock read twenty minutes before midnight. Time to go. Her final shift at the museum went from midnight to eight. She checked her outfit and smiled. It didn't really matter what she was wearing. She wouldn't have it on for very long.

* * *

Peach borrowed a beige sedan from a different retirement community from where he got the car used at the first heist. He assured Tinman it had quite enough muscle under the hood, should it be needed. He also gave everyone tactical flashlights for protection and pagers for communication. Earlier in the evening, he shot out the street light next to the loading dock of the museum. He insisted on bragging about the fact it took only two shots from his slingshot to do the job.

An hour before they were to leave, Tinman did his best impression of Lee Marvin in the Dirty Dozen reviewing the plan. Everyone was definitely on the same page and eager to get at it.

Just before they left, Bones sidled up to Tinman and, with a wink, palmed him two Viagra tablets. He whispered he'd probably only need one. Tinman thanked him and promptly swallowed both. Call it a crutch, but he immediately felt a burst of confidence. He would definitely hold up his end of the bargain now.

As he drove them to the museum, he looked in the rearview mirror and saw Catfish grinning. "What's so amusing?"

"I always grin when there's action," said Catfish.

Peach clapped his hands. "See! I'm not the only one who does that. You oughta give it a try. Calms the nerves."

"I am calm," said Tinman. But after everyone went back to their thoughts, he gave it a try. It didn't help, and he wiped it off.

He parked the car at the end of the side road bordering the museum. They double-checked their pagers, and Bones and Catfish took off. Peach, all in black, slipped into the darkness. As he watched them go, Tinman reached in his pocket to reassure himself his pager was in place. As he did, he realized he was at half-mast and quickly rising. He gulped.

* * *

Ensconced in the security control center, she was surrounded by banks of monitors and tall racks of electrical equipment with lots of twinkling lights. In front of her, were several controls to manipulate the dozens of video cameras placed in and around the museum.

Her job for eight hours was to methodically rotate through the array of cameras in search of any wrongdoing. It was utterly boring and she refused to obey orders. The concept was stupid. The majority of the cameras showed only black. What else are they going to show? It's night! The interior of the museum, except for a few dim lights, was too dark to show any real detail. Everything just looked like inky blobs.

On the other nights she was forced to work graveyard, she spent the time shadow boxing the twinkling lights. Tonight, however, her eyes were zoomed into one monitor which showed the video feed from the exterior camera on the east side of the building. This was where her man would soon appear.

The muscles she'd injected itched and pulsated. She could feel the juice oozing through her veins. A feeling of excited euphoria was rapidly overcoming her other senses. It was like this just before a bout. It was then she would morph from just another human to The Snake. By the time she hit the ring, she was invincible.

Tonight was different. Tonight was lurid with a promise of unimaginable ecstasy. It wasn't often she gave herself to a man. But as she thought about him, she knew she made the right choice. He was worthy of her. Naturally, she wasn't just going to give it up for free. He'd have to fight for it. She giggled coyly. God, she loved the sport.

There he is! No. Who the hell is that?

Two old guys stumbled into view near the northeast corner of the parking lot. Cassandra slammed a fist on the control panel. This could ruin everything. Even with turning off the video recording, she knew she was taking a risk tonight. She couldn't possibly let anyone see her allowing after-hour access.

It looked like the two old farts were in some kind of argument. The guy with the walrus mustache was waving his arms around and pointing at the other.

Come on! Shake hands and get the hell out of here!

Ah! Here he comes! Her man to the rescue. She knew he would take care of the problem. She exhaled. Everything was going according to plan.

* * *

Peach was in position, waiting for the signal from Tinman. He had his kit in his jacket pocket and was eager to get going. If he had it timed correctly, the page should come just about now. And there it was. Everything was going according to plan. He slipped out from his hiding spot, head down, and dashed across the small parking lot leading to the door on the loading dock.

* * *

It was really strange. He hadn't gotten a hard-on for no reason since he was eleven. But there it was. He had to shove it out of the way to get his hand on the pager and send Peach the signal. Showtime.

He made his gestures overly exaggerated to display to Cassie what he was doing. Bones and Catfish looked at him funny and he toned it down a bit. After five minutes of this, they all started realizing it was probably starting to look a little unbelievable. How long does it take to break up an argument between two old guys? Tinman demanded they shake hands and he sent them on their way.

As soon as they were out of sight, he looked to the museum and slowly marched toward it. He could feel her eyes on him. He wondered if he was showing. He didn't want to look too eager too quickly. He stuck both hands in his pockets in an attempt to camouflage the protrusion.

* * *

She could barely contain herself. And from the looks of it, neither could her man. He was only a few yards from the door. Time to go to work.

She leaned over and flipped a red master switch, shutting off the recording function of all the cameras. He stopped just outside the door and looked up at the camera. He waved. She waved back, too pumped up to realize how pointless it was.

She held her breath and pushed the button to buzz him in. Showtime.

* * *

Peach was right on schedule. His wiring was complete. All he had to do was wait for the signal. The electronic lock had been easier to infiltrate than he had imagined and he was forced to stand in full view for longer than he wanted.

Bones and Catfish came into view and darted into the cluster of trees. They were in place. Peach sighed. Come on, brother.

His pager vibrated, he made the final connection, and the bolt slid back. He turned the handle, opened the door a crack. No alarm. He sighed and waited for the next signal.

* * *

It was strangely quiet inside. And dark. Very dark. He felt his way through the little hallway which led to the dining area and the stairs. His eyes began to adjust and he could now see the strange pointed totem sculpture. Above it, floated his giant silver pool ball. The sight was comforting.

Unlike his swelling John Henry. It had never felt so big, and like Jack's beanstalk, it appeared as if the sky was the limit. He stopped at the bottom of the half landing staircase. He looked up and saw a light flick on above the third-floor landing. It didn't do too much to light up below, but enough to illuminate her as she slithered into view.

"Hello," she called down, the huskiness was tangible and alluring.

Tinman tried to respond but the words caught in his throat. He managed a polite wave. He looked at the many stairs he would have to traverse and wondered if he could manage it, given the load he was carrying.

He realized he was looking at her and therefore she wasn't looking at the monitors and thus he needed to let Peach and the others know they were in the clear. He shoved a hand in his pocket.

"Need a little relief, I see," she cooed at him from above. "It's coming darling. No pocket pool. Leave it all for me."

* * *

Peach felt the pager's vibration and grinned. Showtime. He started to wave Bones and Catfish in when he caught a glimpse of a police cruiser gliding down the side road. He flattened himself against the wall and waited.

The car slowed and seemed to be coming to a stop directly across from the loading dock when the dome light erupted, blinking, spinning, and splashing multi-colored light across his face. He made a silent prayer to his guardian spirit and the cruiser sped away, off to spoil some other villain's day, no doubt.

He smiled. Nice to have a friend in low places. He waved to Bones and Catfish and they hustled across the parking lot. Peach swung open the door and the three disappeared inside.

A minute and forty seconds later, after Peach had rigged the door to remain unlocked, they slinked down the long hallway leading to the dining area.

* * *

Tinman glanced to the aft of the ship and saw the Posse appear at the end of the hall and flatten themselves against the elevator. Peach waved. Tinman almost waved back but realized it would be highly impractical. He rearranged himself and started up the stairs.

"Wait!" she cried out. "I want to put on a little show for you. A little teaser before the main feature."

Tinman took his foot off the stair and folded his hands over his tent pole. "I can't wait," he called up.

Cassandra stepped farther out on the landing and seductively swished her hips, loudly humming out her own sexy background music. She was wearing high heels, pants, a button-up shirt, and a cropped blazer.

She started up the first half-flight of stairs. Partway, she shed her jacket, swirled it over her head, and flung it over the edge. It floated down and landed at Tinman's feet. He wasn't sure if it meant he was supposed to retrieve it and bring it up to her, but he had the feeling the answer was no.

She paused on the landing between the two half-flights and the striptease continued, shirt wafting through the air, landing on his head. He brushed it off and peeked over at the guys, who were barely containing themselves. Bones had his hands clasped over Catfish's mouth and Peach was holding his gut, silencing belly laughs.

Cassie started up the second flight, seductively waggling her butt. She flicked off both shoes and Tinman had to dodge the deadly, dart-like heels as they sailed down.

When she reached the fourth-floor landing, she slowly unbuttoned her pants and slid down the zipper. She wriggled out of them and tossed them over the railing. They got hung up on a step just above the third-floor landing.

She was now in a sports bra and he was fairly certain there was a thong buried amongst the bulging thigh muscles. That could wait for further inspection. What was causing heart palpitations, however, is she was covered from the neckline to ankles in tattoos. Until now, she'd managed to keep them hidden, and he wondered why.

She beckoned with a crooked finger. He chanced one last peek at his gang and saw they were now grouped in a quivering huddle, each trying to silence the other. He sighed and started up the stairs. Dammit. Why hadn't he worn briefs? At least he'd be partly restrained. But he was a boxer guy and hadn't worn tighty-whities since he was a boy, and a lot smaller.

As he climbed, she danced, weaving and grinding to her private soundtrack. By the time he reached the final flight of stairs, she was covered in sweat and glistening. Her tattoos came into full view and he saw she was covered in brightly colored snakes. Some of them running the full length of her body—heads licking her neck, bodies wrapped around her midsection, tails at the ankles. Baby snakes entwined her arms. All of them ready to strike. Beady eyes watched him, forked tongues and fangs waiting for their moment.

He didn't think he could get any harder. But now, on top of the artificial stimulants pumping through his veins, he was genuinely aroused and stretching to uncharted heights. And it hurt. Boy did it hurt. He needed relief and soon. He stepped onto the landing and purposefully marched toward her, ready to get down to business. Nothing on earth could stop him now.

She stopped him with a hand, palm out. "In there," she purred, pointing at a room off to the left. Behind her was the entrance to the Sky Room, with the outdoor Sky Plaza beyond.

He followed her eyes and saw a door leading to a lounge area dubbed The Founder's Room. This was reserved for the bigwigs who donated the most money. He understood why she'd chosen this room. These were the people she despised the most. The rulers of the museum.

He happily led the way. She closed the door behind. The lounge had brightly colored couches and chairs, a bar at one end. He turned to her.

"Strip," she panted.

* * *

After Tinman disappeared up the stairs, Peach managed to settle everyone down. He waited until he couldn't hear his brother's heavy steps on the stairs and slipped to the bottom of the staircase. He spied Tinman and Cassie stepping into a side room on the fourth floor. He waved in Bones and Catfish and the three quietly climbed the stairs, exiting on the third floor.

Peach led the way to the gallery that held the baskets. As he entered the room he quickly pulled out his pick set. He motioned to Catfish to remain at the doorway as a lookout. He and Bones crouched in front of the first display case. Peach looked to Bones and winked.

"This is the fun part," he said and got down to business.

* * *

Tinman had intended on undressing slowly, giving Peach and the others more time. But there were urgent needs to attend to and he went at the task with a vengeance. Quickly, he was down to his boxers. There was no way possible to hide the monster jutting out and up from underneath, so he didn't try. For some reason, he found himself wishing he had a camera to take a picture of it. For medical research purposes, of course, not bragging rights.

He turned to her. She eyed him up and down, licking her lips as she went.

"I like it rough. You up for that?" she asked, closing in on him.

"Uh, sure. I'm game. Whatever rocks your socks," he said with a nervous grin.

The left jab was a blur as it sped through space and crashed onto his left cheekbone. It didn't quite knock him to the ground, but he realized it was only a love tap from this crazed Amazon.

Cassie let out a little growl. The steroids were sending jolts through the hypothalamus and amygdala sections of her brain. She wanted more.

"Was that good?" she asked as she circled him. "Make you feel all hot and bothered?"

"Well, I'm certainly bothered," said Tinman, shaking off the blow.

"Nice."

The next shot launched from her lower right side and caught him square in the solar plexus. He folded over, his head bouncing off his towering manhood.

Cassie growled, "You like that, don't you? I like it too. It makes me want to make ice cream, know what I mean?"

Tinman managed to shake his head, and sputter, "Not really."

"Come on, hit me," she demanded.

"Huh?"

"I go both ways. S and M. It's only fair. I abuse you, you abuse me. That's true love, am I right? Just like if I go down on you, then you need to go down on me."

"I thought that's what we were here for."

"Later. Now give me your best shot. That's why you were chosen. For those arms, that long reach. At least four inches longer than mine. Come on! Beat me like a rag doll!"

Tinman held up both hands, palms out. "It's just that I wouldn't want to hurt you."

The knee caught him on the outside of his right thigh and he dropped. Cassie stared at him, her eyes aflame. "I'm not afraid of a little pain. Now get up and kick the shit out of me!"

She lowered herself in a ninja-like fighting stance. Tinman struggled to his feet, took one look, and flew from the room. Lightning fast, Cassie dashed after and blocked his way to the stairs. He turned and burst through the doors of the Sky Room.

Used for meetings and gala events, the glassed-in room was empty except for chairs lining the walls. Tinman grabbed one and like a lion tamer attempted to keep Cassie at bay. She was loving it, thinking her man was finally getting into the game. She thrust, he parried. She soon tired of it, grasping a leg of the chair and flicking it over her head.

Tinman gaped and ran out the doors to the Sky Plaza. Large metal sculptures were strewn around the expansive patio. They weaved around them in a lethal game of tag. Tinman managed to stay out of her reach until she cornered him with only a low concrete wall between him and a crash course on flying.

She closed in, making strange gurgling sounds from the bottom of her throat, like a rabid raccoon. She saw an opening and led with a roundhouse kick. Tinman ducked just in time and she lost her balance. Her body tumbled into the cement wall and for a second it looked as if she might topple over. It was pure gentlemanly instinct that made Tinman reach out, grab her and pull her in.

She looked at him, her eyes glowing. "See. You do love me."

The elbow smash to the top of his head took him completely by surprise. He was stunned but not enough to realize she was gearing up for the final assault. He shoved her a little and headed for the door leading back into the Sky Plaza.

"Come on! You can do better than that, big boy!" Cassie howled as she tore after him. The roid rage was in full swing with total control of mind and body. And sister did it feel good. What a joy not to have to think about the consequences of her actions. She was flying high with her prey in sight.

* * *

As Tinman reached the top of the stairs, his only thought was, "Couldn't it have been a foot fetish?" The heist was now the furthest thing from his mind. He took the first landing three steps at a time. He wheeled around the half-landing and catapulted down the second flight. Unfortunately, he landed on Cassie's discarded pants, slipped, and slid across the third-floor landing on his back.

As he scrambled up, Cassie closed in, preventing him from continuing down the stairs. His mind told him he had to protect the rest of the Posse so he couldn't turn right at the hall and head for the aft. Instead, he turned left, into the prow. As soon as he did it, he knew he was in deep doo-doo.

* * *

Catfish was sure he heard some strange noises coming from above, but he didn't want to leave his post in the hallway just outside the gallery. When he heard footsteps thumping down the stairs, he ducked back inside.

"I think we've got trouble," he whispered loudly to Peach.

Peach and Bones were just lifting the glass case off the first display. They froze, looked at each other, and slowly replaced the top. They crept to the door and the three of them looked out at the same time Tinman wheeled around the corner and headed away from them into the prow.

"You think she's onto him?" asked Bones. Cassie charged around the corner in hot pursuit.

"I'd say that's a pretty good assumption," said Catfish.

Not sure what to do, they watched as Tinman and Cassie did an excellent impersonation of the Keystone Kops. One would dash into a side gallery while the other would miss the turn and have to backtrack. Their heads kept popping out into the hall at different times, then one would spot the other and the chase continued.

"We gotta do something!" said Bones.

Peach nodded. "We'll knock her out and tie her up with something then get back to work. This thing isn't sour yet. It's only one girl. Come on."

* * *

Tinman knew this wouldn't last forever. Cassie was faster and quicker than him by far. He was now in the very front of the prow in the gallery with all the alien depictions. He briefly wondered if perhaps Cassie should pose for a portrait.

At the far end was the balcony overlooking the second-floor mural room. There were only two ways out. Either jump off the balcony and drop at least twenty-five feet to the floor below. Or go back the way he came. He would have to make a dash for it, try and get to the stairs. He peeked around a corner and looked down the hall. The coast was clear, for now. He saw at the far end, Peach, Bones, and Catfish coming his way.

Coming to save him. But he knew they had no idea what peril they were putting themselves in. This was his onus. He had to give them a chance to escape. Like a sprinter, he did some quick breathing and shot out and tore down the hall. As he ran, he frantically waved his arms, trying to get the others to flee.

Momentarily, they stopped, unsure of what he wanted them to do. He was halfway down the hall with only a few yards to go before he reached the third-floor landing. He was going to make it.

Cassie leaped out from a doorway and blocked his path. He screeched to a halt. To the left, no escape there. To the right, out in midair, the very top of his floating pool ball. Cassie was slicing the air with karate kicks, an evil snarl on her face.

It was a no-brainer. He ran to the railing, hopped up on it, and jumped. Six feet. Five. Four. Three. Two. His hands grabbed the cable and his body slammed into the balloon sending it swinging far out over the dining area below. As it began to swing back, he struggled upward so his body was spread out on top of the balloon.

He saw Cassie with a bemused look on her face, waiting for his return, fists up. Peach, Catfish, and Bones were to his right, their jaws wagging.

"HANG ON!" cried Peach.

Tinman wondered why his brother thought he might need some encouragement, but didn't bother to ask. Now that he was safely out of reach from Cassie, however, he was starting to wonder if his present situation might prove to be even more dangerous.

His thoughts were broken when he saw her twirl around and face the other guys. "I see you brought along some of your friends," she said. "That's cool. I'm game. Come on boys, slap me around good and I'll do all of you!"

Peach looked to Bones who looked to Catfish who looked back to Peach. All of them were old school and found the very thought of beating up a woman distasteful.

"Hit her with the lights!" cried Peach, whipping out his tactical flashlight.

Catching on quickly, Bones and Catfish flicked on their strobes and they all focused on Cassie. At first, she was a little taken aback, then she started laughing and dancing around and around like she was in a disco and they were providing the light show.

As he swung back and forth, Tinman groaned. She was invincible. What more trouble could they possibly have. He heard a high-pitched squeal, then a snap. His eyes jumped to the cable which was rapidly failing. He said a little prayer, but since he'd never been a God-fearing man, it fell on deaf ears.

With one mighty, shrill screech, the cable snapped and the balloon dropped. Much to his surprise, he didn't plummet to the ground. The amount of helium needed to fill the huge balloon was enough to slow his descent considerably. He started to believe he may just live through this nightmare when below he eyed the looming pointed totem.

He tried to maneuver the balloon by rocking his body back and forth but to no avail. It was a slow-motion disaster, like being on the Titanic, knowing full well you were going to hit that iceberg and there was nothing you could do about it.

He looked up and saw everyone, including Cassie, staring down in utter disbelief. As the totem pierced the balloon there was a humungous boom that rattled the building. Tinman, wrapped up in the shattered balloon, dropped the last several feet, meeting the ground with a thud.

He only had a nanosecond to register he was alive and nothing was seriously broken before the alarm started. The deafening explosion had triggered the earthquake sensor.

He scrambled to his feet and tore madly at the silver metal wrapping that was slowly mummifying him. He heard footsteps coming fast and prayed it wasn't Cassie coming to finish him off. Several hands starting ripping at the material and soon had him free. It was the Posse to the rescue. Peach shoved him toward the back hallway and they all ran for their lives.

Tinman spied Cassie's jacket at the base of the stairs and swept it up as he went. He was almost out of the dining area when he looked up and saw her on the third-floor landing. She was beating her chest and roaring. She thrust out a finger.

"Get back here you pussy! Come on and fight like a man!"

Tinman accelerated and when they reached the loading dock door it was the four stooges all trying to get out at once. While the logjam was worked out, he slipped on Cassie's cropped jacket. Those damn arms of his were way too long and he was certain the color clashed with his red, white, and blue checkered boxers. But it was marginally better than nothing.

He was last out the door. The mix of alarms, approaching sirens and Cassie howling at the moon made for a perfect waking nightmare. As they raced across the parking lot en route to the getaway car, he noticed he had finally returned to normal size. He breathed easier, just thankful for small blessings.

TWENTY-SEVEN

"HELLO EVERYONE, THIS IS SCOTT FRENLEY, and it's that time again. Another exciting edition of Crime Wave! And are you in for a treat today. Naturally, we had our share of minor crimes and accidents, but it's all too petty to even waste a minute on. Instead, let's jump right to our big story because, folks, this is ridiculous on a grand scale.

"Late last night, police and firemen responded to an alarm at the Nevada Museum of Art. When they arrived they were surprised to find the security guard on duty dressed in nothing but her undies! The rest of her clothes were found scattered around the museum and—lo and behold—a man's clothing was found upstairs in the strictly-off-limits Founder's Room! From what police could make out, the female guard had decided to use the museum for a little, shall we say, extracurricular activity.

"The man was not on the premises and his identity is unknown. This is because when the authorities attempted to arrest the guard she put up quite a fight. In all, she managed to get the best of three police officers, two firemen, and a police dog, after which she fled on foot. Now that's one tough little lady!

"The police are now searching for the guard who is wanted for illegally allowing an unauthorized person access to the museum and damage incurred during said incident. Apparently, a giant Mylar balloon that was on display was punctured when it fell from its cable and landed on a metal sculpture. It's not clear how this may have happened but police speculate the perpetrators may have literally been swinging from the chandelier, so to speak, during their sexual liaison.

"The man is also wanted for questioning, but police say until they can question the guard further, finding said man will be quite difficult, if not impossible. Apparently, the guard turned off all video recording devices before beginning her illegal shenanigans.

"Representatives from the museum say the guard has been released from her position. Ooh, what a surprise! They are thankful none of the valuable items in the museum were found missing. In particular, they mention they are most grateful the famed Dat So La Lee baskets were not harmed or stolen. On loan from the Historical Museum, these baskets are purported to be the most valuable items in the museum, each fetching upwards of a million dollars!

"For a basket? What's the deal with that? Maybe I should quit this broadcasting gig and take up basket weaving! What do you think folks? I know, I know, you'd miss me too much. Aww. I love you guys too.

"Anyway, for those interested in viewing these famous baskets, too bad! They're on their way across the country for a national tour and won't be back in Reno for over a year. And that about wraps it up for Crime Beat.

"One last thing for regular viewers, you may have noted this is our second recent story dealing with security guards who have seemingly lost their minds. Could it be the stress of their jobs? In the case of the campus guard, did the anxiety over people parking illegally push him over the edge? And this latest guard, was the pressure of staring at a bunch of empty video monitors all night so overwhelming it drove her to the brink of insanity? Perhaps we'll never know. But in this reporter's opinion, no job is so important it should land you in the pokey. Unless, of course, you're a thief!"

TWENTY-EIGHT

SHE HIT THE TV REMOTE, turning off the news. Her face was even more blanched than normal. Her baskets were leaving her?! For a year! To a thirteen-year-old that's an eternity. She was quite sure she would not be able to endure it. Every weekend, for months, she'd forced her mother to take her to Reno to see them. Now they were gone.

Of course, there were still the ten baskets at the Nevada State Museum in Carson City. But those had been off-limits to her for over six months, ever since that mean curator told her she was a pest. A pest! For wanting to see her heroine's famous works? It wasn't her fault the museum refused to put them on permanent display and they were locked up in some vault. These baskets were the property of the people of Nevada and should be seen.

Their excuse was almost too dumb to believe. They didn't have the space! In that gigantic museum? How much space did it take to display ten baskets? She knew the real reason they were locked away. They wanted to keep them all for themselves. In her opinion, the state shouldn't even have them. They should belong to the

Washoe Tribe. The tribe that created her and Dat So La Lee.

But that wasn't going to happen anytime soon. She knew the history of how the state bought them. They were legally theirs. So she was forced to pester the mean curator to let her into the vault so she could commune with the spirit of her idol. Nearly every day after school she would go to the museum and beg to see them. At first, the curator was excited to see such interest, but after several months she suddenly became a nuisance.

She wished she was a master criminal and could break into that vault. Have the baskets all for herself. Who better to be the keeper of these masterpieces?

She paced around her little room in her mother's mobile home. The two lived on the reservation next to the historic Stewart Indian School, where for ninety years the whites attempted to anglicize her people, even forbidding them to speak their native tongue. The only good thing about where she lived was the house was located on a street named after Dat So La Lee.

Molly's obsession with Dat So La Lee began when she first became aware she was an outcast. Half-breed to be exact. Her mother had slept with some white guy from Carson and she was the result. The name of her father was kept secret from her and the rest of the tribe. She didn't care. She wished she could drain all her blood and separate out the white stuff.

It was her peers who tormented her the most. She didn't look like them with her lanky frame, pale skin, and hair, so she became the perfect target. The Elders were kinder and it was from them she figured out how to combat the barbs and scorn she received from children her age.

She decided she would be the truest Indian on the reservation. She studied hard, day and night, to learn the history and traditions of her people. She even immersed herself in the endangered language and became one of the few young tribe members who was semi-fluent.

Her salvation, however, came when she began to study the ancient art of basket weaving. It was then she discovered the world's greatest weaver, Dat So La Lee. Once she found her, she spent all her free time learning everything there was to know about her life and craft.

She knew her given name was Dabuda and learned how she revived the Washoe tradition of weaving after the Paiutes had forbidden it for many years. Abe and Amy Cohn, owners of an emporium in Carson City, first recognized her great skill in the late 19th century. They employed her to create baskets for sale in their store and they quickly became very popular, some fetching upwards of $50.

Molly found out that at the time, it was an incredible price to pay for a basket. The buffoon on the news had no idea what he was talking about. A million dollars nowadays was a small price to pay for a work of genius.

Her baskets became so renowned, a grouping was displayed in the 1919 St. Louis Exposition. Claims are that she only made between 120 and 300 baskets, and out of those, most were held by anonymous collectors. Hidden away. Hoarded. Meant only for the eyes of the rich.

The history of Dat So La Lee was fascinating to her but not so much as her craft. She was awestruck when she discovered how the baskets were made. The technique was called coiling, using rods of willows for the core and expertly split willow for the outside. The light background stitching was done using the soft part of the willow found just under the bark. The dark stitching was made using bracken fern roots, soaked in ashes. The red highlights came from stitching very fine red willow shoots. All materials had to be gathered at specific times of the year and meticulously prepared before even beginning.

Her technique was unique in using three-rod coiling without interlocked stitches. Every inch had at least thirty-five stitches so that one row could easily require up to 1000. One of her largest baskets boasted more than 50,000 and took a year to make. The thought made Molly's brain swirl.

She walked to her dresser upon which sat her temple. A picture of Dat So La Lee, all 300 pounds of her, hung prominently. Beneath were scholarly articles about her, pictures of her baskets and splays of willow shoots. Off to a side was Molly's first attempt at basket weaving. She started it shortly after discovering her superstar, well over a year ago.

Even to her eyes, it was not a pretty sight. The stitching was amateurish and the design unclear. Her mother told her it was beautiful. But her mother lied. It was ugly and she knew it. The degikup design that Dat So La Lee favored, required a graceful slope, small at the bottom, bulging out in the center, and narrowing at the top. The designs are perfectly spaced and aligned evenly. Molly's basket was deformed from birth, with a wobbly base and squashed sides.

From the start, it had been a disaster. She was determined to mirror her mentor and use the old techniques. It nearly cost her a couple of fingers trying to strip the willow. She had ugly scars to prove it. She couldn't get the hang of the stitching either. She was not into denial. She knew early on she stank at basket weaving. Still, she persevered. Thus, her regular pilgrimages to the museums.

She felt if only she could stare at the genuine articles long enough, the magic would transfer into her mind and fingers and she would finally succeed. Now they were gone. Except of course for the one.

She thought about that. Yes. There was the one. But for her to be with it, she would have to take drastic steps. As she lay on her bed, she wondered if maybe it wasn't all that irrational a plan after all. What did she have to lose? She was not accepted by her generation and her mother didn't understand her. Wouldn't it be better to spend the days in her champion's embrace? Learning the old ways. Perfecting the techniques. Finishing her damned basket.

The thought was so comforting she closed her eyes and dreamed about how wonderful it would be.

TWENTY-NINE

THE CUE BALL NICKED THE FIVE BALL, caromed into the seven, sending it down the table where it collided with the nine which crawled its way into the corner pocket.

"You are the luckiest bastard in the world!" shouted the tourist.

Tinman smiled weakly. He knew otherwise. Either way, at least he'd found a little action to take his mind off how unlucky he really was. It was over three weeks since the travesty at the art museum and though the physical wounds had healed, a few mental ones still throbbed.

"Christ, I thought this would be cheaper than the casinos. You're killing me here," said the tourist. He had a pronounced beer belly and florid face which was getting redder every time Tinman beat him.

"You should've been here last week," said Tinman. "I couldn't sink a ball to save my soul."

"Lucky me."

Tinman had to be careful here. He needed the mark to call for another game at a higher stake. If he was too pushy, he'd shove him right out the door.

The guy studied the depleted contents of his wallet and said, "I got enough for one more game. Forty bucks."

Tinman whistled low. "I don't know. I'd rather stick with what we've been doing. Twenty bucks is the most I've ever bet. I mean, forty bucks on a single game. That's big league."

"Get over it! You've already won three times that. I think it's only fair, don't you," said the tourist, aggressively closing in.

Exactly the response Tinman was looking for. He acted accordingly, grinning nervously and looking cowed. "Well, I guess you're right. Okay. But I really shouldn't. This is when things usually go bad."

"Boo-hoo. Your break," said the tourist as he racked up the nine balls.

Over at the bar, Bones and Catfish couldn't have been happier. Ever since the failed heist, Tinman had been so morose they were starting to worry. Peach, too. He couldn't stop talking about how unfair it all was. The plans were perfect and it was only dumb luck that screwed things up.

Nobody blamed Tinman for his plan, except himself. They all told him there was no way to anticipate the guard would be some sadomasochist. But he knew they were being soft on him. He wished they'd give him crap over it, like he gave Peach over the first heist. At least then he could stop flogging himself.

Bones and Catfish knew Tinman was fretting over money and two weeks earlier offered to include him on the whiz down at the Bowling Stadium where the annual PBA World Series was wrapping up, but he declined. Now, as they watched him ply his trade, their hearts were happy. He was back to work.

Tinman waited until the tourist finished racking then stepped up to the table. He placed the cue ball ten inches to the right of the head spot and prepared to break. With the correct top-right English, he should be able to sink the one in the left side pocket.

The front door swung open unleashing a flurry of light snowflakes that swirled around in the entranceway like a swarm of angry moths. Peach hustled inside and stamped his feet.

He spotted Tinman and blurted, "I been looking for you! Tried the clubhouse first. We need to talk."

"Hold on a minute, bub. Can't you see we got a game going on here," said the tourist. "Wait your turn."

Tinman didn't like the tone of his voice and felt like swatting him with the butt of his cue, but action was rare and he didn't want to chase him off. He said to Peach, "I'm on a lucky streak here. If I take a break I may lose it."

The tourist immediately sang another tune. "Maybe I was being a little rude. Why don't we take a little break and then get back to it."

"You sure?" asked Tinman.

"I think it's a good idea. I need a smoke break anyway," said the tourist, reaching for a pack of cigarettes stowed in his shirt pocket.

Amber, sporting a furry, red Christmas hat, was at the end of the bar, cleaning glasses. She said without looking up, "Outside."

"The casinos let you smoke!"

"Outside," Amber repeated pointing a finger at the door.

"Fine," barked the tourist.

As he grabbed his jacket and headed outside, he mumbled under his breath how unfair life was for smokers. Amber, a reformed one, ignored him. As soon as he stepped out into the light snowfall, Peach hustled to the door and locked it.

"What are you doing?" cried Tinman. "I wasn't finished with him yet! You know how hard it is to find a decent chump these days?"

Peach was a bundle of nervous energy, his normal breezy manner gone. "How much did he have left to take?"

"Forty bucks," said Tinman.

Peach whipped out a small wad of bills, pulled out a fifty, and flicked it on the table. Tinman would have preferred taking it from his mark, but he pocketed it nevertheless.

"What the hell's so important it couldn't have waited?" asked Tinman.

Peach cocked his head to Bones and Catfish and they slid off their stools and dutifully joined the conversation. Peach eyed Amber, making sure she was busy with her private thoughts.

He motioned for the others to lean in close and then said, "I know where they got more baskets."

No one said anything for several moments, a flurry of emotions buzzing around inside each of their heads.

"I thought there were only the ten," said Bones.

"We thought wrong," said Peach, hurriedly, like if he didn't say what he had to say quickly he'd forget what he had to say.

"Where?" asked Tinman, his heart pounding.

"Another museum," said Peach.

The other three groaned loudly. The tourist started banging on the door, his blurred face pressed to the glass.

Amber looked up. "Hey, aren't you going to let that guy back in?"

"He's a troublemaker," said Peach.

Amber said, "In that case," and strutted around the bar, heading for the door. She reached up, yanked down the roll-up blind, blocking the man from view, and sauntered back to the bar. The banging continued for several seconds, then stopped for good.

The Posse reconvened. Catfish said, "I'm not too high on these museums anymore."

"Amen," said Bones.

Tinman felt even more distaste for museums than they, but the thirsting for the baskets was not yet quenched. "Spill it," he said.

Peach nodded quickly. "It was a fluky thing. Pepper, you remember her? Okay, so she tells me she has to do some research in Carson, specifically at the Nevada State Museum."

"I went there once on a field trip," said Amber.

Everyone shot her a look, amazed at her dog ears. Like a four-man football team, they hunched into a huddle. Peach continued in almost a whisper.

"So anyway, she invites me to go along with her and I figure it would be fun to invite Sage as well."

"You took two of your girlfriends to a museum?" asked Tinman.

"Why not? They both love culture and they both love cultivating me. Besides they're not my girlfriends, their FWBs. You know, friends with benefits. It's the wave of the future for unattached guys like us. You should try it."

"Pass," said Tinman.

"Suit yourself. By the way, they hit it off great," said Peach.

The other guys shook their heads in awe. Tinman said, "Too bad you didn't have Ginger. You could have made a good pumpkin risotto."

"She couldn't make it," said Peach. "Had to work. But the combination does sound yummy. Where was I? Oh right, so yesterday the three of us go to this museum and it's a real beaut. All kinds of interesting things. What I don't know beforehand is Pepper has an appointment with this bigwig curator. He's going to show her some artifacts or something. So when he arrives, he offers to show all three of us. Here's where it gets good. This guy takes us into the bowels of the museum, strictly off-limits to the public. Before I know it, he's letting us into this giant vault. I'm thinking, this is the first time someone actually invited me into one."

"Must have felt odd," drawled Bones, thoughtfully.

"It was," said Peach, remembering the moment. "But pleasant, nonetheless. So this curator starts droning on about this and that and I'm slipping away, you know. Until he mentions Dat So La Lee."

Eyes flashed from one to the other. Peach, still all business, went on. "And there they were. Ten more baskets. Just sitting on a cabinet. Apparently, when the state bought the ten in Reno, these came with the package. They've been there all along since we first stole the four. Well, I'm so juiced up I'm feeling like I got to take a leak. I mean this guy is letting us hold these things. And he told us a lot of interesting stuff about Dat So La Lee. I had no idea. I'll tell you about it another time."

Tinman's mind raced. The riches were still out there. Was it worth the risk? So far, there seemed to be a curse on them. He said, "How do we go about it?"

"We don't," said Peach. "Definitely out of reach. The part of the museum they're stored in used to be a bank. They bought it and converted it to fit their needs. But they kept the vault. And what a doozy. Time-lock. Walls two feet thick. Around-the-clock security with at least three guards patrolling and watching monitors at all times. It's impossible. And I don't say that lightly. Believe me. I want in there as bad as you."

He looked around at the baffled faces staring back. Tinman snorted. "You chased off a sucker to tell me that?!"

"No, not that. There's more," said Peach. "When the curator was showing us around the vault he pointed out some other weaver's baskets that were found buried under the ground for like a couple hundred years. In perfect condition."

Tinman shook his head in frustration. "What are we supposed to do, start digging holes hoping we find some?"

"Not at random, no," said Peach. "Thing is, I know where to dig."

"You sure you're feeling alright, kid?" asked Catfish.

Peach said, "Dat So La Lee asked to be buried with one of her baskets."

Dead silence. Peach went on. "Get it? I figure she's only been in the ground less than a hundred years. So the basket has to still be good. It's only one, but a million split four ways is still a pretty good haul."

The blank faces made him nervous but he muscled on. "So early today, before the snow started, I drove back down to Carson and found the cemetery and her grave."

"You cased a graveyard?" asked Catfish.

"Purely out of curiosity, mind you. And personally, I thought it was pretty rinky-dink for being the last resting place of such a famous weaver. But it's perfect for us. Out in the middle of nowhere. And there it is. What do you say?"

Bones looked to Catfish and said, "I believe the boy is talking about grave robbing."

"Technically, no, "said Peach. "Robbery refers to using a gun in the act of a crime. So in reality we'd be just grave burglarizing."

Spontaneously, Bones and Catfish broke into hysterical laughter, slapping Peach on the back and pounding their feet on the floor. Catfish was having trouble breathing.

Amber, feeling left out, asked, "What did I miss? What's so funny?"

Bones, on his way back to the bar, said, "Nothing, honey. Peach here just told a dirty joke."

"Ooh! I love dirty jokes!" said Amber.

This sent Bones and Catfish into another round of guffaws. Amber had a snit fit when she realized she wasn't going to be allowed in on it.

Back at the pool table, Tinman and Peach stared hard at each other, both wondering what was so funny.

* * *

Tinman was working on his third crossword of the night. He thought about going down to the clubhouse and practicing, but his heart wasn't in it. After Peach dropped his bomb, Catfish and Bones made it known they were above digging up a grave. They also made it clear they raised him and Peach to know better than to even think about it.

After that, everyone predictably decided to make it an early night. Now, if he could just stop thinking about it. He concentrated on his puzzle.

The next clue was, "Entered into a plot?" Eight letters. Fourth letter an 'O'. Last letter a 'D'. Question mark meant they were being cute.

He tossed the puzzle book to the floor. He decided he'd just sit and think about what he was going to make for Dez' Christmas party. It was two days from now and he, as usual, was responsible for the main dish. He didn't mind. He liked cooking and at least this party did not require a mandatory buy-in to the poker game that would no doubt be part of the festivities.

After beating the tourist today, he had enough money to get whatever he would need to make his dish. He never cooked traditional holiday fare, because he wasn't at all sure what that was. He leaned back, mentally running through his repertoire.

From the side of his eye, he saw the latch on his door lock twist. Before he could even lean up in his chair, Peach strolled in, shaking off snow from his jacket and boots.

"That's damn unnerving," said Tinman.

"Sorry," said Peach, as he pocketed his pick set. "Force of habit."

He wandered over to one of the metal chairs, plopped down, and said, "Snowing to beat the band out there."

"I saw."

"Practically nobody out."

"I bet."

"News says it's gonna be a doozy. No shadowing from the mountains, so we're gonna get dumped on. They say it might take a couple days to clear up. They already closed I-80 over the passes."

"Mm."

"Snow like this will keep everybody off the roads."

"Smart."

"Yup. Everyone's just gonna stay tucked away in their homes. No venturing out."

Tinman watched him watch him. He said, "Night like this, a person could run down the street naked and nobody would see him."

"Night like this, person could do just about anything and nobody'd see him."

Tick. Tick. Tick.

Peach picked up the crossword book and turned to the dog-eared page with the current puzzle. "Got ya stumped?"

"A bit."

"This long one here, huh? Oh, they're being cute with the question mark. Eight letters. Has to be . . . entombed."

Tinman was the first to leap to his feet, rushing to the closet. "You think your car will make it?"

"No way in hell."

Tinman froze, his coat half on. Peach grinned and said, "But I borrowed the perfect ride. An original Range Rover Classic, 1976, before they added the four-door option. This baby will go through anything. 3.5 liter V8. Permanent four-wheel drive, excellent ground clearance. No power steering, though. Not standard until after 1981. No doubt, it'll do the trick."

Tinman continued his dressing through Peach's recitation and now turned to him, with hat, gloves, and coat on, and asked, "Where did you manage to find that?"

"I been eyeballing it down at one of the ritzy homes off Huffaker. Rich guy must have bought it as a status symbol because the dude never drives it. Anyway, he leaves it in a little side garage away from the house. I happened to take a drive down there after the pool hall and saw him and his wife packing up their ski stuff. Guess they figured if they were going to be snowed in they may as well be in Tahoe."

"Makes sense."

"Sure. But guess what they drove up there in? Some ugly Mercedes SUV. I mean if you're going to go play in the snow, why would you leave your Range Rover at home? And if you're going to buy a Mercedes why get an SUV in the first place? Why not get one of those new SL

Roadsters. Now that's a sweet-looking ride. That says Mercedes Benz, am I right? Not some SUV any manufacturer can make. Hell, did you know they make a Mercedes station wagon? How dumbass is that?"

He was still babbling as Tinman shoved him out the door and down the steps.

THIRTY

THE FIRST THING MOLLY DID after deciding to kill herself was to find out the proper way to go about it. As she began to research, she was amazed at how many people wondered the same thing. She was even more awestruck at the number of ways people had come up with. It comforted her. Knowing so many had come to the same conclusion somehow validated her decision.

To be fair, she felt she should give each method of self-destruction an in-depth examination. After all, you only get to do it once, might as well make a production out of it.

The most obvious and, therefore, the most popular way to do oneself in was with a gun. This was also the easiest to rule out. She didn't have a gun.

Harikari was next to go. Who has a sword just lying around?

Poisoning. No poison. Well, rat poison, but really that's beneath anybody, isn't it?

Self-immolation? Overkill.

She wasn't a coward. No more than most and a lot less than many. It's just that she wanted the whole thing to be dignified.

That's why she ruled out drowning. She knew when the water started filling her lungs her instincts would cause her to react, fight back. Despite her decision. Then she would look like an idiot. Flailing around. Trying to live when the point was to die!

In the end, she settled on hypothermia. For the most part, her research told her it would be relatively painless. The onset usually brings on uncontrollable shivering and confusion. She was quite sure she could handle both. As it progresses, the body becomes numb and eventually just quits. It sounded peaceful and definitely dignified. No thrashing about or fighting the inevitable.

She also liked the fact Mother Earth would be the one doing the job. For a week, she had been praying for the right conditions, and tonight the Great Spirit had smiled down on her. The temperatures were dropping and snow was falling.

Her mother left earlier in the evening for a night of gallivanting and Molly knew she wouldn't return home until the early morning hours. Everything was going according to plan.

She decided to give up the ghost at her favorite place on earth. It was a short walk because her most cherished spot was just down the road from her home. She'd not worn a coat or any warm clothing since that would be pretty stupid. She only brought one possession, her unfinished basket; she didn't know the rules but was hoping to bring it with her to the Great Beyond, where her heroine would help her finish it.

Now as she lay on her back, her basket perched on her chest with snow slowly covering her, she knew she made the right decision. She felt a slight shudder and smiled, knowing hypothermia was slowly taking her away.

* * *

"Stop the car," said Tinman.

"What's up?" asked Peach.

"We forgot tools. How dumb can we be?"

"In the back."

"Huh?"

"Tools are in the back. Two shovels and a pickax. I stopped at Harbor Freight before I got to your place," said Peach. "They were getting ready to close early on account of the snow, but they let me run in quick. Did I tell you how much I love that place?"

Tinman looked to his brother. "You had me all figured, huh?"

Peach smiled back. Tinman shook his head and stared out at the increasing snow. There was a chance Interstate 580 to Carson might be closed so they opted for the old highway and were just leaving Reno. There were few cars and almost no snow plows. As a small city with a small budget, Reno preferred to let the white stuff melt rather than spend a ton of money on clearing it.

Though they had to go well under the speed limit, the Range Rover was having no trouble getting through. They were silent for several minutes but neither felt like being stuck with their own thoughts for the entire drive. Particularly when the only thing they could think about was the distasteful act they were about to perform.

"How about a little music?" asked Peach, reaching for the radio. He clicked it on and twirled the tuning dial looking for a station that wasn't intent on playing insipid Christmas music. He stopped at a classic rock station where The Beatles were just wrapping up, "Money (That's What I Want)."

The next song began and Peach let out a whoop. "Van Halen's, 'Running With the Devil!' Now how fitting is that?"

Tinman lurched for the radio and clicked it off. "Let's just talk."

"Okay, you want to talk about what we're going to do with the money?" asked Peach.

"I'll worry about how to spend it after we get it. I don't want to jinx us."

Peach shrugged, disappointed in not being able to daydream. They drove along without talking for a couple more minutes, then Peach said, "How about if I tell you what I learned at the museum. About Dat So La Lee. It's really interesting."

"Seems fitting."

"Okay, so first off, she was probably the first case of obesity in the country."

"Knock it off."

"I'm not joshing. I mean this lady was enormous. But what a huge talent."

By the time they reached the ranch country, the snow was a foot deep and Peach had covered Dat So La Lee's early history and her association with Abe and Amy Cohn.

"So she never got any of the money for the sale of all these baskets?" asked Tinman, drawn into the story despite himself.

"Like an allowance, but basically she got the little cabin to live in and that's that."

Tinman frowned, not liking this. "Nothing more than an indentured servant."

"You could say that. I couldn't. Because I have no idea what it means, but if you say so."

"Keep going."

Twenty minutes later, Peach finished telling how after Dat So La Lee died, Abe Cohn's second wife sold twenty baskets to the State Legislature. At the time, she considered them junk.

"Fifteen hundred bucks! That's all she got for twenty baskets? What an imbecile." said Tinman.

"That's it."

Tinman shook his head in disgust. "Damn shame."

"You got that right. Especially when I tell you what's so special about these baskets."

A short time later, the snow was falling so hard, Eilley Bower's Mansion could barely be seen sitting back from the road. It didn't matter, because neither of them was trying to see it. Tinman's eyes were fixed on the side of his brother's face as he focused on the road and continued his tale.

"You mean to say, she was doing this all from scratch?" asked Tinman.

"Yup. Only branches, roots, and bark. And get this. Her only tools were her teeth, fingers, and a sharp piece of glass. I mean, I don't see how she got even one good knot an inch, much less thirty-five or so. There's this one basket some knucklehead took the time to actually count the total stitches. Take a guess how many."

"Five thousand?"

"Bzzz. Not even close. I was so impressed I remembered exactly. It was 56,590."

A lightning bolt could not have pierced Tinman's mind more. Even though he prided himself on his discipline, he simply couldn't fathom the perseverance and the patience of this lady. His eyes spontaneously teared up, in awe at seeing something grander than the imagination can conger.

"Wild, huh," said Peach. "It was called, hold on a sec. I'll get it. Okay, it was, Myriads of Stars Shine Over the Graves of Our Ancestors. Hey! That was it. I'm sure of it. Anyway, some of these baskets took her over a year to make."

"Why did she call it that?" asked Tinman in a hushed voice.

"Huh? I don't know. But some believe she was inspired by dreams, and the patterns on the baskets have some sort of meaning to her people."

Tinman turned and looked to the sky, the snowflakes plummeting down like shooting stars. "I've heard of that kind of thing."

"So anyway, now her baskets are the most valuable in the world, and she's the most famous of all weavers. Too bad she didn't get to see that."

"She was after something else. Something more important."

"What's more important than money and fame?"

"The perfection of beauty," said Tinman.

They drove on for a while, with Peach periodically glancing at Tinman for an explanation. Finally, he said, "I don't get it."

"Remember how hard I practiced to learn the massé?" asked Tinman.

"Two years. And I remember thinking how nuts you were since you can't use that shot while hustling. Any sucker sees that they're running for the door."

"That's right. But I wanted to know how to do it. Because when it's done correctly, it's the most perfectly beautiful pool shot in the world."

Peach was struck by the words and the tone. He stared at him, so transfixed he almost ran off the road.

They skirted Carson City to the east and turned onto Snyder Avenue. It was very dark. The road had not been touched by any plow. The Range Rover crawled along, shoving snow to the left and right. At one point, they passed a little gravel and dirt lane cutting off to the side and Peach pointed. The sign said, "Dat So La Lee Way."

Peach said, "We're getting close now. The old Indian School is just up a ways. We're looking for a little flagpole off to the left."

Tinman didn't answer. He was staring at the window, his muted reflection frowning back.

"Quite a coincidence, don't you think?" asked Peach.

"What's that?" asked Tinman, quietly.

"This is the exact same day we first stole the baskets all those years ago."

"Are you serious?"

"Yep. Life is funny, huh?"

Peach spotted the flagpole and turned off the road onto a dirt path. The falling snow subsided so only light flakes swirled in front of the headlights. He drove a few yards and stopped. Directly in front was a low field fence surrounding a small graveyard. A metal gate hung loosely like it might fall from its hinges if used.

To the left, was an old historical marker noting this was the place Dat So La Lee was buried. At the bottom read, "Myriads of Stars Shine Over the Graves of Our Ancestors."

The two brothers were silent for a long time.

"You ready for this?" asked Tinman.

"No."

"Let's go home."

Peach nodded, then turned to him. "Since we're here, let's at least go see her. You know, pay our respects."

Tinman looked over with a smile. He nodded and the two climbed out.

* * *

The shivering had stopped once the snow had completely covered her. She could feel her breathing, however, so she knew she wasn't dead yet. Along with the numbness came a deep peace. It wouldn't be long now.

Her mind was wandering into places it had never ventured. She was wondering exactly how it would all occur. She'd heard tales that spirits would visit her and escort her to The Other Side. Of course, she couldn't be sure that was true, because no one who had actually seen these spirits was still alive.

Still, she hoped it was true. It would be very helpful to have someone show her the way. She wondered if once she arrived her idol would be there to welcome her. If not, she would have to ask around and find out where she hung out. It would be so nice if they could be neighbors so she could spend every day studying the craft.

Were there days where she was going? Or was it just endless time? Was there food? She hoped so. She'd skipped dinner and her stomach was growling.

Crunch. Crunch. Crunch.

Or maybe her stomach was crunching. No. What was that?

Crunch. Crunch. Crunch.

They were here. It was the spirits come to lead her away! Yes. She could definitely hear them now.

"Where is she?"

"There wasn't any snow before. But I'm pretty sure she's over here."

Crunch. Crunch. Crunch.

They were looking for her. But they were going in the wrong direction! Why couldn't they see her? Perhaps because she wasn't quite dead yet. She held her breath, hoping to speed up the process.

"I'm sure she's here."

"Well, it's starting to snow again. We can't look forever. We'll come back another time."

NO! Don't leave! You can't go without me! I'm right here. Stay!

Crunch. Crunch. Crunch.

They were so close now. If only she could give them a sign. Yes! That was it! Let them know she was ready to go. Show them. Show them. Show them!

She sat up, snow falling from her head and shoulders. She thrust out her basket and said, "Here I am!"

The two spirits, looking strangely like humans, spun around and saw her. Their eyes popped out of their heads. Their mouths gaped. They screamed. She beckoned to them. They screamed again and ran off into the darkness, disappearing from view.

Molly called out to them, but they were long gone, back to the heavens from where they came. She sighed. What did she do wrong? She turned around and dusted the snow from Dat So La Lee's marble tombstone, her etched name now clearly visible. She kneeled in front of it.

"Can you hear me? I'm the one who visits you every day. Please help me. I want to be with you and learn your secrets. But the spirits have left and I'm still here, in my favorite spot, but without you. Have I chosen wrong? Is there some other path I should be on?"

She bent her head and felt like she may cry. Suddenly, she noticed her silhouette forming in the snow atop the grave. She looked up. The clouds parted. And for a fleeting moment, the stars shone brightly down.

They were so bright it made her eyes swirl but she refused to look away. Then they started to move. Up and over, half loop and back down, tighten. Up and over, half loop and back down, tighten.

That was it! She saw it now as clearly as the flickering stars. This was the secret. The way to correctly form the three coils. She had discovered the non-interlocking stitch.

She threw herself at the tombstone and hugged it. It was cold. She was cold. In fact, she was probably close to freezing to death. She couldn't die now! She had been given a sign.

She jumped up and shook off the snow. She stamped her feet and patted her arms, forcing the blood to work again. As she started for the cemetery gate, the skies closed up, swallowing the stars. Heavy snow again began to fall.

It didn't matter to her. Dat So La Lee Way was only a short walk. And the way she was feeling she could practically float home. Her path was clear. It was now her job to continue her heroine's legacy. To show the world once again the true essence of beauty.

THIRTY-ONE

"YOU KNOW NOBODY'S gonna believe us."

"That's right. Because we're not going to tell anyone. Ever."

"Good idea."

The angry blizzard unleashed its full might, howling and dumping its heavy load, doing its very best to bury the Range Rover as it crept northward to safety.

THIRTY-TWO

TEK WAS ALLOWED TO GO TO THE CHRISTMAS PARTY because all Christmas parties are required to have at least one token kid, and Dez requested Tinman drum one up. He was currently the only one not in the apartment. Tinman, Peach, Dez, Catfish, Bones, Angel, Malice, and Rudy were all inside staring at the locked door.

"Why didn't anyone else take this bet?" asked a suspicious Dez.

Everyone shrugged and studied the pretty ceiling. The bet was fifty dollars Tek could unlock the apartment door without being inside. He barely stepped outside to prepare when Dez started getting antsy.

"Well come on already! Hey! Are you still out there kid?" she called. "I'm trying to get back to the game here! It's okay if you want to chicken out."

"Speaking of which, the chicken curry you brought is amazing," said Angel. "What are the little green balls in it?"

"Makhuea," said Tinman. "Thai eggplant. Most of the restaurants cheat and use the regular stuff."

"It makes a big difference," said Angel. "Mm-mm good."

"And the stuffed shells are killer," said Malice.

Everyone enthusiastically agreed. "Thanks," said Tinman, hiding his pride.

Their attention was drawn back to the door when a thin piece of plastic appeared at the bottom gap. It was about the size of a playing card and had a series of creases on its surface. Attached to the back was a piece of fishing line.

It just sat there for a little bit and Dez rolled her eyes at everyone. Just then, like magic, it began to fold at the creases until it grew into something that resembled a large bug with four wire legs. At the end of each leg was a tiny upside-down rubber cup.

Everyone drifted in closer. One of the legs lifted off the ground and waved at them. They all instinctively waved back. The robot turned to the door and started climbing straight up, the "feet" of the legs functioning like suction cups.

The room was utterly silent, no one dared even gasp— thank goodness. Twenty seconds later, the robot reached the doorknob. The little head examined it, and the front legs went to work. Like a stick insect breaking down a leaf, it quickly turned the latch on the handle lock.

It moved higher and with one leg, slid the chain lock off. Pivoting, it headed to the floor. When it reached the bottom, the legs collapsed underneath and the entire thing unfolded itself until it was a flat card again. There was a yank on the fishing line and it disappeared.

Tek stepped inside to a loud round of applause, with everyone demanding an explanation. He quieted them and held up the robot.

"This, lady and gentlemen," he began, "is referred to as an untethered, self-folding, origami robot."

"I remember those things," said Malice. "But they were paper and you had to fold them yourself. I never could figure out how to do the crane. Sucks."

"Well, this is made of a heat-sensitive polystyrene composite constructed of five separate layers. The middle one is a thin sheet of copper that's been laser-etched to create electrical connections between the various on-board motors, actuators, micro-batteries, and the microcontroller. I installed an on-board heater which when activated causes the robot to self-assemble. Simple."

"I got a few words of that. How about you?" Peach asked Tinman who shook his head dumbly.

"I also included a micro-video camera so I can see what the lock looks like from outside, and also to see if anyone is watching me break-in."

"Okay, that part I get," said Peach.

"What about the legs?" asked Bones.

"They're made out of Nitinol, or muscle wire," said Tek. "Technically, it's shape-memory actuator wire."

"I knew I shouldn't have asked," said Bones.

"I control them wirelessly with this controller," said Tek, holding up a small black box with a mini-screen, some dials, and a joystick. "I still have some tweaking to do. The legs are strong enough to do locks like this but I need something stronger for stiff deadbolts and stuff like that."

"Well, I think you did a bang-up job just as it is!" said Peach, grinning proudly. "What do you call it?"

"What else? The Mule Tool 2.0," said Tek.

"Mule Tool? What the hell is that?" asked Dez.

"Inside joke," said Tinman. "I think you owe the man here fifty bucks."

"Well this is totally unfair! He's a ringer! How was I to know I was going up against some baby Einstein?"

Everyone stared at her. She huffed and puffed then grudgingly forked over the money. Tek pocketed it and the guys all slapped him on the back.

"Fine. Now you," Dez said, pointing to Rudy, "back to the game."

"My pleasure," said Rudy, hurrying back to the poker table.

"I'll bet," she grumbled. Looking back to Tinman she said, "And thanks a lot for inviting this guy, he's a ringer, too!"

Tinman shrugged and Dez marched to the poker table. The poker game started with Bones, Catfish, Rudy, Peach, and Dez, but two hours into it, Rudy had cleaned out everybody but Dez, and he was closing in on her.

Tinman, Angel, Malice, and Tek opted for The Game of Life. They now headed to the other side of the living room to resume play on the dining table. Bones, Catfish, and Peach were kibitzing.

"Okay, who's spin?" asked Angel.

"Mine," said Tinman. He spun the spinner, got a six, and landed on a Stop Space, reading, Spin for Baby.

"Oh for chrissakes. I already got married and now I have to have kids? This game is for straights. College, Graduation, Career, Night School, Marriage, Family Path. Retirement. How am I supposed to relate?"

"It would be nice if they made a game like this for people like us," said Tek. "Call it Life of Crime."

"Right!" Angel agreed. "You could land on spaces like Fooled the Parole Board."

"Tapped Into a Loaded Mark," said Catfish.

"Knocked off an Armored Car," added Peach.

"Worked the Whiz with a Shade on Your Side," said Bones.

"Huh?" said Tek.

"It means you're paying a dirty cop to look the other way while you work," said Tinman. Tek nodded and filed it away.

"Okay, spin already, I'm next," said Malice.

Tinman groaned. "Alright, I can squeeze out of this if I get a one, two, or three. Come on baby." He spun the spinner and landed on the nine. "Triplets! Shoot me now!"

Everyone cracked up. Dez yelled over, "Can it! I'm trying to concentrate here."

"Relax," said Tinman. "We're out of here anyway, Tek has a curfew."

"No, I don't," said Tek.

Tinman mouthed the word, clubhouse.

"Yes I do," said Tek. "Mother will be worried."

Tinman stood up and stretched. "Angel, Malice, good seeing you. And thanks again for the help with the pool table. You're welcome anytime."

"We know," said Angel. "Peach already gave us a key to the clubhouse."

Tinman shrugged. "Bones, Catfish, you want a ride? Tek's treat."

Tek had convinced Peach and Tinman to let him be the chauffeur for the night, claiming Garshasp had sufficiently trained him to drive. He swiped his mom's car for the evening, saying it was only fair since she stole it from his father after he went to jail. Peach and Tinman accepted the logic and the way over had been accident-free.

"Nah, I think we'll stay and watch," said Catfish, heading for the poker table with Bones following. "Not often you get to see the high and mighty come crashing down."

"Oh yeah? Wanna lay a side bet?" barked Dez. "This time I got him."

This grabbed everyone's attention. The pot was huge. The game, Seven Stud Low-Card-in-the-Hole Wild, with one more down card to go.

Rudy's up cards looked like he was going for a spade flush. Dez with a pair of kings up was either after a full house or four of a kind. Dez dealt out the last down card. Rudy didn't even look at it before pushing in a large pile of cash, enough to wipe out Dez if she called.

Dez eyed him closely. "Where did you learn to play like this?"

Rudy said, "Under the highway."

"What?"

"I run a bi-weekly game. Currency is cans."

"You play for garbage?"

Rudy looked up from his cards and stared hard at her. "Those cans are what keep us alive. We're playing for survival, lady. That's real poker."

"Hey! All I'm trying to do is survive," said Dez.

Rudy leaned back and did a slow scan of the plush digs. Dez followed his eyes and squeaked, "This is all for show! Like a stage set."

"Uh, huh," said Rudy looking back to his cards. "You calling, or what?"

Dez fingered the necklace Peach had given her. Peach noticed and elbowed Tinman who nodded and grinned.

Dez said, "Catfish, you said this necklace was probably worth a pretty penny, huh?"

"No surprise there," said Catfish.

Dez grinned, unclasped the necklace, and threw it into the pot. "I think that'll cover it."

Rudy picked it up and examined it. Peach tapped Tinman on the shoulder and cocked his head to the door.

"Okay, we're heading out," said Tinman. "You want a ride Rudy?"

"He's not going anywhere! Not until I get my money back," said Dez.

Rudy grinned. "I'll get a cab, thanks anyway. I keep going the way I am, I won't have to dumpster dive for a year."

"Come on, come on, is it a bet?" demanded Dez.

Tinman and Tek walked to the door with Peach behind. As they were about to go out, Peach turned back.

"Hey Rudy," said Peach. "If I were you I wouldn't touch that bet. Might burn your fingers, if you get my drift."

"I knew it!" bellowed Dez.

Rudy quickly flicked the necklace over to her and said, "Thanks, Peach. Like I said, you're a good fella to have around."

"As I keep telling everyone," said Peach, and closed the door behind him.

Dez held the necklace up and Catfish fastened it back on her neck. With a flick of her hand at the pot, Dez said, "Take it. I'll live to fight another hand."

Rudy swept in the pot. Dez tossed her cards and said, "Where is this game you play?"

"Under the I-80 overpass on East Fourth. Wednesdays and Saturdays. You should stop in, be my guest of honor. From the looks of it, your game could use a little boning up."

Catfish and Boncs tittered. Dez shot them a look, turned back to Rudy, and said, "Shut up and deal."

* * *

Tek insisted on having Peach and Tinman sit in the back of his mom's SUV like he was a real chauffeur. The roads were still a mess after the big snowstorm. The roads hadn't been cleared and with all the traffic, much of the snow was now hard-packed ice.

"Hey Tek," said Peach. "Where'd you get the money to make the robot?"

"Mom doesn't know it yet," said Tek, "but I found the password to her secret account where she stashed all the money she stole from my dad. I figured I should get a cut of the action before she blows through it all. I transferred a bunch of it into a personal trust fund and I'm the only signatory. Well, actually, William Trenner, is the only signatory."

"William Trenner?" asked Peach.

"It's a fake identity I've been setting up the last couple of years. Amazing what you can do when you're a hacker."

Peach turned to Tinman. "We're in the wrong business."

Tinman shrugged and said, "What else is new?"

Tek asked if it was alright to turn the radio on and the guys gave him the okay, as long as it wasn't a rap station. He tuned to a rock station and turned up the volume.

Peach moved closer to Tinman and said in a low voice, "I've been thinking maybe we overreacted. I mean, at the graveyard."

Tinman shot him a look. "What are you talking about?"

"The way she sat up, holding out her basket, almost like it was a gift. You know, for what we'd been through."

"You're nuts."

"Probably right. Didn't look all that good, anyway. All mushed up. Like it wasn't even finished. Not much of a consolation prize."

Words escaped Tinman so he just shook his head and looked out the window. He had worse things to think about. Money. There was no hiding from it. He had to find a way.

Peach, reading his thoughts, leaned in and said, "We need to square you with the city. I can't stand seeing you like this. What's the damage?"

"Three grand will get them off my back. Until next year."

Peach pulled out a sheaf of cash, riffled out three thousand—leaving very few bills—and placed it on Tinman's lap.

"Merry Christmas," said Peach. "That about taps me out from my last heist, but it's worth it."

Tinman stared at the money. "You can't do this."

"Sure I can," said Peach. "I've got to get back to my normal job anyway. This basket thing has tied me up since I hit town."

"I'm not taking your money."

"Well, I'm not taking it back."

Tinman sighed and stared again at the money. "What about we call it a loan."

"You call it whatever you want," said Peach. "Say, I've also been thinking—"

"You sure have been doing a lot of thinking!"

"Thanks," said Peach. "Anyhoo, for a long time, I'm thinking I could do better if I wasn't a lone wolf anymore. If I had another inside guy, the jobs could be a lot bigger."

Tinman raised an eyebrow. "I don't think I'm cut out for it."

"Sure you are. I can handle all the mechanics, but you're the mastermind, casing out the job, making sure we cross all our t's and dot those pesky i's. It's what you're good at." He glanced at Tinman who had a skeptical look on his face. "Look this isn't welfare, brother. You don't know it yet, but you're just what I've been looking for."

Tinman thought about it for a while. He'd been secretly thinking the same thing but didn't want to appear presumptuous. But if Peach thought he had the right stuff, maybe he did. Maybe there was a way out of this abyss. A new start. A new path.

"Would we hit the road?" he asked.

"If we hear of something juicy. But the more I hang around, I think we could keep plenty busy right around here. Reno's changed. More money, and more coming in from what I gather."

Tinman nodded and thought some more. He said, "If we do this, I pay you back first haul we get."

Peach grinned wide. "Well naturally. Plus lots and lots of interest." He nudged him playfully.

"We're probably going to need a wheelman," said Tinman, already on the job.

"See, that's what I'm talking about! You're always thinking. And you're right."

"Bones and Catfish are terrible drivers, so they're out."

"Yeah, not easy to find. Especially one you can trust in a pinch."

Tek was halfway through an intersection, when another car, going too fast for conditions, blew through a red light and headed straight for the SUV. Tinman and Peach reacted quickly, both opening their mouths to warn Tek. Tek was on top of it. He stomped on the gas and simultaneously yanked up the emergency brake while spinning the wheel hard to the left.

The SUV fishtailed, its rear end spinning out and away, just clearing the oncoming car by inches. Tek dropped the emergency brake and finished the 360-

degree revolution, ending up facing the way he'd been going.

"That was radical!" yelled Tek.

Tinman and Peach were flattened against their seats, faces pale.

"It really works! Garshasp warned me about all the red-light runners in Reno, see, and he taught me that maneuver. But we never had a chance to practice it for real. But damn, it really works!" He turned up the music and continued down the road as if nothing had happened.

Peach swallowed hard and looked to Tinman. "I think we found our wheelman."

Tinman nodded and forced himself to start breathing again. They turned onto Fourth Street just up from the main bus station. To make sure everyone knew it was a bus station, the city decided to hang a life-size bus from some giant poles. It was suspended thirty feet from the ground and angled like it was headed for heaven.

Peach stared out the window. "Hey look! The old Wonder Lodge. Remember when we lived there?"

Tinman nodded. "We were thirteen, spent almost six months. One of the long-term places."

"Right. I think I even remember the room number. 310, wasn't it?"

"Corner room."

"Sure brings back memories," said Peach. "What a couple of wild things we were."

"Hell-bent."

On the radio, Charlie Daniels started picking out "The Devil Went Down to Georgia."

Tinman grinned and didn't ask to turn it off.

THIRTY-THREE

IN ROOM 310 OF THE WONDER LODGE, Hobie had most of his impressive gun collection laid out on the queen bed. Cassie was armed with the rest, a SIG Sauer P320 semi-automatic in one hand and a Walther G22 rifle in the other.

In room 310 of the Wonder Lodge, Hobie had most of his impressive gun collection laid out on the queen bed. Cassie was armed with the rest, a SIG Sauer P320 semi-automatic in one hand and a Walther G22 rifle in the other.

She strutted around the room wearing only her snake tattoos. Hobie, lying at the head of the bed, surrounded by the rest of his guns, wondered how he had gotten so lucky after all the recent bad luck he'd had.

"I like being a fugitive," said Hobie.

"Too bad we didn't do more to deserve it," said Cassie.

"That can change."

Cassie grinned, knowing what was coming. She'd had the same thoughts ever since she met him here, hiding out from the law as she was.

"I think we blow this town and show the world what we're really made of," said Hobie.

Cassie slithered in next to him. "Go on a tear, huh?"

"Exactly," said Hobie. "Like Bonnie and Clyde. Now those were real crooks, not like these petty little thugs today."

They fondled each other for a while. Cassie laid her head on his chest and said, "Hobie and Cass, knocking the world on its ass."

He raised her chin. "That's poetry."

"Bonnie Parker was a poet," said Cassie. "Why not me?"

"I'm getting hot," said Hobie.

"Me too." She ditched the guns, stood up, and beckoned him.

Hobie got to his feet, flexing his muscles. "A little foreplay?"

Cassie grinned coyly and nailed him in the jaw with a blazing left jab. Hobie shook it off, feinted with his left, and caught her square on the side of the head with a haymaker.

She lifted herself off the ground and fell into his arms. "Finally, a real man."

Hobie smirked. "Ready or not world, here we come."

From the Author

I want to personally thank you for reading this first book in the Tinman series. I hope you enjoyed it. If you'd like to spread the laughs, no better way than to post a review at the site where you bought the book. As an independent author in this online age, reviews are my lifeline. Please help my efforts to continue writing and living this dream, by contributing your thoughts on this book. All opinions are welcome.

The other books in the series, in order, are **Shady Deal**, **Calling the Shots**, **Nut Job**, and **Family Jewels**. The sixth book, **Stealing Home** is in the works. I know you'll get a kick out of all of them. You can find release dates and links to purchase all of my books at www.crookbooks.site.

I also recently released two new standalone books, **Switch-pitcher**, a baseball adventure, and **High Jinks**, a romantic comedy caper. Check out the write-ups on my site, or find them at Amazon.

Bonus: I am currently offering two complimentary eBooks to my loyal fans. Just go to my website and you will see the link to get your copies of **Crookbook**, featuring twelve short stories that were instrumental in the development of the Tinman Series, and **Thieves Recipes,** containing some of Tinman's favorite recipes as well as tips on scratch cooking from the crook who cooks. It's a delightful blend of cooking, comedy and crime.

About the Author

Marc J. Reilly has worked in all aspects of film and theater. Along with being a freelance writer, and ghostwriter, he has written several original plays, screenplays, and books. He now concentrates on writing novels, and lives in Reno with the apple of his eye, Peg. His goal is to inspire people to dream big, and live life like it's the bottom of the 9th.

That's all for now. This is Marc, your storyteller, signing off. Keep grinning and long live laughter. After all, life is too short not to get a kick out of it.

Printed in Great Britain
by Amazon